blush:
the unbelievably absurd diary
of a gay beauty junkie

By Harvey Helms

For Meredith!!
You're an absolute
Doll!!
Xo

1

For Jason Rockwood

Very Special Thanks

Kathi Lutton

Kaydee Castricone

Allison Kluger

Betty Confidential

Deborah Perry Piscione

Shaun Marsh

April Daniels Hussar

P J Gach

Diana Kay Eaton

Andy Castricone

Chip Lutton

Rich Smith

Stephen Dolginoff

Jillian Manus

Preface

Since I was 19 years old I've known that I would
release my diary for the world to see. Why now?
A few years back, I was sitting in a movie theater
in Cincinnati, Ohio watching *The Devil Wears
Prada*. I absolutely adore Meryl Streep. Who
doesn't, other than any actress nominated in her
category at the Oscars? About half-way through
the film, when Meryl's character Miranda Priestly
starts continuously dumping those delicious coats
and handbags on Andrea's desk, I realize that I'm
laughing hysterically in places where no one else
in the theater is laughing. Now I know I'm a New
Yorker transplanted to Ohio, but this is hilariously
wicked stuff and incredibly true to life. I've
worked for the Miranda Priestly character several
times in my own cosmetic career.

I look over to my Ohio friend and ask,
"Why aren't people laughing?" He says with a
mouth full of popcorn, "Honey! This movie isn't
believable. It's sickly funny but it's not real life."
After a sip of Diet Coke and a swoosh of my hair à
la Cher, I turn sharply and say, "Oh yes it is!" My
mind instantly does a flashback to she-dragons,
man drama, and lipstick. If this friend didn't
believe the crazy truth of the story, then other

3

people outside of urban cities probably didn't either. As I left the theatre that fated evening, I knew immediately that I had to share my diary, blemishes and all.

Now I know what you're thinking. Most gays and fabulous teen girls keep their diaries hidden till death because of the volatile nature of the dish involved. Totally understandable. My friend and soul mate Jason Rockwell has the only duplicate key to my diary, so that in a sudden demise he can share my legacy with Barbara Walters or the E! Network depending on the deal. But with all the current bullying of gay kids, I feel a certain need to share my story to help them be strong, and realize that life does get better. It may sound cliché, but it does take time, fabulous outfits, the right skin care, perfect lighting when you're photographed, and perseverance. It does get better my special darlings, even though right now the evidence in your lives may point to the contrary.

Another timely reason for penning this book is the digital age of instant celebrity. I know it is my time! And tweeting isn't enough for me; you only get 125 characters and I absolutely hate that! And maybe this has happened to you: either you or several of your friends have said that your life story would make a great book, movie, play, Broadway musical, mini-series, or reality TV show. You can just fill in the blank. You may have gone so far as to cast your movie as I have by asking at cocktail parties, "Who would play me? Who would play you?" Though be careful if you ask; they might say Meg Ryan (which means your plastic surgery is on the noticeably freaky side), or Nathan Lane (which means you're a fabulous flaming queen who in drag looks like First Lady Barbara Bush). But if they say Amy Poehler, then you are hysterically funny, and Bradley Cooper-- yum! Enough said. I love them all.

You may have also said that you have to wait for certain people to die before exposing your diary, because it's so scandalous you'd get sued. I waited until my parents passed, out of love and respect. There's nothing worse than the wrath of a Southern belle; more on my mother Grace later.

Blush is a memoir "traumedy", taken from the pages of my diary, about a boy who has dreams of love and success in a world that seems set against him from the beginning. Little did I know that after accidently tripping into the cosmetic industry, the allure of cosmetics would be so addictive and people could turn out to be so ridiculous. I think this is why we have no memory or ability to know the future when we're born. If we knew what was coming, we'd return to our mother's vagina and immediately redecorate our new vaginaminiums!

I guess I'll be a true beauty junkie till I die, and my will contains a digital picture of what I should look like during the viewing at my funeral. It includes the list of shades and products to achieve my best look, including (but not limited to) the following: my foundation would be Dr. Erno Laszlo Regular Normalizer Shake It in Beige, set with his Controlling Powder in medium; Chanel Sun-kissed Bronzer for face and eyes; Dior Show Waterproof Mascara in black; Anastasia of Beverly Hills Brow Groomer; Revlon ColorStay Eye and Lip liners in brown and nude. And finally, Revlon Fire and Ice Lipstick, one of Charles Revson's very first products. I know I'm a man; however, it's the perfect shade for my finale.

Are the people in this book real? Yes, they are. I've changed some names and the actual timing and dates when my drama happened so that a valium overdose can be avoided. If anyone reading this book sees the story differently, then I suggest you write your own book. If we owe each other apologies for the drama that happened, no worries. Karma has a way of leveling the playing field of life. I hope you're all well and prospering because many things can happen when people interact. Some nice and some, well let's just say, make for great reading. I'm gay, so everything will of course be over-exaggerated! If, while reading the story, you find that I accidentally mistake the shade of lipstick you were wearing at a party where you were tearing me apart, please forgive me. My memory is what it is.

So, my pretties, before you begin to read, my advice is to immediately apply waterproof mascara. You never know when a tear of joy or sadness could ruin your look. I love Lancôme and Dior waterproof formulas. The pink and green tube from Maybelline always work too if you're on a budget. But if you're a true beauty junkie like me, you already knew that.

Loving air kisses for no smudging,
XO
Harvey

HARVEY: THE DIARY PREQUEL

1962-1984

"A girl doesn't read this sort of thing without her lipstick."
-AUDREY HEPBURN
BREAKFAST AT TIFFANY'S

I didn't start keeping a diary until I was about eleven years old, so here's the tea and back story that will give you a glimpse into the prequel of my reality! Harvey B.C.-before cosmetics. Ready? Here we go! I was born gay and there was no closet for me to hide in. Kablam! Gay boy drops out of his mother's womb like an Amex at a Prada sample sale. It doesn't matter what the church or Dr. Spock says, I was gay when I took my first breath. You'd have to walk miles in my high heels to confirm this for yourself. When the doctor first slapped my ass I said, "Oh no you didn't!" And when I speak, a Balenciaga handbag falls out of my mouth. No one has ever really asked me if I'm gay. Wait! I take that back. The only person who ever asked me if I was gay was my mother Grace, and I guess it was out of Southern belle courtesy.

Flashback. It's 1974. Think Harvey Milk. Think Anita Bryant, but not for too long! Think Stonewall. Think Southern boy living down the street from the KKK. Think faggot. Think sissy. Queer bait. Light in the loafers. Queen. Mary, and Friend of Dorothy. I've been called everything. Get it?

I use the word "faggot" in this book because that's the vile word I heard at least five times a day for so many years, and if you're upset reading it I understand. People used this word to make me feel like shit, and it worked. Horrible really. So if I'm lucky enough to be interviewed by Matt or Anne on *The Today Show*, or have my own fabulous Barbara Walters Special before the Academy Awards, I hope they understand there's no disrespect intended when I use that word. I hope you understand too. It was my reality for a long time, and I still hear it occasionally today, depending on what part of the world I find myself.

Coming out? Forced by my mother. I'm eleven years old and I'm reaching in the fridge for something to drink when my mother suddenly confronts me.

"Are you gay?"

"Why yes, Mother, I am."

"Well, Harvey, you'll never be happy."

"Are you, Mother?"

End of conversation.

At her funeral I looked down into the casket and realized that my mother was just a woman with her own problems. She happened to give birth to me, but she had her own life full of drama. Most Southern women are candy-coated evil and I mean that in the best way possible. I love that about them. I have a friend who is a native New Yorker who says that Southern women with those sweet accents can say, "Kiss my ass," and you'll respond, "Why thank you, I'd love to!"

My father McClendon, "Mac," on the other hand, was an alcoholic and always went to bed drunk. He smoked three packs of cigarettes a day, which we all know is bad for the complexion. In his defense, he did use Vitalis Hair Groomer and Old Spice; not that I'm a fan of either, but he did try. I give everyone beauty points for at least trying. Grace and Mac were extraordinarily beautiful people with five children who are cute, but not as beautiful as you'd expect. Sort of like the children of Demi Moore and Bruce Willis. I guess in a nutshell I'll sum up my parents' marriage with something my mother once said to me: "Harvey, if I would have met your father's family before I married him, you wouldn't be here today." Elizabeth Taylor and Richard Burton, or by today's standards Jennifer Anniston and Brad Pitt, have nothing on these two. If you haven't seen the film *Who's Afraid Of Virginia Wolf?* Netflix it. It's the story of my parents, and my childhood. I swear.

It's always been difficult for me to understand why my parents couldn't accept me for who I am. What is the big deal? Being gay is different but it's interesting, and for me it is also genetic. Straight people who say it's not... well... that's another book. I never tried to win my father's love like many gay men do by staying in the closet. No offense to any gay men or women reading this, as we all have reasons for doing what we do to survive. Me? Being so feminine, I was cosmically forced to be myself. Painful yet authentic. I spent my prom helping girlfriends ready themselves for the first big night of their lives.

Me, sissy? Who came up with that word? You can always tell the gays in 1930-40's films. The butlers and hairdressers who look like they would blow away in the breeze. Prissy! Sissy! Pansy! God bless those actors. If you're a young gay today, I want you to know that there are others from another time who made the payment so you can enjoy the freedom you have. If you think things are tense now, go back and read the story of Stonewall in New York. I buy a fresh corsage made of camellias on the anniversary every year. Bette Davis would be so proud.

But even with all the prejudice thrown at me from a very young age, I never accepted a society with attitudes and judgments that said, "I'm better than you." My classmates were forever reminding me of my place in the world by calling me names: Freak, Faggot, and Pansy. I had to stand up to the bullies because it wasn't possible for me to hide. I must have really strong guardian angels since I've made it this far.

One of the reasons I think my mother Grace knew that I was gay early on was due to my love affair with beauty products, which began around age four. I credit her with this because she introduced me to the wonderful effects of using Jergens moisturizing lotion with its timeless cherry almond scent. Delicious. It made me a soft and velvety-smooth toddler. It's one of my favorite memories of my mother. She would put it on my face right before I left for school every morning until I was seven years old. It's not a high-end moisturizer, but I love it. I buy products from every class of trade, from drug stores to specialty boutiques. No snobbery here if it's a fabulous product. However, I do have a trick when I'm short of funds. I keep my high-end products by the sink so when I have guests over and they are in my bathroom they can *ooh* and *aah*. They would never know I am broke because I put my fab low-end products in the back of a closet outside the bathroom. People go through all the drawers and cabinets at parties, you know, so beware and be ready. It could ruin your reputation if you don't!

I also credit Grace with my love of Secret deodorant. Strong enough for a man but also great for a four-year-old. Grace taught me what the right makeup base can do for your skin. She wore Revlon Touch and Glow foundation in a shade called Misty Rose. She would mix it with a touch of water and then set it with Revlon Love Pat Pressed Powder in a coordinating shade also called Misty Rose, but never around the eyes. She said it makes you look older if you put powder around your eyes.

I began wearing foundation at age sixteen when the acne began. My first was Clinique Balanced Makeup in Porcelain Beige. Everybody wore this one because it was in every Clinique gift with purchase for years! I've worn foundation ever since. My all-time favorite is a cult product called Erno Laszlo Regular Normalizer Shake It in Beige. I have used this product on and off for 30 years. You shake this elixir of the Gods—one part pigment and one part fabulous oil-controlling ingredients—and lightly pat it onto your skin using a deluxe cotton pad. If you're a junkie, you know which cotton pads are deluxe and which ones are cheap crap that fall apart because you bought them on sale. Apply two layers for more coverage or extra oil control, allowing each layer to set before reapplying. Instantly pore-less, radiant. Never makeuppy.

Around 1966, my oldest sister Cathy's favorite fragrance was Estee Lauder Youth Dew, in the little blue bottle. Everyday my sister would come home and find her little blue bottle mysteriously in my room. Youth Dew was the leading fragrance of its time. Legend has it that Estee wanted to sell Youth Dew at Saks Fifth Avenue and the buyer said, "Absolutely not! We only sell French fragrances!" Estee wasn't having that so she went to the cosmetic department and intentionally dropped the sample bottle on their marble floors, which of course shattered and engulfed the department with the Youth Dew scent. Customers loved it and wanted to purchase it. The rest, as they say, is history.

I also credit Cathy for showing me what great style is all about because she always looked fabulous! She was "Miss Breck." Remember Dippity Doo? I loved the smell of Dippity Doo. Cathy would hot-roll her hair every night on gigantic rollers as I would try on her prom gowns and cocktail dresses with those fabulous dyed-to-match satin pumps. It's my party and I'll cry if I want to! Cathy first taught me how to dance to that Leslie Gore song when I was five years old. It doesn't get gayer than that, does it? Well, unless maybe if you learned how to slow dance to Connie Francis singing "Where the Boys Are."

I'll skip the heinous drama of high school and fast-forward to 1980 when I decide I want to be a fashion designer. I've always loved clothes and watching the rise of Halston, Ralph Lauren, and Calvin Klein in the 1970's inspired me to do be a fashion designer. I love the glamour of the 70's. The best decade ever, because it truly was the beginning of the American fashion designer as a star! 1980 arrives. The Reagans are in the White House and Debbie Harry's hit "Heart of Glass" is the hot new song. I'm attending the University of North Carolina at Greensboro, finishing my first semester in the Home Economics department, where fashion majors are housed--GAG! The only saving grace about attending this dreadful institution was meeting my best friend for life, Tim Richmond.

Not to be too dramatic, and I know that I have a tiny tendency to exaggerate, but I was almost murdered by red neck jocks in my dorm. This nightmare begins with my gay German fashion model roommate Stephan. Extraordinarily beautiful, and before you ask—no, we never had sex. I hadn't had sex with anyone yet. Stephan and I were harassed 24 hours a day in the dorm and all over the campus. I would walk to my classes as quickly as I could to escape the threatening wrath of jocks and assholes. One night while in my room studying, my friend Tim burst into my room screaming and crying. "They've beat the shit out of Stephan, Harvey! The ambulance came and took him away! The red necks beat him black and blue in the cafeteria! Harvey, they're saying you're next so lock this door and don't leave your room tonight! Do you hear me?" Tim left and I locked my door. I was truly afraid for the first time in my life.

The drama continued the next morning after Stephan's beating, when I woke to 20 guys

screaming, "We're going to kill you, faggot!"
Some of them even pissed on my door! I jumped
out of bed in terror and at first couldn't breathe,
but suddenly I was overwhelmed with the smell of
smoke and I could see fire under my door. The
assholes started beating on my door like they were
going to break it down. My heart was beating so
fast I thought I was going to have a heart attack, so
I ripped the screens off the window and just barely
escaped, wearing only my pajamas.

I ran to the infirmary and begged the nurse
to help me but she looked at me like I was crazy;
my cries were falling on deaf ears. I sat in the
infirmary feeling like a gay visitor from another
planet. After about an hour of numbly staring
forward I called home, and my mother answered.
"Daddy needs to come get me right now because I
can't stay here anymore." Grace didn't ask any
questions. I guess my mother knew things were
bad, and if we spoke about it, that would make it
real. Very Southern of her. If you don't speak
about disgrace it doesn't exist. I'm nearly killed,
and I can't even speak of it to my parents.

Daddy finally showed up smelling of beer
and cigarettes and silently sat outside the Dean's
office while I was fighting for my life inside. It
was sort of like a tribunal in front of the KKK. It

didn't matter what I said. Piss? Fire? Stephan's beating? It might as well have never happened. In the Dean's words, *Harvey, you should make a better attempt to get along with others.* I was livid. I stormed out of his office screaming "Come on, we're getting the hell out of here." Back in my room, Daddy watched while I packed up the rest of my belongings. As we were leaving, the guys who had almost killed me were standing at their doors as we walked down the hall. I turned to look at their faces so that I would never forget that moment. Their smiles said *the fag is leaving the building.* They had won.

Daddy and I drove three hours in silence. I couldn't bear to look at him. When we arrived home I immediately ran up to my old room and slammed the door in shame. My mother came up and said, "Harvey, are you okay?" "No, Mother, I'm not."

I cried non-stop for the next few days as the emotional numbness set in. *Should I just kill myself because so many people don't like the fact that I exist?* I went into total seclusion for a few months, sitting in my room listening to Boy George's first hit "Do you Really Want to Hurt Me?" over and over.

But then, one day, by some twist of fate, magic, or fairy dust, I could breathe. Suddenly there were possibilities where there had been nothing but despair. I decided from that moment forward that no one would ever treat me that way again. *No one*. I don't know where this strength came from, but my inner Wonder Woman emerged and she's been here with her magic gold cuffs to protect me from any discrimination that comes my way ever since.

After the sun finally came out, I decided to attend The American Business & Fashion Institute in Charlotte, North Carolina, mainly because Daddy said I was too young to live in NYC and attend FIT, the Fashion Institute of Technology. All the best designers attend FIT or Parson's. The UNCG incident was still fresh in our minds but we never spoke about it. While at AB&F I began to heal and make new friends. Trust was difficult, but I was feeling better with each passing day.

This was also the time and place where my love for women's issues truly began. Equality for everyone. Women, blacks and gays! We all seemed to be in the same boat, born to live the roles we were given. While at AB&F, I had to work an internship with a department store for an entire semester's grade. We worked with the buyers, store managers, etc., to learn the retail business. Eventually we ended up on the floor as sales associates, which was a great help because I needed the job to help with school tuition and my ever-budding beauty addiction.

The department store was Belk's, a large family-owned chain in the Southeast. The story of Belk's is an entire volume of books in and of itself, so I won't touch that here! Human Resources placed me in the men's department. By some fabulous twist of fate, Tim Richmond had dropped out of UNCG because he'd had enough of the gay bashing as well, and turns up at AB&F. This is also when we meet our other best friend and eventually roommate, Richard Brunson. It seemed like Tim and Richard looked at each other for just seconds and then quickly fell in love.

Richard had been an ordained minister; the night after they slept together, I said, "Tim you are going to burn in hell for sleeping with him!" This was courtesy of my Southern upbringing. Tim and Richard are like Grace Jones and Elton John. As you will see, they are also my quasi mother and father, constantly keeping watch over me and my adventures.

So here we are! Now that I've shared all that gay drama, you're probably screaming, *Harvey, get to the point already!*

Okay, okay!

What starts this crazy gay story about my climb up the lipstick pyramid is so ridiculous that you may have trouble believing it. When I look back or tell the story at cocktail parties, people always say, "Really? You couldn't remember to do that?" No, I couldn't. In department stores most garments have sensormatic tags that, if not removed by a sales associate, set off alarms at the entrance as the customer exits, to deter shoplifting. Here's the problem: I couldn't remember to remove them from the clothes I sold! I would sell tons of clothes and the customers would walk with their new purchases neatly wrapped in white tissue and pristinely placed in a Belk's shopping bag, but seconds later, well, off went the alarms.

When the alarm went off, another sales associate would have to go over to the customer, look at them as if they were a criminal, search their bag, and remove the sensormatic tags. They would also record the sales associate employee number who made the sale and didn't remove the sensor. I was getting 16 write-ups a day. I would hear the alarm and think, "Oh my God! I'm going to get fired!" I would beg other associates, "Please don't record my employee number!" Eventually, the store manager Gretchen Thomas called me into her office. I just knew I was going to get fired and get a big F on my internship.

I walked into Mrs. Thomas's office and surprisingly she was smiling. What? This caught me off guard…and then to my surprise, she said, "Harvey, you've become our top men's clothing sales person out of 100 stores, so congratulations! However, we are going to have lawsuits around you and these sensormatic tags." Her smile disappeared and without hesitation she said, "Harvey, I should fire you but I think I have a solution to our little problem. You need to work in a department that doesn't require sensormatic tags. So after much deliberation I've decided to place you in the cosmetic department. You are officially the new beauty advisor for Ultima II cosmetics."

Now you might think that I thought of that as good news because I love beauty. To become one of the very first male beauty consultants selling behind a cosmetic counter? In the South? There were male makeup artists, but male store consultants were virtually unheard of. Working every day those bitchy, overly made-up beauty queens judging me? Here's what was running through my head: my father is going to kill me and my mother will have a nervous breakdown. I didn't want to lose my job however. I gulped. "I don't know, Mrs. Thomas. Are you sure?"

She smiled and replied, "Trust me Harvey, I have a very good feeling about this—why Harvey, you're blushing!"

"Am I, Mrs. Thomas?" I walked out of her office thinking, *One of the first men to sell behind a cosmetic counter in Charlotte, North Carolina? It won't be so bad, right?*

*"When life is a "real" bitch again, and my old
sense of humor has up and gone,
It's time for the big switch again...I put a little
more mascara on!"*
-JERRY HERMAN
LA CAGE AUX FOLLE

"Tim, I'm not going to do this because it
has *big gay disaster* written all over it and you
know it! I don't care if I'm supposed to start
tomorrow! They can find someone else, so hurry
up and give me a light! I need a cigarette!"

I always smoke Marlboro lights when I'm
nervous and this is definitely one of those
moments! My roommate Tim Richmond hands me
his lighter and thankfully my next gin and tonic.
This is drink number four. Children of alcoholics
always count their drinks. I don't know why.

I remember being a little boy counting the
number of Pabst Blue Ribbon beers Daddy would
guzzle on a daily basis. My other roommate
Richard Brunson, ex-minister and Tim's
boyfriend, keeps saying, "Harvey, you have to do

this 'cause if you don't you'll fail your internship! Besides, you're the biggest beauty queen I know and you're a natural!" Richard is always the calm practical one.

"You're right Richard, all I need is a big fat F on my internship."

With all this current retail drama looming, I decide to relax by applying my Queen Helene Mint Julep cleansing masque. It's like an industrial strength shop-vac for your pores. *Mmmm...* Minty fresh. Masking, smoking, drinking, and pacing the floor, I'm checking every few seconds to see if Queen Helene has dried down on my skin. Tim looks at me and asks, "When are you going to call Grace, Harvey? You better call your mother now because if she hears this from someone else, you'll have hell to pay!"

"Oh, Mother!" I down my gin and tonic, the liquid nerve that I very much need before calling Grace and giving her the news.

"Hello... Mother?" It's never Mom or Mommy. It's always been Mother.

Tim whispers, "Come on Harvey, get this news out fast before she can interrupt!"

I go for it. "Guess what, Mother! I have a new job and I'm going to work in the cosmetic department at Belk's and I start tomorrow and I'm really nervous but excited too!" I take a breath.

Silence. Big breath and I begin again: "So Mother this is a great opportunity and Mrs. Thomas thinks this is a good idea and I think I could be good at it, so what do you think Mother?"

Silence. The first words out of her mouth are: "Harvey have you been drinking? Harvey, how am I going to tell your father about this?!"

I yell back, "Mother, it's the 1980's, for God's sake!" I glance over to the mirror to check out my Flock of Sea Gull's hair masterpiece. Thank you Final Net Hair Spray! Arguing, Grace conveniently says, "Harvey, I didn't raise you to speak to your mother this way. Didn't I get you Barbie's Dream House that one Christmas?"

"Oh Mother! Why are you always using Barbie against me?"

"Harvey, *I* raised you as a beauty queen so this is all my fault!"

I hate it when she does this! Grace becomes the martyr and I feel the guilt! She whimpers. "All this recent unpleasantness must be my fault."

Grace loves the phrase *recent unpleasantness*. Whenever the subject of the Civil War comes up she will always say, "Are we

26

talking about that recent unpleasantness?" But as always my mother, in true candy-coated evil form, will balance all that negativity that she just spewed at me by ending on a positive note.

"Well Harvey, I know that whatever you do you'll do it well. Bye-bye."

She does this all the time; something negative and then something positive (i.e."He's a horrible alcoholic but he has lovely children"). And the big finish with her sing-songy, "bye-bye!"

I mimic her "bye-bye" and slam the phone down.

Tim looks at me and pulls out the gin. "Another?" I nod my head in agreement.

"Tim, obviously this conversation hasn't helped my confidence. It's just like when I was a little gay boy standing in my mother's high heels looking up at her. *Harvey, you take those high heels off this instant before your father sees!* What should I expect? We both know she won't understand. And of course she has to bring up Daddy. *What will he think?* He's not thinking anything, Mother, he's passed out! Tim, obviously my life has not been easy up to this point."

Tim whispers to Richard, "*understatement.*"

"Richard," I continue, ignoring Tim's sarcasm. "I'm called faggot at least five times a day and now I'm going to be one of the first guys behind a cosmetic counter in a department store? You might as well make me target practice for every red neck who shops at Belk's!"

"Harvey, you are going to be great at this!"

"Tim, what about all the products I will have to learn? How will I learn to do makeup? What if I'm not good at it?"

"Well, Harvey, you are more than proficient at putting all that crap on your own face!"

"Shut up you gay bitch! What about standing for eight hours behind a counter? What if I faint?"

Tim takes a big swig of his own cocktail. "Slow down Boy George! I'm going to make you one more drink—then it's off to get your beauty sleep." That will be drink number five? *Hmmm*.

I feel my face. Masque is dry. As I rinse off the minty fresh Queen Helene masque I'm dreading tomorrow, but my pores look refined and ready for anything!

The next morning I try to put my best face forward. Clean, close shave, and a light touch of foundation to hide the blemishes that have erupted from all this stress! Black mascara, applied on upper lashes only. I always think that looks more natural. I spritz a few extra suirts Secret deodorant for my nerves. *Come on, Secret, you're the only thing that has never let me down!* And finally, three layers of Final Net hair spray perfection that even a New Orleans hurricane couldn't muss today!

I finally decide on a lavender shirt, coordinating tie with a conservative grey suit. What time is it? Mother hasn't made our routine morning call. She's got to be freaked out and that's no surprise. With me turning into a new public beauty queen must be too much for her to deal with. Oh well! I'll call her later. As I take another glance at the kitchen clock I start to feel the first day panic. *Come on, Harvey! Get it together or you're going to be late!*

I put myself on auto-pilot, blasting Pat Benatar "Hit Me With Your Best Shot!" and drive to Bojangle's to have a delightful cajun chicken breakfast biscuit with a Mountain Dew. Southerners drink soda or iced tea in the morning as well as coffee. Sometimes both together—we need the extra caffeine rush. I pull into the parking lot in front of Belk's department store at South Park Mall, the best mall in Charlotte, located on the south side of town where all the old Southern money dwells. I turn the engine off and roll down the window letting out a big gay sigh. I sit in the car and smoke a final cigarette before heading in for my first day.

My mind was a flurry of thoughts. *Why should I be nervous? I can sell! Oh dear! I don't think the Bojangle's biscuit was such a good idea and I don't have time to throw up! I'll have to redo my makeup and I can't be late. Come on Harvey, check your look a last time in the mirror. Damn!! Humidity plus stress plus Bojangle's biscuit discomfort equals a terribly oily shine!! Oh my God!! My T-zone looks like an oil spill deep in the heart of Texas! I know! A touch of Coty Airspun corn starch powder and I am matte perfection again. Smoke one more cigarette? No! Come on queen! It's show time!*

I meet Patti Garrison, Director of Human Resources for Belk's, in her office on the second floor. I've never seen her in the store before, so this has to be a big deal if she is involved.

"Good morning Mrs. Garrison." Patti looks me up and down and doesn't utter a word. "I'm a little nervous about today but I..."

Patti interrupts, saying, "That's nice. Please finish filling out your inter-department transfer forms."

Boy she's scary with severe black hair and beyond-white skin. She's young but already looks like an old lady. Her evil isn't candy-coated; it's straightforward satanic evil. And it's all in the name of the Lord. She's what I call *a pretend Christian* who's probably married to the Grand Poobah of the KKK. All her hatred and prejudice is justified by her holier-than-thou attitude and incredible ignorance. She gives you that "I'm going to heaven and *you're* not, you Sodom and Gomorrah sinner" superiority.

By the way she looks at me I can tell that she wants me to fail. No—to be more specific, she wants me first to fail and then to burn in hell. She just keeps grimacing at me. I know what she's thinking, *A man in cosmetics? Absurd!* She is such the Southern homophobe. Just like my ridiculous cousin the (honorable?) senator from North Carolina, Jesse Helms. These two are birds of a feather. More about cousin Jesse later.

Now I know that the only reason I've been given this chance is because of Mrs. Thomas' kindness and the willingness of Stephanie Cape, the Revlon Ultima II Account Executive, to try something different. Mrs. Thomas called Stephanie and told her about me. Stephanie is very progressive and agreed to me taking the line without interviewing me. Stephanie is a bubbly, Goldie Hawn look-alike that trusts Mrs. Thomas. Patti Garrison, however, has other ideas. I heard that Patti looked at Stephanie and simply blurted: "Absolutely not!"

Stephanie held her ground! "Patti, I'll pull the line out of the store if you don't hire Harvey. Don't forget that Ultima II is one of the top three brands sold in department stores. Are you going to go up against Gretchen Thomas?" Obviously she couldn't, so here I am.

Patti continues to look me up and down as I finish my department transfer paperwork. "Are you ready?" She doesn't wait for my reply. Instead she barks, "Let's go!" I almost puke up my problematic cajun biscuit all over her lavender Coret polyester business suit.

Patti is looming behind me while we're going down the escalator, breathing her coffee-scented dragon breath down my back. I can feel her eyes glaring at the back of my head and I can also smell her sickly sweet White Shoulders fragrance. When we reach the main floor we immediately turn right and march over into the cosmetic department. All the beauty vixens are standing at attention. Patti looks at me and says coldly, "After you."

It was kind of like walking down the hall for the last time at UNCG looking at those red necks, except this time the villains are overly made up candy-coated-evil women. The first woman whom I meet is Jean, counter manager for Elizabeth Arden. She is a tall blond glamazon whose makeup is heavy yet impeccable. Big hair. Big nails. Honestly, big everything! Her trouble-making part-timer Tammy, who is about 4'11", is standing beside her with her hands on her big hips. They look at me and simply say, "Hello" in unison.

The Estee Lauder girls are in navy jackets, and the Clinique girls in their signature white lab coats are pleasant enough, but all have a forced cosmetic beauty queen smile on their faces. Any minute I'm expecting them to say "God bless America" or "I want world peace." However, there is one Clinique girl who doesn't look like Clinique. She's sort of goth-meets-grunge but in a hypo-allergenic fragrance-free kind of way (if that makes any sense). She looks at me and winks knowingly.

"Well! Will you get a load of *him*?" The voice came from somewhere over in the fragrance bay. Just so you know, cosmetic companies call their case locations *bays*. The most revered women in cosmetics work the fragrance bays. Whose voice had I heard? Katherine. Tall, conservatively dressed, and not a hair out of place. She also looks like she's been smoking cigarettes since Queen Elizabeth I first discovered tobacco from the American Indians. "Good luck young man! You have a lot to learn."

It seems as though I've been walking for hours down this reception line. I guess if I would have known what was waiting for me at my bay I would have chatted with everyone a little longer to try and escape my fate. No such luck, though, as I finally end up at the Ultima II cosmetic counter. Trying to be perky I proclaim, "So this is my new home!" Patti Garrison grimaces but receives a page over the intercom and has to leave. No words of encouragement like, *Good luck* or *Call me if you need help.*

As I walk behind the counter I can see a beauty advisor standing with her back to me. She doesn't even turn. What a reception! Were these Southern belles raised by she-wolves? Where's the Southern charm and grace? Mrs. Thomas has a good feeling about this? Good for whom? I spy a mirror and do a quick hair check. Still fabulous. Thank God I was having an exceptional hair day.

As I bend down to look into the skin care case I get a sudden chill. I look up and there she is, looming. DEBBIE. I only know this because of her name tag. She's the skinniest woman I have ever seen in my life and this includes those people in National Geographic who haven't eaten in months. I give her a half-smile and say, "Hello", but she turns back to a display case and starts wiping down the glass cabinets in her bay. Debbie is the Revlon beauty advisor. Revlon is considered very ghetto because of its low price point and the fact that you can purchase it in "a drugstore near you." Debbie's anorexic before the medical term or practice has even become popular, or at least addressed in public. The most astonishing thing is that she wears Lucille Ball Lucy Show ice-blue eyeshadow. Hideous unless you are a Las Vegas show girl, or Lucille Ball herself, of course. She's cold as ice and her eyes always seem to be looking past me as if I don't exist at all. From this moment on I can only think of her as "ANOREXIC BLUE EYESHADOW DEBBIE."

The very first words out of her mouth to me—well, not exactly *to me*, because she's looking right past me—are, "I'm going on break." I immediately think, *For what? You don't eat.* As she is walking away I realize that I'm here in this cosmetic bay all by myself. What if a customer comes? What do I do? Critique their makeup? Tell them the anorexic bitch will be right back? Stand here and continue thinking that everybody I just met hates me? I'm feeling so fidgety that I have to do something, but what? I decide to look, feel, and smell products so I will look like I know what I am doing.

I look up and everyone is watching my every move. For a minute my inner beauty junkie is in heaven because of all the products lined up in a pristine row waiting to be enjoyed. At that same moment I realize that Katherine in the fragrance bay is right: I have a lot to learn.

As I'm looking for a tissue to wipe the cream off my nose (I stuck it too far into a jar of Revlon's miracle cream Eterna 27), I see an older Southern lady who looks like a cranky spinster that probably owns twenty cats, walking quickly toward the Revlon Counter. This will be the first woman I wait on in this department. She looks dehydrated and maybe a little drunk, too. *Come on Harvey, take a breath. You're on!*

"Hello, Ma'am. How may I help you today?"

No one has taught me anything about anything, let alone the appropriate Belk's greeting. This woman slams her purse down on the counter and asks in a raspy exacting voice, "Where's the Revlon Girl?" She and I stare at each other for a million seconds.

"I'm the Revlon girl." I laugh nervously. She doesn't.

Instead, she just stares at me, the old battle axe! "WELL" she says. The next 20 minutes arc hell as she keeps breathing hard and tapping the counter with nails that I think are, quite honestly, a little young for her to be wearing. She keeps saying *"WELL...!!! WELL....!!! WELL!!!?"* I was ready to faint.

Here's what ended up on the old bat's list:
- Moon Drops Moisturizer
- Misty Rose Touch and Glow
- Love Pat Misty Rose
- Love That Red, Love That Pink, Persian Melon, and Orange Flip lipstick
- Base Coat, Top Coat, and Fast Dry Spray for nails.

"I'm sorry Ma'am, but I can't find anything in this huge bay! It's my first day and I don't know where anything is!"

"You actually work in this department young man? I know the Belk Brothers are crazy from marrying their cousins, but this is ridiculous!"

I see her mouth moving but I stop listening because I catch a glimpse of my reflection in a mirror; my Final Net hairspray has lost its control. My fabulous doo is now in my eyes, matted against my forehead just like Jane Wyman's bangs in the TV show Falcon Crest. My bangs are hideous! I'm trying to smile and I think I even pee a little.

I try to keep her calm. "Ma'am, I'm sorry, but we're out of everything you need today. Why don't you come back tomorrow and maybe then we'll have what you need?"

"Look here, young man, you don't know what you are doing and you don't belong in this department. Makeup is for girls, not boys! Didn't your mother teach you that? Where's the regular girl? You know, the skinny one! Cat got your tongue? Boy, get me the department manager."

Department Manager? I don't even know who the department manager is. I look over to glamazon Jean at Elizabeth Arden.

"Jean, what is the department manager name?"

"I've already called her, Harvey. She's coming." So, enter Connie, the cosmetic manager, petite, older woman with an incredibly sweet face. How does she handle all the beauty divas? She has just arrived for her shift, so I didn't get a chance to meet her earlier. "What's the problem today, Mrs. Jones?"

"The problem, Connie, is your staffing here. A man selling behind the counter? I've used Revlon since before you were born and I've never had such terrible service!" Connie's eyes keep getting bigger and bigger as this old woman continues screaming about me and the service. "What is a man BLAH BLAH BLAH? He doesn't BLAPPITY BLAH BLAH BLAH! How could you BLAPPITY BLAH BLAH BLAH? Where is BLAH BLAH BLAH?"

Connie now has the calmest look on her face even though this old witch is really screaming. I also suspect that she has dragon breath like Patti Garrison from a mix of Maxwell

House Coffee, Wild Turkey Bourbon, and Milk of Magnesia.

Out of the corner of my eye, I see Anorexic Blue Eyeshadow Debbie returning from her break. God, I can see her hipbones through that white trash silk dress she has on. Now my humiliation will be complete! This girl who probably lives in a trailer from the wrong side of the tracks is going to end my cosmetic career before it really begins.

Dragon Breath Battle Axe points her boney little arthritic finger. "That's her! The skinny one!"

"Why Mrs. Jones, what's wrong? You look so upset!"

The old bat begins by asking why a man is selling Revlon, and continues with how I didn't know what I was doing... *blah blah blah.* Here we go again. Anorexic Blue Eyeshadow Debbie replies, "That's okay Mrs. Jones, I'll be glad to help you." There's nothing worse than a smug anorexic bitch with blue eyeshadow making me feel worthless. She mutters under her breath—yet audibly enough: "Mrs. Jones, you *know* a man doesn't belong in the cosmetic department."

Mrs. Blah Blah Blah nods in agreement, and Connie finally asks, "Are you happy now, Mrs. Jones? Thank you for shopping at Belk's and please don't hesitate to let me know when I can be of assistance again."

Debbie quickly finds every product that was requested and rings the sale. I feel like I'm going to cry, so instead I leave the counter and go to find Connie's office. As I walk past the beauty divas they each turn their backs on me. Oh no! It's the first day and I'm already taking the cosmetic walk of shame to the manager's office. This feels as bad as having toilet paper stuck to your shoe as you leave the rest room, making the whole roll follow you wherever you go, which if you've noticed typically only happens in a very public place like a restaurant or disco dance floor. Connie's office is in the back, behind the ladies dresses' section. I notice some lovely new Oscar De La Renta jackets on my way back there. Love, love, love Oscar!

I reluctantly knock on the door.

"Yes?"

I slowly poke my head in.

"I've been expecting you, Harvey. Sit."

"Am I fired?"

"No. First, it's nice to meet you. Second, it's your first day. Third, Mrs. Jones is in here complaining at least once a week. She wanted me to fire Debbie last week for being out of Make Mine Mauve lipstick. So it's nothing personal."

"Thanks, Connie. But I don't know if the cosmetic department is going to work out for me... I've only been here a few hours and I've already gotten a complaint. Plus, the girls don't seem too thrilled to have me in the department."

"People don't like change, Harvey, and let's face it, you're different... I know I'm not the first person to point that out to you!" We both break out laughing at the same time. "You know, Harvey, Mrs. Thomas wants this to work, even though Patti Garrison has been against it from the beginning."

"What about you, Connie?"

"Honestly, Harvey, the cosmetics industry isn't for the faint of heart. I have a business to run. You have one month to prove yourself, just like anyone else who works in my department."

She gives a curious smile. "It's just lipstick, kid."

I take a deep breath as I begin to relax, but before I get to comfortable in myself Connie gently points out one last suggestion.

"Oh, and by the way, Harvey, you could use some oil control."

I slowly walk back to the cosmetic department pondering what Connie has said about my lack of oil control and the one month to prove myself. When I arrive at the Ultima ll counter I pretend to just clean the display cases so that if anyone approaches the counter they won't think I actually work behind the counter. In fact, I am so embarrassed that I take my name tag off so customers won't think I am an employee.

Driving home after that first day of beauty hell, all I can think is, *Have a DRINK!* Tim and Richard mercifully take me out to our favorite gay disco, The Odyssey. There are only two gay bars in Charlotte. The other is Scorpio's, a lesbian bar that welcomes gay men on Wednesday and Thursday nights. The Odyssey is our haven from the homo-hating world! After hours of dancing we finally come off the dance floor loving Prince's new hit 1999.

Wow! 1999 seems so far away from 1982! "Tim, what do you think we'll be doing in 1999?"

"The same thing we're doing now! Dancing and being fabulous!"

"Honestly ya'll, this has been the worst day of my life. I wish you could have seen that skinny smug bitch!"

Tim hands me a drink. "What's wrong with you queen?! Don't let those evil, overly made-up witches get you down. Let's make Debbie and Patti's life miserable!"

Richard, always the sensible one, just looks at me. "Don't give up Harvey. Miss America would never give up, would she?"

"Oh! Richard! You just had to bring up Miss America!"

Tim, lighting a cigarette, adds, "Yes Richard, that's true. But I still think we should spread rumors of Anorexic Blue Eyeshadow Debbie around her trailer park." We burst out laughing. It's the first time that day when I feel OK.

Driving home, I can't stop thinking about that heinous Revlon customer. What have I gotten myself into? I've got to call Mother. I don't want her to say, *I told you so! Bye bye!* So I'll tell her a little white lie: *Mother, there was no "recent unpleasantness" today. Patti Garrison is the biggest bitch I've ever met, but she does look lovely in lavender polyester.*

I guess the apple really doesn't fall far from the tree.

*"I always say shopping is cheaper
than a psychiatrist!"
-TAMMY FAYE BAKER*

Every day it's the same thing. I go to work, wait on crazy women with bad breath who give me grief, and then go home to my roommates Tim and Richard where they let me vent while pouring cocktails down my throat as fast as I can drink them. *Blah blah blah, uppity bitch. Tim, please make me another Long Island Iced Tea—or blah blah blah, please my favorite gin and tonic."*

Tim, Richard, and I have lived together for a year so far and we love it. We currently reside at The Farrington's, a high-end apartment community for the young and upwardly mobile. There's a strange Southern belle named Rebecca who lives directly above us. Her father is a senator or something significant in the government. Rebecca reminds us of this every time we see her and yet she's always so vague about what "Daddy" actually does. Her Southern accent is so sticky that we can barely understand her. Believe it or not,

there are different kinds of Southern accents…
Rebecca's is from Mississippi, the Deep South, so
her accent is as thick as Brooke Shield's eye
brows and as slow as the line at the Honey Baked
Ham store at Christmas.

She sashays down to our apartment at least
once a week, rings our doorbell, and says: "Can
one of you gay boys please highlight my hair
tonight? My hairdresser, that big gay bitch, can't
squeeze me in! Look how dull my hair is, and I
have a date tonight! Thank you *so* much."

We always give her the same blank
disgusted look and say the exact same thing:
"Rebecca, just because we're gay doesn't mean we
know how to highlight hair. We can see how you
would think that—because our hair is so
fabulous—but you need to go to Eckerd's drug
store and buy Revlon's Frost and Tip kit and do it
yourself. It comes with easy instructions." (I
personally know this because I've done a quick
Revlon highlight many a time. Better than that
dreadful Sun In Spray which always leaves hair
brassy and dry. Or as we say in the South, "fried,
dyed, and laid to the side.") Rebecca always
releases a dramatic Southern belle huff and stomps
back up the stairs. Now we all know that some
gays love doing hair and I take nothing away from

them. I love fabulous hair stylists too. Unfortunately some gays just aren't born with the *whip-up-a-quick-highlight-or-hairdo* gene.

Every day at the beauty counter I'm tortured with the exact same questions and ridiculous comments: *Why are you in cosmetics? Isn't it strange for a man to sell blush? Do you have a lover? Are you the man or the woman in the relationship? What's it like to be gay? God burns homosexuals, you know.*

Some days, I can't take it anymore. I need air! The mix of blunt questions and too many fragrances is making me dizzy! One particularly annoying day I decide to go out the employee entrance at the end of my break and get some fresh air. The goth Clinique girl is leaning against the wall, smoking a Virginia Slim cigarette. While we've smiled at each other from across the bays, we've never actually formally met. She looks at me, blowing out a puff of smoke, and says, "This humidity is giving my hair a hard-on! My name is Sue."

"Well, I'm no stranger to big bangs and Final Net hairspray. My name is Harvey. It's nice to meet you."

"Oh, I know who you are. My brother is gay and I totally understand what you're going through."

So, question. Why is it that all straight people know one other gay person and thus feel like they are part of a special club? I love it when they ask me if I know so and so just because he's gay. It's like all gay people must somehow know each other. "You must know him, Harvey! He's a hairdresser?" (There we go again with the hairdresser thing.) Or they say, "I have a guy I want to fix you up with. He's a hairdresser." (Well at least I could have million-dollar highlights for free! Something to consider…)

It's nice to finally have the possibility of a friend in the department and she's definitely a misfit like me.

"Sue, how did you get that job at Clinique? Clinique girls always look like freshly scrubbed virgins..."

"I know, right? One of my mother's friends is my Account Executive. It's total nepotism." Sue has on a very pale foundation with extremely dark purple eyeshadow, blush, and lip color. Well applied and perfectly blended. Most Clinique girls barely have on mascara and baby pink lip gloss.

Wow, she must be a great salesperson because Connie is tough about sales!

"Between you and me, Sue, I don't know if I'm going to make it in cosmetics. Patti Garrison and that Debbie…" She shoots me a look and says, "Oh, you're going to make it all right, Harvey. You're the most interesting thing that's happened here in years. I'm going to teach you the ropes, but first Missy, you need to be exfoliated." First Connie's oil-control suggestion and now this! The nerve! Don't these girls know how fragile a beauty queen's ego can be? "That sounds painful Sue!"

"Who cares if you're prettier, queen! And let's get the oily shine and break-out under control. What's with this boring gray suit? You need a fabulous navy suit with an outlandish tie! I also think you should be blonder. So much to do! We'll take care of Satan's daughters Patti and Debbie soon enough, after *I* give *you* a makeover and turn you into a fabulous beauty advisor."

It's at that moment that I wonder if Sue practices witchcraft. With one last drag of her cigarette she grabs my arm. "Come on, Gorgeous. I think we'll start with Clarifying Lotion #3." I follow her thinking, *"Hmm? That sounds painful but delicious!*

Over the next few weeks, Sue beats cosmetic knowledge into me relentlessly day after day. I haven't attended Ultima II Beauty School so I'm a blank beauty canvas! Sue starts everyday with, *"Repeat after me: CLEANSE. TONE. MOISTURISE."* My head is spinning! There are so many things to remember. I hear Sue's voice at night while I'm sleeping whispering important beauty mantras into my ears. *Don't sleep in your makeup. Always wear sunblock. Don't pick at blemishes. Use a masque to purify your pores. Anti-aging. Lift. Firm. Exfoliate. Retexturize. Hydrate. Penetrate. Epidermis. Dermis. Fragile eye area. Sebaceous glands. Hereditary. Free radicals. Anti-oxidants. Hypoallergenic.*

In between lessons, I am having other "first" experiences. One difficult lesson was about taking a return of products from somebody else's line, especially concerning returns in the fragrance bay. I took back a bottle of Chanel No. 5 because the customer complained that "It smells like bathroom toilet paper!" She didn't have her receipt but I thought, "Well, if it smells like toilet paper..."

Katherine, the head matron of the fragrance bay, came back from break to hear the news. Jean, the big rat from Elizabeth Arden, screamed, *Harvey took a fragrance return from one of your customers!* The whole department immediately went dark and I think I heard a small explosion. Katherine stomped over to my bay, fuming.

"Harvey, we don't take returns from a customer without the receipt. We try not to take returns at all."

"Katherine, the customer said that she'd bought the fragrance from you but really didn't like it."

"What do you know Harvey? You prissy little know-it-all! I knew you were a mistake the moment I laid eyes on you!"

I will never make *that* mistake again. Who knew Chanel No. 5 could be so dangerous?

I haven't had the chance to do a full makeover on a customer yet. I've tested lip color or eyeshadow on women without demonstrating the full cosmetic works. This will be my next big lesson from Sue.

"Harvey, the more you put on them, the more they buy, but you have to know what you're doing, including which products and in what order. You need to know how to skintype. Choose color. Blend. Blend. Blend. They have to look more beautiful and glamorous than when they sat down in your makeup chair. And always end a makeover with a spritz fragrance. Get them addicted to your fragrance so that their husbands will come back at Christmas and buy your gift sets." So evil, but so smart.

Sue does exquisitely beautiful makeovers and she's as fast as lightening! When she finishes her masterpieces, the women look in the mirror, crying joyfully, "I've never looked this beautiful!" There are others who do makeovers in the department, especially at Elizabeth Arden, and their customers look in the mirror and cry, "I look like a whore!" That's always fun. *Bless your heart, ma'am*. That's Southern for, *you poor dumb bitch*.

One early Tuesday morning Sue abruptly approaches my counter dragging a short brunette by her arm. "Harvey, this is Amy, and she needs to purchase the Ultima II Translucent Wrinkle Cream." Amy looks at me curiously. Pointing to one of my new color displays she asks reluctantly, "Are these new Ultima II colors?"

"Yes, these shades have just arrived."

Then out of the blue Sue more or less pushes Amy into my makeup chair and says, "Harvey is going to give you a new summer makeover to update your look, Amy."

I'm shaking because I'm so nervous and I hope that Amy doesn't notice. It's really scary; sort of like your first time with sex. I have to find out what she likes and how she likes it. "Do it like this, not like that. That feels good. Stop! Don't do that! Please! Not in my eye! You're being a little rough!"

I finish the look with a light spritz of the Ultima II fragrance Ciara. Oh, the aura of Ciara! Sue swivels Amy around in the chair and looks at my work. Looking in the mirror, Amy says, "Well, if I had a headdress I could work in Las Vegas."

Ouch. I was expecting tears of joy and rapture; I had spent *an hour* on this woman.

Anorexic Blue Eyeshadow Debbie is standing there and bursts out with her sinister laughter. "Amy, when you're ready for a beautiful makeover I'm here at Revlon."

Sue looks at Debbie while remarking, "Yes Amy, you can try Revlon but you can also buy it at *a drugstore near you* when you're out of tampons or toilet paper!"

Debbie doesn't even flinch. She leaves the counter and spreads her poisonous gossip at every bay, letting the other lipstick vixens know about my makeover failure. Amy doesn't buy one thing other than the products she came in for.

Sue grabs my arm. "Don't worry! Your makeovers will get better the more you do them, Harvey. Screw Debbie! Revlon is getting thrown out of here soon anyway. I heard that from my Account Executive last week. Come on, let's go to the break room and celebrate your first makeover!"

Having composed myself with crunchy Cheetos and Cheerwine soda pop, I try to walk back to my counter with my head held high. I get a whiff—actually more than a whiff; it's like a nuclear explosion—of the Estée Lauder fragrance Private Collection, which has permeated the entire store. Strangely, Debbie actually looks a little excited. Maybe she accidentally ate a carbohydrate?

Sue whispers to me ominously, "Here she comes, Harvey."

"Who? Who's coming?" As I turn around, there are six women huddled together talking nonstop. They walk towards us as a single group, smoothly like they are floating on air and then they begin to part like the Red Sea in the Ten Commandments. When these six overly made-up women separate, they reveal a little surprise. Is it her? No! *Yes*! It is.

Tammy Faye Baker from PTL. Tammy Faye is the wife of TV Evangelist Jim Baker, whose show Praise the Lord! is on TV 24 hours a day saving souls and begging for money to build the biggest church ever in the world. Tammy Faye cries daily, with mascara running—no, streaming—down her face, begging for money to help the church. Her favorite song is "*I'm gonna have a little talk with Jesus! Tell him all about my troubles!*" She's a little pixie of a thing, or as Tim would say, *she's no bigger than a minute!* Tammy Faye has on more than her fair share of makeup, complete with huge mink false lashes. Her makeup is not applied very well but as I look at her I somehow know that there's a beautiful woman under all that makeup.

I literally can't move I'm so star-struck. Is she going to come over here? God, I hope so. Do I have time to call my mother? Thank God Las Vegas Headdress Makeover Amy has already left. Where's Sue? She's probably gone outside for a cigarette, which is okay I guess; okay because it's obvious that neither Tammy Faye nor the six glamazons in tow would prefer the natural look of Clinique.

Tammy Faye and her entourage are standing in the middle of the department being welcomed by our manager Connie. Anorexic Blue Eyeshadow Debbie looks at me, or at least the closest thing to looking at me "Harvey, Tammy Faye likes Ultima II, Estée Lauder, and Elizabeth Arden."

"Well, Debbie, it makes sense that it would take three cosmetic companies to create that signature look!"

In a twinkling of the eye, Tammy Faye and the ladies of the Christian coalition are standing in front of me staring and smiling. What should I say? *Hello Ladies! How's Jesus?* I think better of it. "Hello Mrs. Baker, how can I help you today?"

One of the glamazons says in a sugary venomous way, "We've never been waited on by a man before! Look girls! There's a man selling cosmetics!" Which is actually Christian code for: *I didn't know that Belk's would hire a queer, who's also going to burn in hell, to sell Ultima II! Look, y'all!*

Tammy Faye looks at me with her big false eye lashes and signature smile, complete with cackling laugh and says, "You're just darling! He's darling. Isn't he just darling?" The glamazons nod their heads reluctantly in unison. Tammy bats those lashes at me and asks, "What's your name Sweet Pea?"

"Harvey Helms."

She turns to the entire department like she is on her TV show and raises her hands, I guess up to Jesus, and proclaims: "The Lord calls us to help each other in any way we can. He blesses all those who seek him." She then turns back to me and swings her petite hand toward me. "I'm glad to meet you, Harvey. Call me Tammy Faye." I gently shake her hand while admiring the gabrillion dollars' worth of diamonds she is wearing.

It's just as Debbie said. It takes three cosmetic companies to give Tammy Faye her signature look. Ultima II Beautiful cream makeup, set with Elizabeth Arden's Flawless Finish Compact Foundation, Fresh Air foundation, and Private Collection fragrance from Estée Lauder. Her mink lashes are custom and she wears two sets on top with one and a half on the bottom, and of course gobs of mascara. She never removes her makeup (or at least that's the legend).

Tammy Faye bought seven of the following products for her and the Christian Coalition entourage: Beautiful Cream makeup in Aurora Beige, #2 loose powder, Midnight Mauve/Prairie Mauve Eyeshadow Duet, Ginger

Plum Frost and Sahara Rose blush, Sparkling Bordeaux and Ripe Sienna Plum lipstick, Black & Pearls Eyeliner, Under makeup Moisture Lotion in Mauve, and Procollagen Anti-Aging Complex for Face and Eyes. $1,500 dollars later, it was wrapped in tissue, bagged, and in their hot little beauty-addict hands! Debbie didn't lift a finger to help, so I was sweating like Miss Piggy.

I was about to thank Tammy Faye but she surprised me by grabbing my hand and kissing it!

"Harvey it was a great pleasure to meet you today and the Lord and I thank you for your lovely service. You know, Harvey, you kind of remind me of some of our lovely boys who sing on our show. You should come to PTL for one of our Holy Sunday services! May Jesus bless and keep you safe!"

I've seen the show a million times and she isn't kidding! But those PTL singing queens are in Jesus' closet and won't be coming out any time soon. With a little tear in my eye and a wave of my hand, I call out to her.

"Goodbye Tammy Faye! Hello to your husband Jim and Jesus! Enjoy your Ultima II!"

And just like the Book of Revelations says, *She was gone in an instant.* A hundred thoughts buzzed in my mind all at once. *Oh my God! I just waited on Tammy Faye Baker! Tim and Richard will die! My mother will faint! I have to call Stephanie! Wait! Damn it! They'll never believe me! I should've gotten her autograph!*

As Tammy Faye is leaving, Sue walks up.

"I smelled the Private Collection, so I left," she explains. "How did it go---must have been good seeing how many Ultima II bags they were toting away." She took a deep breath before continuing. "Well, at least you're not burning in hell, Harvey!"

I roll my eyes at that one. I'm proud of my first big sale. "I guess I'm one of Tammy Faye Baker's personal beauty advisors now," I say.

Sue looks at me with a mix of condescension and fear.

She whispered sharply, "You saw how much makeup she had on, didn't you? I wouldn't announce that so loudly."

When Sue and I turn around, the entire department, including Connie, Debbie, and Patti Garrison are standing there. Patti, with a raised evil eyebrow asks, "So? How did it go with Tammy Faye?"

I see my chance to be vindicated, to stand up to those witches.

"No big deal, girls. Jesus wants me to be Tammy Faye's new beauty consultant. She loves Ultima II, and that is my line, isn't it? Now if you'll excuse me, my shift has come to an end." And with that, I turned to go outside for a cigarette!

Patti huffed toward the escalators while the others scattered, whispering as they departed. Debbie stood there like a zombie as usual.

For the first time since I started in this department, tonight when I said *See you tomorrow, girls,* they all sort of half-smile and realize that I am here to stay. I guess Tammy Faye had the cosmetic gods bless me. As soon as I get home I call Mother. When she answers I sing, "*I'm gonna have a little talk... with Jesus / Tell him all about... my troubles.*"

"That's nice, honey. Mac, Harvey's gone crazy but maybe there's hope after all, 'cause he's singing about Jesus!"

HARVEY'S DIARY:
AUGUST 25, 1984
"The Brat Frat Pack?"

"When you stop talking, you've lost your customer.
When you turn your back, you've lost her!"
-ESTEE LAUDER

After the Tammy Faye Baker incident, or TFB, as it will come to be known, my makeovers are improving with everyone I assist and I'm starting to feel more confident. I picked Michael Marin's *Makeover Magic* book with his fabulous before-and-after photos so that I can improve my skills. The most amazing transformation is Phyllis Diller. Her *before* look is like a little Jewish man from New Jersey while the *after* look is full-blown Las Vegas Phyllis. Makeup truly is an art form; in taking a woman who is a blank palette, and turning her into great beauty, I'm beginning to discover how makeup can transform someone's life. Especially having just completed makeovers on a girl with severe acne and an older woman who had been burned in a fire; these makeovers changed my life as well because I found a way to help people feel better about themselves through the art of beauty. It's at this point when I realize that I want to be a master makeup artist. This is what I want to do with my life!

When I get all warm and fuzzy like this, Sue comes over and slaps me back into reality! "You sell makeup Missy! Estée Lauder says *"If you don't sell, it's not the product that's wrong! It's you! Never stop talking!"* Sue is always quoting Estée to drive her points home. "You better sell tons or it's back to the men's department with you. Oh that's right, no men's department you dizzy queen who can't remove sensormatic tags! It will be worse! *Housewares*???"

Sue is supportive in a loving, hard-core sort of way. Life's interesting, isn't it? This goth Clinique girl is my fairy god-sister and now even Katherine the Fragrance She-Dragon is warming up to me (or at least she smiles at me now. I flatter myself in calling this progress). My sales are increasing everyday, which is great because in this industry if you don't meet your quotas you're simply out. You have to push. If you come across a beauty advisor who does slow makeovers or says *It's okay, you don't have to buy anything*, chances are she (or he!) won't be here the next time you come shopping.

With practice, my makeovers go from my customers just buying the one obligatory product to sometimes purchasing everything! With all of Sue's training, I finally make a sale over $500! Sue told me I couldn't count my $1,500 sale with TFB because I didn't work for it. TFB asked for the product; I didn't have to recommend or demonstrate anything. Sue says that's what *Clerks* do: "Clerks work in drugstores and we beauty advise in department stores. That's why we are called *beauty advisors*." Sue's so serious about this that sometimes it scares me.

Fresh back from lunch one day, I'm inventorying my skincare products when the phone in my bay starts ringing. Debbie is touching up her nails and acts like she doesn't hear it. That Revlon Quick Dry Nail Spray is gagging me! I'd give the extra skinny ice princess a snide look, but it's such a waste of time. Instead, I pick up the phone.

"Good afternoon, Belk cosmetics. This is Harvey, how may I help you?"

"Hi Harvey! It's Stephanie. Congratulations on Tammy Faye! Mrs. Thomas called me with the great news! Does she really wear that much makeup?"

"Yes she does, Stephanie, $1,500 dollars' worth!"

"Listen Harvey, the other reason I'm calling is that you're booked to go to your first beauty school. Your trainer's name is Mark Cooper. He's also your Account Coordinator who facilitates special events for North Carolina. Please be at the Adams Mark Hotel downtown at 8:00 in the morning sharp. Call me tomorrow night so we can talk about what you learned! Okay? See ya. Oh and don't be late!"

I scream across the department: "*Sue! Guess what? I'm booked to attend my first beauty school!!*" *What should I wear? Who is this Mark Cooper? Will this further my career?* I've graduated from AB&F with my degree, and decide that although I love fashion, it is official. I am totally addicted to cosmetics. So much so that I now believe I have liquid eyeliner running through my veins.

Sue, hearing my news, excuses herself from a customer, and literally runs to my counter.

"Sue, you left a customer waiting!" I gasp.

"I know, but your first beauty school is a life-changing event and besides, she only wants information and said she's not buying today. So, listen up, Missy! First of all don't be late, or the trainer will lock you out. Second, raise your hand at every question and kiss their ass as much as you can. They'll say glowing things to your Account Executive and possibly give you extra free products. Three. See who the trainer adores and make friends with them. You only want to be with the winners! And four! Most importantly! Don't associate with any troublemakers, like the people who ask *Why is this product discontinued?* or *When are you coming to my store?* It will leave a black beauty mark that you'll never survive. Understand?"

Oh my God! So much beauty pressure that I just know a pre-beauty-school zit is coming!

After work that night, Tim, Richard, and I visit our favorite gay bar and several gin and tonics are soon running through my veins. I love The Odyssey because we can be openly gay without the threat of harm or harassment, although sometimes outside the club rednecks lurk, waiting to kick some gay ass. This night our friend Judy McGibony is out with her frat boyfriend Bryan, who's very tall, blond, built, and gorgeous—very much like Robert Redford in "The Way We Were." (You know, the 1970s movie starring

Barbara Streisand? If you don't, buy a box of kleenex and netflix it. Yep, Bryan is that fabulously sexy.) He's out with some of his new frat brothers as a dare. *"Dude, let's go to a gay bar!"*

I want nothing to do with them because it makes me think about those jerks at UNCG who would have burned me alive had they gotten their hands on me. I can be myself here at The Odyssey, and these guys are definitely not going to make me feel like I'm the freak. Tonight *they* are the freaks; they're on my turf. Tim and I are laughing with Judy when Bryan comes over and in his most condescending voice says, complete with limp wrist, "What are you girls talking about, your makeup?"

I instantly raise an eyebrow a' la Joan Crawford! "Bryan, we're talking about what a stud you are!"

Bryan actually blushes. "Whatever, man." He quickly walks back to his frat brothers at the bar.

"Don't worry, Judy, I'm not after your boyfriend; I just knew that crack would send him running back to his boys!"

It's beyond late and Tim and I are on the dance floor jumping around to Cyndi Lauper's

"Girls Just Want to Have Fun," when I see Bryan and the Brat Frat Pack staring at us. "Tim, what's wrong with these guys? I feel like we're in a gay zoo being stared at. Doesn't it remind you of UNCG?"

"Harvey, that nightmare is *over*, darling. Plus I think some of those boys want to come out of the closet, but are too afraid. Now stop worrying about it or you'll have premature wrinkles and need a face lift by the time you're twenty-five! Just keep dancing! It burns calories!"

As it gets close to last call, I look at Tim and sigh. "Cinderella's got to go, honey, because you know tomorrow is a historical day! My first day at beauty school!"

"Okay Helena Rubinstein, just one more cigarette and you can go."

As I put the cigarette to my lips, a hand appears in front of me with a lighter. As I look up, I see a blue-eyed stranger with the lighter saying, "Please, allow me." He's very tall and handsome in that Kennedy sort of way. As he's putting his lighter back in his pocket, I realize that he's one of Bryan's frat brothers.

I quickly say, "Thank you for the light. Tim. I'll see you and Richard at home."

As I'm walking to my car, I think *Blue eyes!* Yummy, but he's a straight jerk, isn't he? It's brat frat boy dare night and he's straight, right? He did light my cigarette. Is there such a thing as love at first cigarette lighting?

HARVEY'S DIARY
AUGUST 26, 1984
"Harvey Goes To Beauty School"

"In the factory we make cosmetics,
in the store we sell hope."
-CHARLES REVSON

"Good Morning! I'm leaving for work!" I hear Tim yelling at me through my bedroom door, but I just grumble and roll over. "Get your ass out of bed, queen, or you'll be late for your first beauty school!"

I sit straight up in bed and immediately remember Sue's four golden first-beauty-school-day rules! Quickly jolting out of bed all I can think is *Coffee first!* On the way to the kitchen I look in the bathroom mirror and spy two new zits. Oh God, not today! Well, I did have an omen about zits yesterday so I must be turning into a skincare psychic due to Sue's cosmetic wizardry! I do feel a bit hung over as well after dancing the night away.

After two cups of coffee and three cigarettes while standing in front of my closet trying to decide what to wear, I decide it's time to try to conceal these monster zits. Sue taught me to use a brush for a more natural look, so no big beige concealer lumps for Beauty school! On my third attempt to make this concealer look natural, I start to think about blue-eyes frat boy. *Who is he? Does he really like me or was it a frat house dare? Oh Harvey, stop thinking about him or you'll be late!*

While applying one more coat of mascara I'm startled by the phone. "Damn it! Mascara everywhere! I pick up the phone while trying erase this mess. "Hello Mother."

I drink four more cups of coffee and smoke what I'm sure was at least ten cigarettes while she spews her recent unpleasantness. "Harvey the Lord is cursing me because my children never do anything I say! Your sister Iris is smoking that marathon again, I just know she is because she gets that crazy dazed look in her eyes!"

"You mean Marijuana, Mother?"

"That's what I said, Harvey, so stop correcting me. Oh, you made me forget what I was saying!"

"Mother, you were talking about marathon."

"Oh… yes... I think your brother Gary is in jail again and I just don't know what to do. I've done everything possible to raise you kids right but—"

"Mother, today is my first day at beauty school and I can't be late!"

Grace quickly inserts: "Well, don't tell your father, because I've had just about all the problems today I can handle!"

Ugh. "I have to go, Mother. I'll call you later." If I had said *Mother, I have cancer and only have three months to live,"* she would probably have said, "Well, don't tell your father, because you know how he hates cancer." *Forget it.* Time for me to get dressed.

After trying on about ten ensembles, I decide on a conservative navy blazer with pin-striped Calvin Klein trousers which Sue suggested. I wish Tim and Richard were here so we could play fashion show! Meanwhile Boy George is blaring on the stereo.

"KARMA KARMA KARMA-KARMA KARMA CHAMELEOOON / WE COME AND GO / WE COME AND GOOOOOOOO."

I love Boy George because he got me through my UNCG nervous breakdown and now he's right here with me again on the first day of my first beauty school. Not to mention, his makeup is flawless!

As I look in the mirror I think *Very smart first day of beauty school ensemble. Professional yet artistic.* As I'm rushing trying to find my car keys the phone rings again.

Mother!? "Are you smoking, Mother?"

"Well, yes, if you must know… because I'm very upset and I didn't get to finish telling you everything, you had to get off the phone so quickly. I think your father is seeing another woman! Harvey, you know it's that woman from the 8th floor!" My mother smokes but doesn't inhale when she's mad at my father. She keeps a pack of Winston cigarettes in her top vanity drawer.

"Oh Mother! Daddy is not! Stop smoking and I'll call you later. God!" I hang up.

The thing is, I'm sure my father is having an affair with a woman named Louise. She actually called me to say that she was pregnant with Daddy's child. They met in the mental ward on the 8th floor of the mental hospital, hence my mother is always saying *that woman from the 8th floor*, where my father had to have shock treatments for depression. My daddy is an incredibly handsome depressed alcoholic. What a nice love-story right? Two forbidden lovers have their brains zapped and live happily ever after? I'm also sure that Iris is high and Gary's in jail.

I will never tell my mother any of this. She knows. But as with all candy-coated evil Southern belles, we just pretend that it doesn't exist in order to save our pride. In the South, some things are just better left unsaid and/or unconfirmed. Besides, if Grace admits to knowing, I'm afraid our family will end up on the 11o'clock news looking like white trash because my mother zapped my father and Louise with an electric cattle prod while they were screwing in my parents' bed. The camera will cut to my sister smoking "marathon" at some ghetto bail bond place trying to get money to help my brother get out of jail.

The only thing that's worse than this is every year the winner of the National Hog Hollering Contest, from Charlotte, North Carolina, gets broadcasted on the local news and on The Tonight Show with Johnny Carson. National Humiliation Contest is what they should call it. Tim, Richard, and I typically strike up a chorus of *"Oh No!" every time it happens.*

It's like that time the three of us went to see a Dionne Warwick concert at the Charlotte

Coliseum and she stopped the show because the popcorn man was being too noisy. North Carolinians love a snack! That popcorn man was just doing his job and Dionne stops singing and screams, "PEANUTS! POPCORN! COME'ON CHARLOTTE GET YER PEANUTS!" Tim, Richard and I were so embarrassed to be from the South right then. Of course, if I was the peanut man I would have just told her to "Walk on By". I felt so guilty buying my popcorn after that---but a queen needs a treat you know!

Where was I?

Completely flustered from my mother's call, I try to apply an extra layer of concealer to completely cover the blemishes. I'm nervous about venturing into downtown Charlotte this morning. I'm embarrassed to admit this but I've never even been downtown. My parents never took us anywhere but Myrtle Beach when we were growing up and I hate driving, so I'm terrible with directions. If you say left I will go right. Anyway, I have so much on my mind already, what with the adultery, pot, jail and triple zit concealing action!

You see where this is going. I'm late to my first beauty school. Sue's Rule # 1 is broken. I keep driving down the wrong streets and begin to sweat. I hate sweating. Every Southern beauty queen knows that sweat is the biggest villain in keeping your look fresh. Is my makeup separating? Oh my God! My white dress shirt is wrinkling. Oh my God, my life is over! After ten more cigarettes and a quick foundation touch-up, I finally arrive.

I walk through the lobby of the hotel. So big. Where do I go? A really cute bell-boy says "Can I help you with something? *Hmm?* I thought. Better be professional! After quick directions to the Promenade Room, I'm walking down the hall, nervous as hell. *Should I knock? Should I just go in? No. Knock. No. Go in. No...*

As I'm arguing in my mind, the door opens and there's a tall gorgeous man staring down at me. "Please come in. You're late."

A room full of women—fat, thin, tall, short, young, and old; every type is represented. They all have on a little too much makeup and their eyes are mesmerized by that sophisticated man in the front of the room, who just reprimanded me for my tardiness. He's dressed like an ad out of GQ magazine. Is that an Armani suit? Cufflinks! He's a vision.

"I'm Mark Cooper." He stops speaking and all the beauty queens turn and look at me expectantly. Mark Cooper reaches for a cigarette and lights it. He's silent. I immediately start blabbering: "My name is Harvey Helms and I'm from South Park Mall and sorry I'm late, but—"

"Please take a seat, Mr. Helms. In the future please remember that the training begins at 8 o'clock."

All the girls release a bout of coy giggling under their breaths. They're totally flirting with Mr. Gorgeous, the bitches.

I see one open chair and as I quickly take my seat I hear a whisper: "My name is Sherrill Webb."

"Harvey Helms," I reply automatically.

Mr. Cooper stops speaking and glares at us. Sherrill and I straighten up in our seats. Sherrill's a beautiful girl with short chestnut hair and well-placed highlights. She's wearing one of those expensive designer pant suits that are so popular for the professional woman today. Perhaps it's an Oscar? Ralph? Somebody chic! She whispers, "I work for Ultima II at Eastland Mall." Eastland is the #2 store for Belk's, just under my #1 store at South Park Mall.

"I'm at South Park."

"I know, I've heard about you."

"Sherrill, do you think we'll get some free products today?"

"I hope so!"

"What's for lunch? Will Mark validate our parking? I love your pant suit."

Mr. Cooper raises his voice. "Charles Revson, the creator of Revlon, named Ultima II after his yacht. It's the biggest in the world."

"Is that girl named Debbie still on Revlon Harvey?"

"Yes, do you know her?"

"Not really, but we're constantly having Revlon returns from her customers. I think they're afraid of her."

Sherrill and I start giggling and can't stop. It's like when you're in church and can't stop laughing. Mr. Miller is not amused. He has one of 70's mustaches that I can't stop staring at. Awkward.

At the break, Mark Cooper comes over to me. "So, Harvey, you're at South Park? Well, you're going to have to work diligently to get those sales numbers up because Miss Webb from Eastland has been beating you for the last three months. How long have you been on the line?"

"About three months," I begrudgingly say.

"Well I hope you pay attention today so that you can remain on the line. Look at Miss Webb. Doesn't she look like a cosmetic professional ready to be promoted? Harvey, cosmetics is all about *image*."

As he walks away, Sherrill approaches me. "Sherrill," I say sadly, "Mr. Miller says you are ready to be promoted and that I'm in desperate need of a makeover."

"Don't worry, Harvey, Mark doesn't like competition and you are the only other man here."

I'm sort of happy anyway, because I keep Sue's Rule #2, associating with the winners!

Mark brings us back to reality: "All right, girls, break is over. Oh, *girls and Harvey*. Now let's speak about the most important thing a woman can do for her skin. Who knows the answer?" Everyone's hand except mine goes up. "Miss Webb?"

"Use a sunblock every day!"

"Correct as always, Miss Webb. What product makes a woman most loyal to you and Ultima II?" All hands but mine are up once again. "Mr. Helms?"

I'm quickly trying to remember everything Sue has taught me. "Fragrance?" I respond reluctantly.

"Fragrance!? Who taught you that? No Mr. Helms, it's not fragrance. The correct answer is *foundation*. Please take good notes today since you need to get the sales at South Park up!"

I break Sue's Rule #3 about raising my hand at every question so I decide to sit in my chair with my mouth shut for the rest of the class. I was so excited about coming to this beauty school and now I wish that I could crawl under the table. I automatically break Sue's Rule #4 about associating with trouble makers because I guess I turned out to *be* the main trouble maker! Better stay close to Sherrill.

We're served dry chicken and vegetables for lunch, after which Mr. Miller takes us through Makeover 101. He demonstrates the cosmetic steps in a completely different manner than Sue taught me. I don't dare say a word. *"Always apply the eye makeup before the blush."* Sue taught me to build the skin tones first, including blush, before adding eye and lip color. I'm staying with Sue's method.

When the training's finished, Mr. Cooper says, "I wish you girls good luck in getting your sales up and making women more beautiful. That's especially true for you, Mr. Helms."

Before leaving I turn to Sherrill, my new best beauty friend other than Sue. "Let's stay in touch!"

"Absolutely, Harvey! It was great to meet you!"

As we're about to leave the room, Mr. Cooper hands each of us our school gratis in a white Ultima II bag with gold tissue paper. I lose my way again driving home which is the icing on the cake of my day. I'm so disappointed because school is supposed to be exciting and uplifting. Instead it is a total downer! (Except for meeting Sherrill of course!)

When I arrive home I immediately pick up the phone to debrief Sue about my first day of beauty school experience but her answering machine picks up instead. *"If you know who you're calling, don't leave a long boring message."* Beep.

"Hi Sue! Well I survived my first school and it wasn't great because I arrived late and the trainer hates me but I'll tell you more tomorrow. Oh and the beauty advisors at Eastland mall hate Debbie too! Bye! I love you!"

Where's Tim? I want a Long Island Ice Tea. Sifting through all the liquor bottles trying to figure out how to make one, I remember my gift from beauty school and open the bag, ripping the tissue away. *What the—?* A few of the products look like they've already been… USED? WHAT!!!! Mark Cooper gave me used products? I feel like calling Stephanie to tell her what happened but Sue magically appears in my mind.

It's funny, Sue's makeup always looks softer in my visions. *"Harvey, this is just like Debbie and Patti, so don't say anything and beat him at his own game."* That's what Sue would say. And Sue is right! Maybe I will grow a mustache! I pour myself a gin and tonic because obviously Tim is running late and I don't have the slightest idea how to concoct a Long Island Ice Tea. Better call Mother and see how many cigarettes she's smoked and if there's any news about love on the 8th floor.

HARVEY'S DIARY:
SEPTEMBER 15, 1984
"The Epilady Lady"

*"It's not what something's worth.
It's what people think it's worth."
-CALVIN KLEIN*

What had been new and horrifying has now become routine, even effortless. I arrive at work and check my makeover schedule for the day. Next, I see if any product has been returned and take it up with the advisor who took the return. Then step out in front of my display cases to make sure they are immaculate. Check my inventory to see what is out of stock. Evaluate whether I need to check with Stephanie for an order or call the dock to see if any shipments have arrived from Revlon's Edison New Jersey factory. Make follow-up phone calls to see how customers are enjoying their products and possibly get a phone order to meet my daily sales quotas. Set up my makeover station, placing brushes, alcohol to clean brushes, and cosmetic testers before use. (You don't want a customer coming back complaining she got a cold sore, pink eye, or herpes from any tester!) Clean my hand-held mirror to use during makeup instruction. Check my look from head to toe thoroughly in the mirror. Hair jacked up? Check. Skin matte? Check.

Then out in front of my counter with the special product of the day to entice women to my den of beauty. I sometimes spritz a fragrance in the air. You know the dreaded spritzer girls and boys that hunt you down to try their fragrance? Yes… I've become one of them… And we know it's annoying, but it works! I might be promoting a new color look, miracle moisturizer, self-tanning cream, cellulite-reducing gel, body exfoliator, or just myself doing fabulous before-and-after makeovers. We are all out in front of our counters competing with each other. But most importantly, I check with Sue about the latest store gossip or try to hear if any new cute guys have been hired in other departments!

Every now and then a vendor will come into the store to demonstrate a new product. Products that aren't an entire cosmetic line are placed on free-standing shelves near our cosmetic counters in the department. Products like Pantene, Vitabath, Claire Burke… you know, the room spray mainly sold at Christmas to make your house smell like a

Christmas trees or Grandma's homemade cinnamon apple cider? Ah, and also the new fragrance Krystal, named after Linda Evans character on the cult TV hit Dynasty.

The Epilady is one of those products and it's scarily close to my counter, so I have to help sell it. Connie comes up with Sue in tow saying, "Okay you two, the Epilady Lady is coming in to demonstrate and sell this new wonder product."

Sue and I grab the box and say in unison "THE EPILADY".

"Wow! Look, Harvey! It says *No more shaving. Absolutely painless hair removal guaranteed!*"

"Okay Connie, we'll be glad to help. Does it really work?"

Connie gives us her *Kiss my ass* look.

As we are talking, the Epilady Lady shows up. "Hi, ya'll! My name is Robin and I'm here to introduce the Belk customer to this miraculous new hair removal system. Where should I set up?"

"Right over here, honey. My name is Connie and I'm the cosmetic manager."

Under her breath, Sue murmurs, "She is the tallest, blondest, most Southern ex-beauty pageant contestant that I've ever seen, y'all."

"Sue, she's definitely candy-coated evil but she seems a little nervous." I call over to Robin: "Don't worry honey! We'll help you with anything you need. You pull them and we'll ring them through the register up for you."

Robin smiles as she's setting up her table. It's like she's an actress getting ready for her performance. "That is so nice of you, Sue and Harvey."

Robin makes sure that all is in order and then pulls out her pressed powder compact to check her lipstick. She rubs a little spinach off her teeth. One more *swoosh-poof* of that teased, ultra-bleached, beige-blond hair and the compact goes back into her pocket. She pops a tic-tac into her mouth and slowly starts to look around the department like a wolf seeking an innocent little bunny rabbit that she can sneak up on and grab for lunch. Robin's eyes are laser-locked on three women shopping together over in Misses dresses. In a blink of an eye, she lifts the Epilady and pushes the on button.

"Sue," I hiss, "the Epilady sounds like one of those electric carving knives you use on Thanksgiving!"

Robin begins to lift the Epilady up higher and higher.   Amazed, Sue provides more commentary. "She's raising up the Epilady like it's the baby Jesus in the Christmas pageant."

Finally, Robin seductively walks over to these three unsuspecting victims and in a mesmerizingly lazy Southern drawl says, "Good afternoon ladies. Would y'all be interested in never having to shave your legs again?!"

The three exchange nervous looks and giggles. *Never shave our legs again?! That can't be true? No more shaving?"*

Robin purrs, "All you need is *THE EPILADY*." Robin's voice becomes as light as a whisper. "It's painless and removes the hair instantly." These women lean in to hear Robin whisper and Sue and I hear them say *OOOOOHHHHHH!* We then see Robin grab one of them by the arm and say "What a lovely blouse. Can I use your arm to demonstrate Epilady's painless effectiveness?" Robin doesn't wait for the woman to agree. She quickly rolls that sleeve up and presses the Epilady into the woman's skin. For the next three hours, Sue and I see Robin repeat this process and it always ends up the same way. Screams, and then blood. Sue steps over to the table after each demo to remove the bloody tissue evidence.

We haven't sold one Epilady but we have gone through about five boxes of Kleenex! Connie finally comes over and looks at Sue and I. "I heard screaming."

Sue and I point at Robin. Connie sighs and rolls her eyes as she goes over and looks down at some of the bloody tissues from the last customer. "Robin, honey, I don't think the Epilady is right for the Belk's customer, so why don't you just head home early. Thank you so much for coming in today." Good! Sue and I have had enough of the Epilady. Thank God it's the end of our shift. As I'm packing up to leave for the day, the phone rings and Anorexic Blue Eyeshadow Debbie answers. "Belk cosmetics. Hang on. Harvey, it's for you."

"Who is it?"

She shoots her hideous blue eyeshadow eyes at me. "I'm not your secretary, but… it's a man."

I grab the phone. "This is Harvey, how can I help you?"

There is a brief silence and then a deep voice says "Hi Harvey. This is John. John from the other night."

What John from other night? I don't remember a John. "I'm sorry, I don't remember meeting you."

"Yes you do, I'm a friend of Judy and Bryan. I lit your cigarette before you left?"

Silence. "OOOHH, yes, I remember, Blue Eyes!"

"Harvey, I got your number from Judy and I hope you don't mind. I—well, this may sound strange, but—I want to go out on a date with you."

Longer silence. "You're asking me out, John? Is this another dare from Bryan trying to get back at me for being a smart-ass last night?"

John, very gently says, "No, Harvey. I think you're really cute and I guess I'm telling you I'm gay too. My frat brothers don't know."

"Oh. Well, John, if you're asking me out then I would say you're definitely gay. When do you want to go out?"

"I'll meet you at The Odyssey tonight? Around 9:30?"

A big gay sigh, and then: "Okay John. You don't mess around, do you? I'll see you there at 9:30 tonight. I hope this isn't a joke!"

At home I call Mother immediately to tell her to stay away from the Epilady, as well as any of her friends that want her to try it. I'm suddenly really afraid that she'll use it on my father!

Tim waltzes in and throws his bag on the counter. "Why are you smiling, queen?"

"Well, Tim, if you must know, John the frat boy with the gorgeous blue eyes, who lit my cigarette last night, asked me out!"

"What? Okay, that just cracks my face Harvey. Is he really gay?!"

Richard comes in and looks at both of us. "What are you two up to?"

Tim smacks Richard on the head. "It's not me. Harvey has been asked out by one of those quasi-gay frat boys from last night."

Richard looks skeptical. "Oh Lord, Harvey!"

"I have to get ready, you two! Tim, should I mask? No! Have a drink first? Maybe apply a deep hair conditioner? No! Smoke a cigarette!"

Tim snaps at me. "alm down, queen!"

"Oh and Tim, be ready to leave by 9:00 and have that Jet Grape hair jacked out to the high heavens! I need your support just in case this is another frat joke."

Now with gin and tonic in hand, while multi-tasking with face mask and deep hair conditioner, I'm wondering what to wear? I scream upstairs. "Tim, what should I wear? My Calvin Klein jeans and a pink IZOD knit shirt? Is preppy best on a first date with a frat boy? *TIM*?"

Tim screams back. "That's fine Liz Beth!" Liz Beth is his nickname for me when I'm prepped out in Ralph Lauren or IZOD.

"What shoes?"

"Queen, please. He's not going to care. He wears wrinkled clothes!"

Loafers with no socks. Very collegiate. I have to look good. I haven't been on a date ever. I'm nervous. Does he really like me? This is the time I need to call my mother and have her say, *He'll love you honey no matter what you have on. Is he good enough for you?* But I know I can't because it will never happen that way. Before leaving the house I spritz some Oscar De La Renta fragrance and re-spray my hair three more times. I must have re- powdered my face as many times too.

Tim finally screams, "Come on, it's time to go or you'll be late for Frat Boy!"

There's a line at The Odyssey to get in and the music is pulsing inside and people are dancing on the sidewalk. We are a little late because of me, and as I look around at the crowd I don't see John. Not that I would know exactly what he looks like. I know he's tall and has beautiful blue eyes. "Tim, do you see him? Do you think he'll stand me up?"

Tim is silent. Oh, I'm nervous. "Tim do I look okay?" Tim shoots me a look. "Tim!"

"You look fine, Harvey!"

"Tim, *fine* describes hair texture and expensive jewelry. What about my hair? Too big?"

Tim pushes me over to Richard. "Richard will you please do something with YOUR child?" Richard pats me on the back as we finally get to enter the club. "It's okay Harvey, he'll be here, don't worry. ""Tim and I head straight for the bar and in unison say, "Gin and tonic please! A double!" I start rocking because they're playing one of my favorite new Michael Jackson songs: *Billie Jean is not my lover, she's just a girl who says that I am the one! But the kid is not my son!*

Tim looks at me. "You better get it together, Blanche! Here he comes."

I take a quick gulp of my drink. "Are you sure? "

"Yes, queen, that's him!"

Without one word, or a *Hello*, or *Good evening*, John walks over and kisses me. I mean a real kiss. Before I have time to react or even enjoy my first real John kiss, I hear "That's sick, man. John, what the hell are you doing with these queers!"

I turn and see his frat brothers. I look at Tim before turning to John, absolutely horrified. But before I can speak, John pushes me behind him and says, "Sorry guys, I asked y'all to come tonight so that I could *come out*. I'm gay and I like Harvey."

What? I feel like we just walked in and it's *Kiss me then kill me*? I grab John by his long arms and pull him to face me. "John, you really like me?"

"Yes Harvey, I really like you."

Tim puts another drink in my hand and says "Heads up, honey, mean drunk frat boys at 3:00."

Oh, hell no! I made a vow to myself after UNCG that no one would ever treat me like this again. "Back off you straight assholes!" I bark.

Then Tim steps in front of me and adds, "Come on, boys! I will take off my shoe and beat the crap out of you! Who's first?" Tim can really do an incredible shoe beat-down!

The frat brats back up and start moving toward John, and I immediately fear for his safety. One guy screams, "John, we showered together, man! You've seen my dick!"

Tim raises his glass and says "Hmm!" I give Tim a look that says *Not now.*

I thought they were going to hurt John, but instead they turn their homophobic wrath on me. "It's your fault, you faggot! You made John a switch-hitter you queer!"

Are you kidding me? I push Tim to the side. "You can't make anybody gay, you simpletons!"

One of the frats is apparently confused. "Simpletons? What's that?"

The head frat boy shouts, "That's it, John! You're out of the fraternity! No faggots allowed! You're all sick and you'll burn in hell!" Another frat guy pleads, "Come on John! You're not gay, man! You're my frat brother!"

"Sorry guys. I am gay."

"We're out of here, you faggots!"

At this point I realize that the music has stopped and everyone in the bar has circled us. As John pulls me into him and kisses me deeply, the entire bar breaks out into applause and whistles. *"You go girl!"* Tim takes a gulp of his Long Island Ice Tea and says, "You just can't do anything without a little drama can you Liz Beth?"

I look up at John as he looks down at me with those big blue eyes and sexy smile. As I hear Marvin Gaye's song *Sexual Healing*, John pulls me to the dance floor and engulfs me in his arms just like in the movies. I've never felt this way. So this is what romance feels like? I want more. I'm in John's strong arms swaying to the music and as our bodies are pressed together I whisper into John's ear "The next time you almost get me killed will you give me a little advanced notice, please?"

He whispers "Yes my love," then he lightly kisses my neck.

I don't ever want this moment to end. I pull John's ear closer to my lips and whisper, "Have you ever heard of the Epilady?" John's smile somehow melts the day away.

HARVEY'S DIARY;
FEBUARY 13, 1985
"There's a new man in town"

"I survived because I was tougher than anybody else!"
-BETTE DAVIS

"Tim, John and I have been seeing each other for six months so do you think it's okay if we have sex? You know I'm not a slut! I've made him wait so long! Do you think I'm a slut? I love him."

"Wait, did you say *love,* Harvey?"

"Yes, I guess I did. Tim, I didn't know that love could feel this way. Is six months too soon? I don't care."

"Well if you have butterflies dancing in your stomach while you wait for his calls, maybe you are in love."

"Tim, you know it's a miracle that I can even begin to feel this way after watching my *Who's Afraid of Virginia Wolf* parents all these years. I've never seen my parents kiss or embrace; in fact, I've never even seen any semblance of love. I've only seen arguments and the aftermath of my mother in emotional shambles. I don't want my life or my relationships to turn out like theirs did."

"Slow down, Harvey!"

"Tim, my family is so dysfunctional and John's from a prominent family in Winston Salem where his father is the Match King. You can open any pack of matches and you'll see DD Beene and Sons, Winston Salem, North Carolina. Hey! Look at me, Tim! I'm the First Lady of Matches!"

"Harvey, I'm calling your mother. You're officially crazy. And, I can't believe you two haven't had sex yet! And what, may I ask your Highness, are you waiting for? An invitation from the Queen?"

"I don't know why, Tim, but I'm glad he's a gentleman and wants to take his time. I know he respects me and I'm looking forward to sex when the time is right."

"Look, Doris Day, you better not let Rock Hudson fall through your fingers just 'cause you're a prude!"

"I'm not a prude, Tim, but I must say good girls do wait until they're married."

"Well since you already live in the imaginary world of *"Harvey-land*, you better give him a good ride on the roller coaster, if you know what I mean!"

"Tim! I don't understand you! We'll continue this after work."

Tim leans in and kisses my cheek. "Okay Doris."

Hmm? No call from Mother today. That's interesting. I wonder if something's wrong. And then, I laugh out loud. *Of course something's wrong Harvey! There's always something wrong.* I'll call her tonight. Can't wait to tell her about John! Well, maybe not. It will be one more thing that she can't tell Daddy and selfishly I also want to keep John protected in my back pocket. I'm always afraid about anyone meeting my parents because I never know what will happen. No recent unpleasantness for me today! I want to remain Cinderella as long as I can!

As I drive to work, I notice that the season is turning to Spring. Winter just flew by and the trees are beginning to bud. The air has that crisp warm bite that signals that it's almost time to pack sweaters away for their summer hibernation! As I get out the car, I notice that the wind has picked up and storm clouds are forming. Walking into the employee entrance, Kevin the security guard, whom I've had a little boy crush on, says laughingly: "Hey Harvey, you've finally got some competition!"

"What? Oh Kevin, you just like all those pretty girls better than me!"

I clock in and go directly to my counter thinking about what Kevin just said. *Competition?* I put my bag into my personal drawer, and as I look up I notice that the department is completely empty. The evil Lauder girls, who never leave their counter, are nowhere to be seen. I sometimes think that they sleep here overnight so that they won't miss a sale. They don't pay any mind to us humble folks or think of those of us who've got smaller lines as competition. They're elitist. Estée Lauder is the Queen of the brands and these Lauder girls fiercely compete with each other because Estée has the most full-time and part-time beauty advisors in the department.

Twelve gorgeous cut-throat girls, to be exact. A grandmother of one of the girls passed away and Sue overheard another Lauder girl say *"She'll be out for at least a week so* we *can make more money."* No chance for that because the girl was back the next afternoon right after the funeral. Ruthless. If they don't meet their Night Repair Serum quotas, they get sacked. No exceptions. It's so heated sometimes that I feel sorry for the girls who think that working in cosmetics is just about being pretty. You have to sell and compete or you hit the pavement. Connie was right! The cosmetic department isn't for the faint of heart.

Just as I'm thinking about her, Connie comes walking up. "Where were you?" I'm blank. "You were supposed to be at our breakfast this morning to hear the announcements about changes in the department."

"I didn't know about the breakfast, Connie!"

"Harvey, Patti Garrison sent the invites out and—" Connie stops and looks up to the ceiling. I am about to ask a question when I see Patti Garrison walking towards us.

"Connie, I think something's wrong with Patti."

"Why is that," she asked.

"Because Connie, Patti is smiling."

Standing behind Connie is Anorexic Blue Eye-shadow Debbie and a man whom I've never seen before. This mystery man is heavy set with big—no, *really* big—dark hair sprayed into place like MGM's tap dancing star Anne Miller. His black eyes are heavily made up with an uppity expression of *Kiss my cosmetic ring, I've arrived."* Debbie has a *How the Grinch Stole Christmas* smile on her face, so I know trouble is brewing.

Patti says, almost singing, "Oh Harvey, I'm so glad you're here!"

Patti almost has her next word out of her mouth when Debbie blurts out, "Harvey, this is Alberto Scala and he's the new beauty advisor in our bay for Charles of the Ritz. He has much more cosmetic experience than you or I, and Charles of the Ritz will probably be taking your display cases soon with his incredible sales record."

Oh my God, the world is coming to an end! Debbie actually looked me right in the eyes for the first time! "Okay Debbie, so we have another beauty advisor working in our bay."

Debbie looks at Patti. "Sorry Patti, I couldn't help myself."

These two have such a strange dysfunctional relationship! Patti turns to me. "Sorry you missed our little celebration for Alberto this morning, because we are so excited to finally have a man in the department." Patti looks at Alberto lovingly. Finally happy to have a *MAN* in the department?

"Alberto *Sca-lah*"—Patti's attempt at an Italian accent is brutal—"Meet Harvey Helms."

Alberto stands there with that uppity look on his face as I stick my hand out, but he's not having that. Patti looks at Alberto. "Harvey is on Ultima II; you know, your competition?"

Alberto, arching one of his over-plucked eyebrows above his heavily made-up eyes, replies "Ultima II? From Revlon? That's not competition. Henry, just so you know, if I was an animal, I'd be a cat! Sleek, fast, and ahead of the the pack." I look at him and think, *More like a fat Italian tabby cat who drinks too much milk and somehow got into his owner's mascara.*

I automatically know deep down in my soul that Alberto's one of those crazy people you see sometimes wearing a black cape when it's not Halloween. "My name is *Harvey Helms,*" I say, correcting him as slowly as I can.

Patti claps her hands together. "Well, Alberto, we have things to do, beginning with your register training facilitated by yours truly! "

WHAT THE? Patti is all over him! My first day was like being marched to the firing squad and this fat overly-made-up cat gets a party and personal Patti register training? Connie looks at me and shrugs her shoulders. As they walk away, Alberto turns back to the entire department for a proclamation: "I hope I can bring some color, some glamour, to make this dull department the best ever. I love you all, Ladies!"

As they disappear up the escalator, I look at Connie with really big eyes. She just rolls hers back at me.

Where the hell is Sue? I need to go outside and smoke ten cigarettes just like Mother does when Daddy is out of control, but Connie stops me by grabbing my arm. "Wait Harvey, there's more news."

Debbie then pushes Connie out of the way and says, "Harvey, I know that this will not come as any surprise to you, since you've probably noticed that I've been gaining weight and have gotten to be as big as a house, but I'm six months pregnant and will be taking my maternity leave starting today. "

"WHAT!? Debbie, you're pregnant?"

Connie places her index finger on my chin to close my mouth that has obviously dropped to the floor. Six months pregnant? She's so anorexic that I guess she doesn't have to hide it. I wonder which trucker has knocked her up. And for that matter, how will she make room in her trailer for the baby?

Thank God, Sue pops up from nowhere with a huge fake smile on her face. "Sue, there's a new man on Charles of the Ritz who thinks he's a cat and Debbie here is six months pregnant and leaving soon to have her baby."

"I know, Harvey. Debbie, here's a little parting gift. When I heard about your good news at the breakfast, I felt bad because we didn't have a gift for you."

Okay, now Sue is acting like she's from another planet. *Can this day get any weirder?* With Debbie leaving and Alberto entering, I momentarily think that tensions in our bay are going to go from bad to worse. I do have a revelation about Patti though. Maybe it's not the presence of a man in the department that she despises; maybe it's just the fact that I was forced on her by Gretchen Thomas and Stephanie. Is this her sick way of getting back at me choosing Alberto Scala as her vengeance?

If I could've seen a crystal ball at this moment, I probably would've had the same notion that Glenda the Good Witch in the Wizard of Oz bestowed to Dorothy after she sees the Wicked Witch of the West for the first time in all her blaze of glory. Dorothy says to Glenda, *I thought you said she was dead?* Glenda looks back and says *That was her sister, the Wicked Witch of the East, this is the Wicked Witch of the West, and she's worse than the other one was.* I definitely feel like I'm trading one witch for another.

We all stand there just staring at each other. Sue winks at me as Debbie looks at her gift and begins to unwrap it. As she pulls off the last of the paper Debbie coos "The Epilady! Pain-Free Hair Removal System. Thank you, Sue." Connie starts choking uncontrollably and as I pat her on her back, Sue and I smile at each other and chant "THE EPILADY!"

*"Love is a fire. But whether it's going to
warm your hearth,
or burn your house down, you can never
tell."*
-JOAN CRAWFORD

"Richard, I know it's still cool for April—but a fire?"

"Harvey, you know how I love having a fire lit whenever we can because it just makes everything so homey!"

"Okay *Grandma*, I'll watch it, but keeping the fire lit can't be that hard!"

"You need to be careful, Harvey, because you know how accident-prone you tend to be."

"I'll ignore that comment, Dick!"

"Harvey, I only let my mother call me that! I'll be back after picking up Tim from work in about thirty minutes."

I light a cigarette and stare at the waning fire, thinking about my relationship with John. It's been so magical… up until last week, when John took a trip to see his brother in Los Angeles. He didn't call me at all while he was out there, and all of the sudden he's back in Charlotte singing Madonna's new hit song *Borderline* and looking tan, having used Clarin's Self-Tanning Milk. *Tanning Milk?! John just came out, how could he already know about Tanning Milk? He's only been gay for two minutes!* He has Hollywood in his eyes and I have fear in mine.

As I'm staring into the fire, imagining all those gay Hollywood temptresses putting their hands all over my John, I realize that the fire's starting to die down, so I put a stack of newspapers on the top of the wood and it fires up immediately. *See, Richard! It's not that hard.* The lit newspaper slowly begins to levitate because of the wind and all of the sudden it disappears up the chimney. My brain goes into panic mode. *Harvey, the freshly fire lit newspaper is going out of the top of the chimney onto the roof!.* PANIC MODE! *It's got to be on the roof! Where else could it go?*

I run outside and yes, it's definitely burning on the roof!

Think Harvey! A bucket! I run back in the house, grab a bucket, fill it with water and run back out to throw it on the burning roof. Up the water goes, then down all over me*! Shit! The* *ladder!* I run to the back and see that a huge spider is on the ladder! *Spider? Yikes!* I look and spy the water hose. *Harvey, why didn't you think about the hose in the first place? You're so crazy!*

As I pull the hose to the front and start watering the roof, Rebecca the crazy Belle from upstairs comes down in her Laura Ashley robe. "After you're done watering the roof, Harvey, can you give me a manicure?"

"Can't you see that I'm busy, Rebecca?" Having extinguished the fire, I go back in the house soaking wet, sit down, and light a cigarette. As Tim and Richard walk in, Rebecca follows them from behind, pushing our front door wide open. "Harvey, since you're done watering the roof..."

"Rebecca, there will be no manicures this evening!"

Tim and Richard burst out laughing. Richard says "So, keeping the fire lit is easy, huh? Harvey, the roof is fire proof."

"Okay Richard, I'm over it! Stop laughing! I need to talk to you two about John! Stop laughing, Tim! Never mind you queens!"

Back in my room, I call my mother, crying about John. She whines right back. "I don't know why you want a man, Harvey, they're never faithful. Just look at your father with that woman from the 8th floor."

"Mother!"

"Harvey, why can't you stay single and go back to the Baptist church? I'd love to tell your father that you're going back to church! Are you still singing about Jesus like you were a few months ago?"

"All right Mother! Let's have it your way like we always do. I'll call Tammy Faye as soon as I get off the phone with you! Satisfied?"

My mother did what she always does when I get fresh with her. First the big Southern belle dissatisfied sigh. Then let the guilt trip begin. "Well, that's all right, Harvey. I won't bother you ever again."

"Mother, don't hang up!"

Of course she does. I'll give it about an hour and call her to apologize. I walk back out to make a gin and tonic, and Tim starts laughing all over again. "Shut up, Tim!"

"You were watering the roof, Harvey?" He can't stop laughing.

Back in my room with gin and tonic in hand, I try my mother again. She answers the phone with the most manufactured, sickeningly sweet "*Hello*" you've ever heard. I swear when she's mad at me her hello has six syllables. "Why Harvey, I wasn't expecting to hear from you again this evening."

Exhausting! "Mother, I'm sorry for hurting your feelings. I have a lot going on right now, that's all. Call me tomorrow morning." One day I just want to say to my mother *Can't you just listen and support me in the things that make me happy? I love John. Don't I deserve love, damn it*!? Grace would never hear it. Anyway, John is making me nervous and I'm worried that he met someone in LA. Then the most horrible thought appeared. *Am I turning into my mother?*

I grab hold of myself. *Don't think about it anymore. Go to sleep and forget it.* No use. I can't sleep, so I start obsessing about my other problems. On the cosmetics front, it's been a few months since Anorexic Blue Eye-shadow Debbie left to have her baby, but we eventually threw her a baby shower/farewell party in the break room right before she left. With all those beauty queens in that small break room, you could smell so many fragrances that it was like a whorehouse with really bad lighting, complete with vending machines.

Now normally, you'd hear all these Southern belles just drooling over each baby gift, saying things like *Isn't that the most precious thing you've*

ever seen? and *That's just made for a little Angel!*
Sue and I sat in the back so we could see every
minute of this ridiculous circus. As Debbie
continued opening gifts, they kept turning out to
be the same thing. Disposable diapers. It was a
little awkward by the tenth gift. A few times
Debbie did open boxes of baby formula, and Sue
blurted out "Thank God! At least the baby will get
to eat!" Connie stood up at the end and handed
Debbie an envelope with some money she'd
collected and said, "I guess a new mother can't
have enough disposable diapers."

Right. 28 boxes of them, to be exact.

After the party, we all walked back to our
respective counters wondering what would happen
to Debbie. I want to know who will take her place
on the Revlon counter. But more importantly,
who's going to help me with the new cat? Oddly
enough, Alberto Scala is standing in our bay at his
end where Charles of the Ritz is located. Sue and I
stand there and look at each other.

"It's okay Sue. He's just going to ignore me
just like Debbie did."

"Maybe not, Harvey. Here he comes."

"Harvey, is it?" Before I can speak, he
continues: "I like my coffee with cream and one
Sweet-N-Low, please." Again before I can speak,

he returns to his end of the bay and starts examining his eye makeup in the mirror.

Sue nudges me. "I'll take a Diet coke!" I smack her arm. "Don't worry, Harvey, except for the old ladies who buy Revenessence from Charles of the Ritz, Alberto won't be doing much business."

Debbie comes back to the counter to double-check if she's left anything behind. She opens three drawers but there's nothing left. She looks at me and Sue with an emotionless expression and in true Anorexic Blue Eye-shadow Debbie fashion, she exits right past us without saying a word. Not one word. I do give her points for not displaying any fake emotions. No candy-coated evil, but I guess I expect something from her. One last insult? Funny; for a second, I think I might miss her. Go figure.

Revlon is removed from the bay the day after she leaves. The end of an era. Anorexic Blue Eye-shadow Debbie is finally gone, and I think I can sleep now.

HARVEY'S DIARY:
JUNE 5, 1985
"The Witch from Black Mountain"

"The most beautiful makeup of a woman is passion.
But cosmetics are easier to buy."
-YVES SAINT LAURENT

It's been a few months since Debbie exited stage left—and the new Diva on Charles of the Ritz settling in and not living up to the initial hype from Patti Garrison. With things settling down a bit, I'm now focusing on developing a bigger name for myself. I never see Patti Garrison anymore, which is another miracle of Debbie's exit. My business is growing every month and I have a larger customer following, thanks to Sue. Women come into the store requesting "Mr. Harvey at Ultima II."

Even those above-it-all Lauder girls are frequently sending over to me the difficult makeovers, like the women scarred with severe acne, burns, and birthmarks. They also send a few crazies whom they don't want to deal with. Actually more than a few. At least one or two a week. I adore the crazy women because their lunacy makes the day pass faster and gives me great material for fun cocktail conversation.

Today, a super nut comes up to the counter and just stands there staring. Not at me; just staring into space. She's beyond pale, with hair all the way down to the floor in sort of an ashy chlorine-bleached blonde shade. This woman is a little extra scary because after observing her for a few minutes, I notice that she doesn't blink. Mother always says *People who don't blink are crazy.* (And of course you know she added, *Just like that woman your father met on the 8th floor. She never blinks either!*) This quasi Crystal Gale look-alike also has these teeth that are crooked and an interesting shade of yellow I haven't seen before.

She finally stops staring into space and opens her mouth to speak. "A medicine man whom I met on the top of Black Mountain had a vision and told me that I needed to come here and get a makeover cause I'm going to be a famous model. He said he could tell by the whites of my eyes that I will be famous!" She then places her hand on her heart. "I swear that since I met him, they keep getting whiter every day."

"Wait here a minute, Honey," I tell her. "I'll be right back." I walk over to Clinique where Sue is doing a product inventory. "Sue. Don't ask any questions, just come with me."

Back at my counter, this woman repeats to Sue everything she'd said to me, repeating the same dramatic gesture of hand on heart. After a few seconds, Sue takes the woman by her hands, looks her straight in the face, and says, "Normally when the medicine man from Black Mountain sends girls in here with the whites of their eyes as white as yours, he wants them to go to Elizabeth Arden cosmetics. It's right over there, sweetie. Good luck with your modeling career!"

I look at Sue, then glance over to the Arden counter. Our future crazy model is telling Jean the glamazon what she's told us. Jean looks at her like she's crazy and says something back to her. The woman turns from Jean and points at me and Sue. Jean glares at us as we start to laugh at her.

"Harvey, that will set Miss Jean straight; last week she sent me this picky, depressed woman with *beyond bad* breath, who didn't leave my counter for two hours and only bought one thing." Sue turns and smiles at Jean, muttering under her breath, "Don't screw with a Clinique girl, you Elizabeth Arden Bitch." Then she spots someone quite different. "Is that your Account Executive Stephanie?"

"Where?"

"She's right over there looking at the Lancôme bay. Who's that she's with?"

"I don't know, but he's as gorgeous as Superman's Clark Kent!"

"Harv, looks like you have a surprise store visit. He's probably someone from Ultima II. Corporate loves to surprise us to see if we're working, chewing gum, blabbing to our boyfriends on the phone, or just sitting around reading magazines. Look busy! Quick! Grab the Windex and look like you're cleaning! They love that! Find me later."

The two of them walk up and Stephanie says, "Hi Harvey! How are you? I love that you keep everything so clean!" Air kisses on the cheek. "Harvey, meet Rick Jordan. My boss and Regional Manager."

Six foot four and the spitting image of Clark Kent wearing these incredibly sexy horn-rimmed glasses and has a voice as deep and sexy as the singer Barry White. "Hello, Harvey. Your color case looks exceptional! Congratulations on your sales increases. I live in Atlanta Georgia but I've wanted to meet you for a few months. How are you liking Ultima II?"

"I love it here, Rick!" I must look like a fool; as he walks around looking at my merchandising, all I can do is stand there with big eyes saying *Yes Rick! Yes Rick! Total beauty orgasm!*

"Harvey, you keep this business growing and you'll have quite a career at Ultima II."

Stephanie winks at me as I shake Rick's hand. She gives me another air kiss. "We're off to Eastland Mall to see your sister Sherrill Webb! I'll call you later, Harvey."

As Stephanie and Clark Kent leave, Sue comes running up with about eight women behind her. The women are asking: "So, is Mr. Gorgeous with Ultima II?"

"He's *my* Regional Manager," I sneer, "so back off you beauty bitches! He's mine! Or, at least he's my Regional Manager! Rick Jordan!"

They sigh in unison and walk away. Sue laughs. "I know two of those girls will be renaming their vibrators *Rick Jordan* tonight."

"Sue, the visit went so quick!"

"Well Corporate normally doesn't stay long 'cause it cuts into their cocktail time!"

"Sue, Rick told me that if I keep growing the business, I'd have quite a career! What do you think?"

"Harv, the biggest compliment I can give is that I have nothing left to teach you. Now that you've graduated from AB&F, you're definitely ready for what's next. But being promoted up from behind the counter can take quite a while, unless someone high up in the New York headquarters notices you. Mr. Gorgeous may help you, but let's face it, Harvey. We live in Charlotte, North Carolina, and New Yorkers think we're hicks. We're probably screwed. Sorry, Honey."

Later that day I walk in through the door at home and throw my bag on the kitchen counter. Tim's laser-focused in some cookbook, whispering to himself "*Onions, mushrooms, and celery.*" He looks up from the book and quips, "Okay. What's wrong with you?"

I slide onto one of the bar stools. "Nothing."

"What's wrong with you, queen? And don't say *nothing* because everyone has stepped on my last nerve today and I'm not in the mood for *100 Gay Questions*. Tell me or I won't make you a Long Island Ice Tea. Is it John?"

"No."

"Is it Patti?"

"No."

"Is it the man who thinks he's a cat?"

"No. Tim? Do you think we're going to live in Charlotte for the rest of our lives?"

The doorbell rings and Tim rolls his eyes. "Wait here." He opens the front door and standing there are two young, clean-cut guys dressed like Mormons. "Hello Sir. Can we come in and tell you about Jesus today? Don't worry because Jesus loves black people too."

Tim puts his hand on his hips and screams "*What?*"

I run over to the door. "Sorry boys, we got some Jesus from two other guys yesterday!" I slam the door quickly so that Tim won't be put in jail for killing children. "Tim, make us a drink and I'll tell you what's wrong."

Tim starts pulling out the liquor bottles, cussing about religion under his breath. "Tim, I just don't think we're ever going to get out of the South. I don't... "

Richard comes walking in saying, "I just ran into the cutest boys selling Jesus. I almost asked them in." Tim yells "*That's it*" and he stomps to their bedroom and slams the door.

Richard is dumbfounded. "What did I do?"

I start to cry and bellow out "*Nothing*, Richard! It's just that we're going to be stuck here in Charlotte forever, that's all! FOREVER!" I run to my room and fall on the bed. After a good long cry I decide I should mask my pores but then don't because I'm too depressed. Even beauty won't help me tonight. No messages from John for weeks. Where the hell is he? Damn that tanning milk! Even beauty products are working against me!

"Men are like mascara. They run at the slightest display of emotion."
-KABLIR BEDI

It's another *I'm going be stuck in this redneck town for the rest of my life* Wednesday and I'm down on my knees cleaning my skincare cases, when the phone rings. I start to get up but I hear "The Cat" running to answer the phone. Alberto loves to answer the phone. His boyfriend Jack, who sounds exactly like Mickey Mouse, calls the counter every two hours. Alberto sickeningly answers the phone: "Belk Cosmetics! Most Expert makeup Specialist Alberto Scala. Can I help you be more beautiful today? Oh. Harvey, it's for you," whereupon he drops the phone on the counter. "It's a man. He says he's the President of Ultima II."

" Alberto this has to be Sue playing a joke!"

Alberto rolls his eyes and returns to sticking his face in the mirror again. I make my usual *kiss my ass* face at him and put the receiver to my ear.

"Hello, this is Harvey Helms. How may I help you?"

"Harvey, this is Stanley Noland, President of Ultima II."

"Really? Is Sue there with you?"

"Sue?" At that moment I see Sue with a customer at her counter. Clearing my throat, I quickly blurt out, "I'm sorry Mr. Noland, go ahead…"

"Harvey. I spoke with Rick Jordan and I wanted to call and congratulate you on your spectacular business results! It's just incredible what you've accomplished. Ultima II is the #2 brand just under Estée Lauder in your store! I've always known that Belk South Park had huge potential if we could find the right beauty advisor. Listen Harvey, we want to keep the sales increasing by sending you our National Director of Beauty Michael Cope. "

"What's a Director of Beauty? I mean what does he do?"

"Michael Cope will fly in from California and orchestrate a beautiful makeup event in your store. He'll do the makeup consultations for you but you have to book the appointments."

"He'll do my makeovers for me, Mr. Noland?'

"Yes!"

I thought for a second. This man thinks somebody needs to do *MY* makeovers for me! "No thank you, Mr. Noland, I can do my own makeovers, but thanks for calling." I hang up. *The nerve of this Stanley Noland! He thinks that I'm not capable of doing more makeovers to increase my business? After all I've done?* I'm not just a beauty junkie in training, I'm also a drama princess practicing to be queen. I go back to my skincare case and start to squirt Windex like crazy.

The phone rings again and Alberto looks at me with his evil arched brow but makes no attempt to answer this time. He stands by the phone filing his nails sarcastically cooing, "Aren't you going to get it Harvey? I'm busy."

"Fine. You know what you can do with that nail file—Good afternoon, Belk Cosmetics."

"Harvey, please don't hang up on me. I think you misunderstood. This is a huge reward for you as only a very select group of Stores get the Director of Beauty. Michael is famous and he's done television. He lives in Hollywood—" *Blah Blah Blah. Name drop name drop name drop—* "Stephanie and Rick will be calling you with the dates and all the details. This is a big deal! Boy, you have moxie. I'll look forward to meeting you

in person but until then keep up the good work!"
Click. He hung up on me before I could.

The phone rings again. After I pick it up I hear a voice like Mickey Mouse. "May I speak with Alberto please?"

I hand Alberto the phone. "It's for you. I think it's someone from Walt Disney."

Back to Windexing and thinking that the good news is that Rick Jordan spoke to the President of Ultima II in New York! *Director of Beauty? What kind of title is that?* I just can't let it go. *He's going to do my makeovers? Well let's just see how many he can do.* Alberto, who's plucking his already over-plucked eyebrows says, "What are you up too Harvey?"

"Oh. nothing. I just need to get on the phone and book a few appointments."

Two weeks later, Stephanie eventually calls with all the event details that begin today. Michael Cope likes mineral water at his makeup station, and the Belk Visual team is building a large special event area on a stage for Michael's appearance. Connie has been by the counter for the last month asking, "How many appointments have you booked? Garrison is up my ass!" A full page ad, with Mr. Cope's headshot, announcing his arrival and appointment times for makeovers by this maestro, ran in *The Charlotte Observer* last week.

Sue seems skeptical. "The makeup Guru arrives today? Well. Harvey, you may not be stuck here forever after all. What's wrong with the Cat on Charles of the Ritz? I haven't seen him move from his end of the cosmetic bay and he just keeps pacing back and forth."

I whisper to Sue, "He's not living up to the initial Patti press and his sales are down. Connie is over here every morning asking about his numbers."

"Hey Harv, don't turn too quickly but the frat boy with blue eyes who's been missing in action for weeks has resurfaced."

"John?"

"You got it, baby face. Good luck."

I check my face in the mirror and slowly walk over.

"Hey baby," he says quietly.

Hey baby? Has LA ruined my perfect gentleman?

"This is Barrett Klutz, you know, he's one of my ex-frat brothers."

"Yeah, I think I remember him from the night you came out. Hi,Barrett."

"Listen Harvey, I've been really busy with school and hanging out so I haven't had any time to call since I got back from LA."

Hanging out? I see. "It's been a few weeks John and I've been worried. Not even a call?"

John looks at Barrett." Tell you what, Harvey, let's meet at The Odyssey on Saturday night. Like 9:30? We can talk then."

"Oh. Okay John. I guess I'll see you guys Saturday night. I have to get back to work 'cause my big event starts in an hour." No goodbyes as I watch John walk away, *Saturday night huh? Is it over?* I have a big knot in my throat and feel sick to my stomach.

Connie frantically comes rushing up. "Are you ready?"

"I have one hundred booked appointments ! So Connie, for the next three days, the Director of Beauty will have to do five women an hour, and about 40 women a day. No bathroom time for the King of makeup! Let the games begin! Let him direct my beauty! Hah!"

Connie says. "Well don't kill the poor boy. You know, Harvey, you've changed since that first day back in my office where you weren't sure about staying in cosmetics. Congratulations. Having the Director of Beauty here means you've arrived, my dear. I'm proud of you." She looked at me puzzled. "Are you ok? You look sad."

"Connie, I'll be alright. Will you do me a favor though and double check to make sure his makeup table is perfect and put out the little snacks for our customers?"

"Sure. Harvey, remember that you're young and there are a lot fish in the ocean."

"Yeah, and you don't have time for fishing right now Missy so get it together!" "Sue!"

"Calm down Liberace! Everything will be ok."

"Oh really? John and I won't be. I have this feeling that he's breaking up with me Saturday night."

"Harvey! Put that out of your mind and focus on your career! Where is Michael Cope? Your first appointment will be here in 30 minutes. How big is his entourage?"

"I don't know! Do you think he's going to boss me around? *HARVEY! Bring me my big powder brush immediately! I said Aurora Beige not Tuscan Beige you idiot! Are you color blind?*"

"God. Harvey. You are such a drama queen. Oops, Clinique customer waiting! Gotta go!"

I am staring into space just imagining the worst when I hear: "Hello. I'm Michael Cope. Are you Harvey? I've heard so many wonderful things about you. Rick Jordan said I'd better be careful or you'd be taking my job!"

Michael is a beautiful blond with a handsome face like Fred Astaire. I look past him indifferently. "Where's your entourage?"

Michael starts laughing. "Entourage? It's just me!"

Alberto comes from out of nowhere, wearing his black cape and a black hat with one big fuchsia feather, pushing me out of the way, sticking his hand in Michael Cope's face. "It's such a pleasure to meet you. We must know many of the same people since we are stars in our industry. We must compare notes later! It's so nice that you could come and help our little Harvey get his sales up!"

I took a breadth and said. "Michael Cope, meet Alberto Scala. He represents Charles of the Ritz."

The Director of Beauty was so gracious with that neurotic cat. At that moment the first appointment showed and we were off to the races. All my appointments showed that day and they purchased every product that Michael used in his makeover. After the first day I was in love. Exhausted but in love. My very first beauty crush.

We spent three days together working side by side. Between looking at him with goo-goo eyes and thinking about making John jealous so that he would desperately want to defend my honor, I picked up more makeup techniques that I passed along to Sue. She was totally impressed! Michael did every makeover without complaint, and they were not only beautiful, but personally tailored to each woman. No assembly line of beauty here. We sold the most Ultima II in the history of the store and I actually ran out of most of my inventory.

I couldn't stop crying when Michael left the store, and in perfect Sue fashion, she came to my counter saying "Get over it! Stop crying, Tammy Faye, or your mascara will run!"

"But Sue, he kissed me on the cheek and said *Harvey you won't be working behind the counter for much longer because you are fabulous!*"

"Honey, he probably says that to every beauty advisor he works with and besides, you know that cosmetics industry is the closest thing to Hollywood. So you better toughen up, Bette Davis!"

Toughen up? Crying in the car on the way home, Peaches and Herb's big hit *"Reunited"* comes on the radio and I decide this will be our song. I dry my tears, content to just think. *"I miss him so much and it's only been thirty minutes. How will I live without him? How will I go on? How will I get his job?"* As I pull into the Farrington's, I sit in the car and think about John. Meet him at The Odyssey 9:30 Saturday night? Well at least he's still sort of a gentleman giving me three days' notice to figure out what to wear when I get my heart broken by an ex-frat boy.

"I taught the high society ladies in America
to wash their faces.
There is no skin like Laszlo skin."
-DR. ERNO LASZLO

Time for a little beauty break. Sometimes in life when there's too much drama, I like to take a refreshing little beauty break. It might be applying a favorite masque, a firming serum, an exfoliating salt scrub, or, if really traumatic, a little L'Oreal Preference for a quick hair color change. *Because I'm worth it,* you know. I've been known to tell friends: *If life isn't going your way, it's probably because you're not using enough beauty products. Adding the right firming eye cream to your regimen can change your life!* As a beauty junkie, I discovered a skincare line that will always be a mainstay in my beauty regimen. Ladies and Gentlemen, may I be the first to introduce you to the one and only, Erno Laszlo.

Erno Laszlo was a Hungarian Dermatologist who made his way to the USA and became the beauty specialist of his day to the Hollywood elite, including Joan Crawford and Jackie O. Even the suicide photos of Marilyn Monroe's night stand have a jar of Laszlo Phelityl Cream. Now that's loyalty! You either performed Dr. Laszlo's cleansing ritual as he prescribed or you were excommunicated. Actress Ava Gardner asked the doctor. *How can you tell I'm not following your prescription?* He glaringly replied, *Madame, your skin betrays you!* You couldn't just buy Erno Laszlo skin treatments in those days, you had to be a member of a special purchasing club and everything.

Now you're probably thinking, *Harvey, you sell Ultima II. Why would you use a competitor's products?* Good question. First, I'm a junkie and always looking for newer, better, more delicious, life-transforming products to make me more attractive. Second, I'm very oily and extremely prone to blemishes. What is finally going to clear my complexion?

At South Park Mall, just a few stores down from Belk's, there's a very small, chic specialty store called Montaldo's. Isn't that a great name? Always makes me want to throw a cashmere sweater over my shoulders and spray on some Hermès Eau d'Orange Verte. My sister Cathy purchased her Estée Lauder Youth Dew and

Weejun loafers at Montaldo's. One day on my break, I am passing by and do a double take. They have cosmetics! Now I'd heard that they sell products that you could only get in New York or Paris. I've always been shy about going in, but of course this day I just couldn't resist.

The cosmetic department is located in the front of the store and in the center of the department is a brand that I've never seen before. Standing behind the counter is a mysterious redhead, with her hair cut exquisitely into a 1920's bob, and perfect makeup covering the most glorious skin I've ever seen. As I approach the counter she hypnotically purrs, "Good Afternoon. Are you a current member of Erno Laszlo?"

I reluctantly say, "No, I'm not."

"My name is Linda. Please let me welcome you to Erno Laszlo and a lifetime of beautiful skin."

"My name is Harvey." I can feel Linda casting a special beauty spell over me.

"Please have a seat Harvey. From this moment on, after purchasing your prescribed skincare regimen, I will be your personal Laszlo consultant. You will be asked to present your membership card with every purchase. Before we begin I must advise you to NEVER add or mix any other products with your Laszlo Ritual." She took a dramatic pause and sat down at her special consultation desk full of fabulous black and white marbleized bottles and jars. "First, I will clock you. Your time on the clock indicates how dry or oily your complexion is."

After a few questions and examination of my skin under a magnifying mirror, Linda announced, "Your complexion is set at 3:00. Extremely oily. Harvey, for the rest if your life you will perform your Laszlo Ritual twice a day with midday touch-ups. You must always do what I'm getting ready to show you without fail because it's the only way to achieve the perfect Laszlo complexion. If you have any doubts, any misgivings whatsoever, you cannot become a member of Erno Laszlo Institute."

Sitting silent with big eyes, there's no way I can say no to her or to the dream of the perfect Laszlo complexion. Linda motions me to follow her to her special cleansing sink. "Now Harvey, pay close attention! You must do this exactly as I demonstrate it." She conjures up some Cleopatra trance and channels the following:

1. Turn on the faucet and fill the basin with hot water that is comfortable to the touch.

2. Take your prescribed Special Skin soap and dip it into the water creating a soapy lather. Next, take the moistened soap and rub it into your skin. Begin with your T-Zone, following with cheeks, forehead, and throat.

3. Massage your skin for at least 30 seconds using your hands in circular upwards motions.

4. Splash your skin 20 times with the hot soapy water.

5. Allow sink to drain while turning back on the faucet with hot water and again splash your skin 10 more times with the clear hot water.

6. While your skin is still warm and moist, apply Conditioning Preparation oily skin toner with high amounts of Resourcinol to control oil and kill bacteria, avoiding your eyes and lips.

7. Shake and apply Regular Normalizer Shake It, tinted treatment finisher. A.M. only.

8. Buff with tissue to remove any residue.

Set with Controlling Powder in medium for extra oil control. AM only.

9. Lightly, with your ring finger (this finger is more gentle) pat Phelityl Eye Cream, avoiding your lash line.

10. At night, apply Heavy Controlling Lotion in place of Regular Normalizer Shake It for oil control while you sleep.

"Now Harvey, you're going to complete this regimen in front of me so that I can make sure you execute this ritual properly."

I'm so nervous! It's like a mystical ritual with incredible new smells and feelings. After I finish, I'm totally soaking wet from the splashing but then I look in the mirror and I'm truly shocked. I've never felt this clean, matte, smooth, or this glamorous. Linda looked at me with pride. "Harvey, your ritual is complete. Be aware though, you will see major changes in your complexion over the months to come, and you may experience some breakout due to the state of your pores today."

I leave the store with freshly glowing skin, bags of products, and an optimism I haven't felt in a very long time. This will always be my dirty little beauty secret while I'm selling other brands. I can't even tell Sue that I'm now officially a true beauty insider, a card-carrying member of the Erno Laszlo Institute. *Thank You Dr. Laszlo. Now I know why they call you "The Angel of Beauty."*

***"Before I put another notch in my lipstick
case, you
better make sure you put me in my place!
Hit me with your best shot!
-PAT BENATAR***

I wake up late, hung over and remembering that John didn't show up. 9:30? No John. 11:00? No John. 1:30? After countless gin and tonics, I barely remember anything else from last night except the feeling of abandonment. I hate it when I get that empty feeling in my stomach. I don't want to go to work today because I feel sick and my heart's broken. I did let myself think for a minute that John was in a terrible accident and knocked unconscious on his way to The Odyssey. *But abandoned or not, Harvey Helms, you have to get up.*

I crawled out of my room and slumped onto a bar stool. "Tim, you really don't believe John was in an accident, do you?"

"Krystal Carrington, do you think Blake was in an accident? Don't make me go all Alexis Carrington Colby on your ass this morning!"

I snapped back with, "I'm Sammy Jo, you bitch!" Tim shattered that "John in an accident" illusion. John just didn't show up.

"Tim, I don't want to go to work today, but I have to because I'm meeting my new Ultima II Account Coordinator Janet Russell." Stephanie had called and left me a message.

As I reach for my cigarettes, Tim says, "You need to get over it! He's not worth it!"

"Tim, don't start this morning! I haven't had my coffee or Laszlo Ritual yet! Plus I've been totally humiliated by a man whom I thought loved me, so don't step on my last nerve!"

"Harvey, don't start all of that again!"

The phone rings. "Oh, Mrs. Helms." Tim says it in a super happy, sing-songy, irritating way. I start waving my arms wildly while whisper-yelling "NO!!!! Tell Mother I've already left for work!"

"He's right here, Mrs. Helms. Hang on!" followed by a quiet *"Harvey that will teach you not to mess with me 'cause I will cut you."* Tim sometimes channels Elvira, Mistress of the Dark.

I grab the phone "*What,* Mother?"

"Now Harvey, don't you raise your voice to me, young man, especially with all the problems I'm having this morning!"

"Sorry Mother, what's the problem now?"

"Well, this will only take a second. Now you know your brother is no stranger to trouble. He called this morning from jail and needs $10,000 to get out. Harvey, we can't pay that..." I put the phone down on the counter and pour some coffee. I pick up the phone and hear, "And your father is so depressed he's just gone back to bed." I put the phone down and light a cigarette. I pick up the phone again. "Well Harvey, I know you have to get to work. Have a good day, Honey! Bye-bye!" *Click.*

I'll call her after work. God I'm so late! I literally jump into my clothes, put my brain on neutral, and drive to Belk's. Janet is supposed to meet me around 2:00.

As I slowly arrive at the counter, Alberto Scala is brushing out his kitty mane, spraying it with some really stinky, pee-yellow hair elixir. "God, Alberto, what's that horrible smell?"

"Not horrible. *Medicinal,* Harvey! It's a placenta-based hair conditioning spray, and look at the incredible sheen it deposits in my hair! Oh, and Harvey, some guy dropped this letter off for you a few minutes ago."

Holding my nose I say "Thanks Alberto." It definitely has John's chicken-scratch handwriting and all I can do is just stare at the letter. My *Dear John* letter from John? Not funny. I can't read it now, so I throw it in my bag to cry over later at home. I try to pull myself together. *Now Harvey, you have to get ready to meet Janet Russell, so make sure everything's in order because you don't need any cosmetic drama on top of this man drama.*

Janet shows up about an hour and a half late. "Hey Harvey! Sorry I'm late, Tutti, but Montaldo's is having a huge jewelry sale and Momma needs some new treats! Listen, I need to run to the rest room and then we'll get started, okay? I don't have any makeover appointments today do I 'cause I don't feel like doing makeovers today. I'll be back in a minute. Wait! What is that smell? And who's that?"

Alberto turns and looks at us as I explain. "Never mind about him and that smell is his hair conditioner."

"Oh." Janet picks up a fragrance tester of Ciara and starts spraying in his direction.

"Janet, I think that makes it worse!"

I then see this tornado of a woman, who is the spitting image of a young Elizabeth Taylor, clicking her way up the aisle toward the rest rooms. It's like Janet and I have known each other for years even though we just met and she didn't even introduce herself.

By about four o' clock I realize that Janet has either fallen in the toilet or she's shopping somewhere else in the store. It doesn't matter. I also realize that I haven't seen Sue all day and now all I can think about is John's letter in my bag. I'm about to pull it out when I hear "Honey! Look at this gorgeous bracelet I just bought! Pretty fabulous right? I can't really afford it but I just have to have it! I also found two cute skirts and these pumps. What do you think?"

"Janet, Honey, where did you come from?"

"Lovey I just moved here after working with Ultima II in Florida, to take Mark Cooper's position."

"*What*?"

"Didn't you hear? Well, Mark's been promoted to Stephanie's position and Stephanie's taking Rick Jordan's position because he's the now the new Regional VP. Got it?"

"That was fast! Listen Janet, we haven't sold one thing today and I'm going to get in trouble."

"Don't worry, Tutti, Rick Jordan loves me. At last year's Christmas party he asked—" Janet lowers her voice "—*Janet, can I hum "Silent Night" on your pussy?* Let's just say that I spent the night singing 'Oh Cum all Ye Faithful!' Listen, I need to go back upstairs and get my new skirts so I'll be right back." Janet's clicking her way up the escalator again.

Well! Mark Cooper is now my Account Executive? I haven't seen him or his 70's mustache since beauty school. I have to remember to call Sherrill Webb to discuss this!

As I look up, I see Sue slowly walking to my counter. "*Girl*! Where have you been? It's been a wacky day with my new Coordinator Janet, who looks like Elizabeth Taylor. I think she has a little shopping problem."

"Oh… I think I saw her upstairs trying on furs in the salon. I also saw a drag queen trying on dresses in the Misses department. Harvey, why is it that most of these men who want to be women have humongous Adam's apples?" Sue suddenly gets quiet and starts looking down at the floor.

"Sue, what's wrong? Where have you been all day? Do you want to go smoke?"

"Harvey... I'm leaving Belk's because I've been promoted and I'm now going to be an

Account Executive with Germaine Monteil cosmetics. They wouldn't let me say anything until just now that it's official."

I feel my eyes tear up and the emotion is slowly rising in my throat. I gulp and can't hold back the tears. Sue starts fidgeting with her name tag so she can't look me in the eyes. Wiping the tears from my eyes quickly I blurt out -"I'm so proud of you Sue! It's great! God, I'm so jealous too!" Sue looks up and I can see through all that goth makeup that it's hard for her to tell me this news. "It's okay Sue, you'll come here and we'll still have lunch."

"Harvey, I have to move to Atlanta for the job and I'm leaving Charlotte in two days."

Amazing. I've lost Sue and John in the same day. In this moment I realize that I truly love Sue because she's become one of my best friends and I've learned so much by knowing her, even though we only see each other at work.

I've asked Sue to come out to The Odyssey a few times but I guess bars aren't her scene. If I hadn't met Sue, I don't think that I would've lasted this long in this department. All of the sudden, I feel like I've been hit in the stomach and can't catch my breath. "But Sue…"

"I know, Harvey."

"Oh my God, Sue, I don't have enough time to plan your goodbye party or… "

"Harvey, please no icky goodbye parties. It's not me. I just want to make a clean exit with no fanfare because you know that I hate these bitches! You're the only person I'm going to miss and you'll come to Atlanta. Besides, you know we'll always have THE EPILADY."

We fall into each other's arms and I once more can't hold back the tears.

"Will you stop crying, Miss America! I know, Harvey, you don't have to say it. Me too." She turns to leave. "Don't worry, Harvey, you'll be out of here soon enough, and try not to kill any cats! By the way, what's that horrible odor? Ultima didn't come out with another rank fragrance did they?"

"No, The Cat is refurbishing his mane with a urine-scented placenta spray."

We look at each other like it's the last time we'll ever see each other. Classic Sue breaks the tension. "Harvey if anyone else gets knocked up and needs disposable diapers, I hid two boxes in the stockroom after Debbie's goodbye party!" She kisses me on the cheek and then I watch her walk to the Clinique counter, take off her Clinique white lab coat and place it on the counter for the very last time. Then she's gone.

After waiting a few moments out of respect, I go over and take the coat. Partly because of sentiment, but also because I need a truly fabulous Halloween costume! Can't you see it! TRICK OR TREAT WITH CLINIQUE! *Love it!* Not like when I was a little boy and my mother forgot to buy me a costume at the grocery store. She'd always say *Harvey, this year you're going as a hobo!* I'd just look back and defiantly say, *Mother I don't want to go as a hobo. I hate it! Everybody will laugh at me just because you forgot to buy me a costume!* The Hobo look consisted of one of my father's dress shirts, big pants tied with a rope from the garage, and beard stubble created by lighting a cork with a match and smearing it all over my little face. Those were devastating Halloweens with the most un-gay costume ever in the world!

Standing there dreaming of horrible Halloweens past, Janet comes clicking up. "Honey, where are you?" She's waving her hands and snapping her fingers in front of my face. The clanking of her twelve bracelets brings me to the present. "You look like you need a drink. Actually several drinks. Let's grab our bags and get the hell out of here. Do I need lip gloss?"

Janet and I end up at The Odyssey and she looks like she's in heaven. "I love the queens, Harvey! It's girls' night out!" We're drinking Tequila and dancing to Wang Chung's "Dance Hall Days", just letting this day dissipate into the night air. We come off the dance floor and Janet says, "Here, Tutti, go do some of this in the bathroom. It will make you feel better. Ok?" I look down and it's a bag of cocaine and a straw. It's the hot new drug and I've seen others snort it a few times at parties but I've never actually done it before. For some strange reason I instantly trust Janet, so I go for it.

Sneaking into the bathroom, I'm nervous so I go straight into a stall feeling awkward and clumsy. I hear two drag queens. "Girl, your wig is too hot! Where did you get it? Does mine look like last year's Halloween?" I burst out laughing and the white powder flies everywhere. Feeling stupid, I stick the straw in the white powdered clump and start snorting. After raising my head up and trying to swallow, I hear another queen say "Honey, don't break your nose in there."

My lips, nose—my whole face, really— seems to be going numb and my heart is beating so fast that I think it's going to jump out of my chest. I slam the stall door open and step out. Everyone turns. The drag queen cocks her hand on her hip "Girl, I know it's been snowing in there but did you stick your whole nose in it? Got any more?" He takes a tissue and wipes my nose whining, "Children doing drugs. Where the hell is Nancy Reagan when you need her?"

I stumble out of the rest room to find Janet at the bar ordering us our tenth round of cocktails. She turns and immediately wipes even more excess white powder off my nose that the drag queen must have missed. She starts laughing. "It's your first time, isn't it?"

"I can't feel anything, Janet, and I feel like the room is spinning."

"Harvey, do I need more eyeshadow? I feel like it's fading. Honey, where's the bag? It's time for Momma to make her trip to the rest room."

"What? Janet there's no cocaine left. I thought you expected me to do it all."

The next thing I remember I'm back at home on the couch with Janet watching MTV with Madonna crooning *Like a virgin... Hey! .Touched for the very first time...* Needless to say, Janet sat up with me all night but I don't remember much more. She called me late Sunday afternoon and filled in the blanks of my memory. "You couldn't go to sleep, Harvey, so we watched Madonna videos for hours! And then when I thought you were going to settle down, you handed me a letter, crying and begging me to read it to you. All the letter said was *It's over. I'm sorry. John.* You lost your mind but then you asked me a 100 million times: *Do you like Madonna, Janet? Tell me every reason why right now!* Harvey, I don't think cocaine is the right drug for you. Who's this John anyway?"

"Oh Janet, he's a frat boy that loved me once upon a time, but unfortunately we are not going to live happily ever after."

"I'm sorry, but men are jerks. Listen, Tutti, do you think I should buy those earrings that match the bracelet I bought at Montaldo's? I can't afford it but I really want them!"

I have this sinking feeling that addiction may be Janet's middle name. I burn John's letter late Sunday night, thinking that it would make the emptiness go away. It didn't.

HARVEY'S DIARY:
OCTOBER 10, 1985
"Bend over and take it like a man!"

"In the book of life, the answers aren't in the back of the book."
-CHARLIE BROWN

John was a big blow to my ego, and although it's been about three months since he dumped me, my heart still hurts. The day after I burned the letter, I found out that John was sleeping with that frat brother Barrett Klutz, whom he'd brought by the counter on the day of my big event. *How could he do this to me?* I thought that we loved each other and I don't have any clue how to heal from this. Trust has always been an issue for me with my parents acting the way they do, and, well, honestly, with all people in general because of the homophobia issue. Tim won't even let me say John's name in the house, threatening to lock up the liquor cabinet if I even look like I'm going to say the "J" word.

Work is my solace and I guess the beauty gods are taking pity on me. Just when I thought my life was over, Stephanie calls with unbelievable news!

"Well, Harvey, are you sitting down?"

"Why, has Janet been arrested for shop lifting?"

"No, Crazy! Are you ready for this? I'm promoting you today! Your new title is Belk Director of Beauty and let me tell you, Patti Garrison had a heart attack when I told her, but it's done! Oh! And your work sister Sherrill has been promoted too! Tomorrow, you two will attend Rick Jordan's district meeting at the Marriott on Tyvola road, so be there around noon so we can finalize your Revlon new-hire paperwork. Now you can pack your stuff up, baby, because you're officially finished as a counter girl! Aren't you excited?"

This moment that should be one of the greatest of my life is so bittersweet, because without John, nothing makes sense right now. Putting on a fake smile to sound sincere I say "Stephanie, I'm so happy! Thank you for everything you've done for me!"

"Are you kidding, Harvey? You deserve this promotion with the incredible job you've done, especially with all the obstacles you faced. The dress is business casual for the meeting. See you tomorrow, Mr. Director of Beauty."

I wish Sue was here so I could run to the Clinique counter and tell her the news! While cleaning out my personal drawer and thinking about this dysfunctional place I've grown to love, Alberto Scala appears and kind of staggers over to me, swaying back and forth. "Um, Alberto, have you been drinking that hair elixir?"

He slurs, "I overheard you on the phone. Are you being promoted?"

"Yes Alberto, I am."

"Well, Harvey Helms, you think you are sooooo great and you really make me sick. And let me tell you something else! You're not better than me. Can I help it that my business isn't as good as yours? *NOOO*! Revlon has given you so much support! Hell, a monkey could run your counter with that much support." Then, he belched. No, I mean he *BELCHED*! Before Alberto could continue his tipsy tirade, he fell backwards with a heavy thud, just like in the movies. Standing over him and looking down, from this height he reminds me of a big sad cat passed out on the floor. Looking at him lying there I sort of feel sorry for him and I wonder if anyone has any catnip to revive him.

No surprise, of course, that my last minutes in this department will be as strange as the first when I was escorted down the escalator by the wicked witch. No fanfare, but a call to you-know-who.

"Patti Garrison, please."

I look down at Alberto. *Is he purring*? "Hi Patti, it's Harvey. I just want to say thank you for all the things you've done to me while I was employed here at Belk's. Listen Patti, Alberto *Scalah*, the man you hired, has passed out from a few too many over lunch at TGI Fridays, and he's taking a nap under the counter."

I hang up the phone quickly and drape Alberto's black cape over his passed-out body. As I step over him, I check my look in the mirror for the last time. A little pressed powder and I'm set! God, I wish Debbie was here to see this moment! I grab my box of personal belongings and take a last panoramic view of the department. Katherine the fragrance lady is arguing with a customer about returning a used bottle of "White Shoulders," while the Lauder girls are out front of their counter fighting over the next customer, and the Clinique counter of course looks lonely without Sue. Well, folks, no party for me either because I agree with Sue. I hate goodbyes. I'll call Connie later cause I'm sure she already knows anyway.

As I walk out of the department for the last time, I look up to the heavens and whisper, *Thanks, Tammy Faye*. Sitting in my car, I realize that I've actually become a beauty advisor. I'm half in a dream about the future, and half envisioning Patti Garrison trying to pick Alberto up off the floor.

Walking in through the door at home, Tim and Richard are standing there with big smiles on their faces. "Ok, you two! What did I do now? "

Tim cocks his hip. "Harvey, just cause you're the Directress of Beauty doesn't mean you can be all sassy with me!" Richard pops a huge bottle of champagne.

"How did you find out, Richard?"

Nadine, Richard's mother, who works upstairs at Belk's, had called them with the latest employee gossip. "You know Belk's! Mom said Patti is on the war path!"

After three glasses of champagne, I decide to call my mother. Tim grabs the phone away from me. "Are you sure you want to call her?"

I grab the phone back and raise my glass of champagne. "Dial the number Tim! *Mother!* I've been promoted! My new title is Director of Beauty. Can you believe it?"

"Director of what?"

"Beauty."

I hear her smoking. "Well that's nice, son, whatever it means. Anyway your father has gone off with his friend Huey."

"Who, Mother?"

"You know that bald man that worked with your father at Du Pont? Every time he comes over he asks me for a glass of water."

"Yes Mother, I remember him."

"Well there's something that you don't know. The last time your father went out with him, he came home and... I don't know how to say this...Well.... Your father had doo-doo stains in the front of his underwear, Harvey!"

Complete silence.

I finally break it, "Mother, what are you saying?"

"I'm saying that your father has had sexual relations with Huey! Why else would he have those stains in the front of his underwear? Well *you* should know, 'cause isn't that what you boys do?"

"Mother I'm *not* talking to you about this! I called to tell you that I got promoted and as usual you have to change the subject to Daddy. I have to go."

Tim walks back into the kitchen. "What's wrong with Grace today? How did she take the news?"

"Not a word about my promotion, but Mother thinks Daddy is having anal sex with his friend Huey."

Tim spits his champagne into the air, choking. "Does that mean he broke up with the woman from the 8th floor?"

Oh my God, I swear I'm living in the Twilight Zone. "Oh, never mind Tim!" With more champagne in hand, I decide to apply the Erno Laszlo Hydra Therapy Masque so that I will look refreshed and rested for my first District meeting tomorrow with gorgeous Rick Jordan!

Tim walks into my bedroom and flops on the bed. He can always tell when something's wrong. "What's wrong?"

"Tim, I want to call John."

"Well go ahead, Crazy! Dial the phone, then hand it to me so I can tell him to *Kiss your ass!* Harvey, you're *not* calling him! You know he's turned out to be a big gay whore and don't start crying or you'll deactivate your mask!"

The next morning, I find that navigating to the Marriott on Tyvola Road is easier than it was the time I went to the beauty school downtown. This one's a big hotel too, but a little more casual.

I walk to the front desk and ask, "Where is the Revlon District meeting being held? I'm the new Director of Beauty."

The woman looks at me blankly. "Well I'm the Front Desk Manager," she replies, "and it's in Suite 404."

Approaching Suite 404, I can hear talking because the door is propped open. As I walk in I see that everyone is busy at work. There are some new faces but I see Sherrill and Janet busy doing expense reports, and my old trainer slash new Account Executive Mark Cooper is huddled with other Account Executives whom I've never met. Stephanie and Rick are deep in conversation, but in this moment everyone's head turns from what they're doing and in unison say "HARVEY!"

Rick Jordan, in his deep, dreamy, Clark Kent voice says "Welcome aboard Harvey! Everybody meet Harvey Helms, our star from South Park!" He sticks out his big sexy hand and I immediately blush. I somehow find the nerve to shake it. I'm definitely in love.

Bringing me back to reality, Rick puts on his serious businessman's face and walks to the front of the room. "Guys, now that everyone is here, let's get down to the business at hand. I want to unveil a new sell-through program for Ultima II that will encompass all the Belk Department stores in the Southeast called *The Belk National Makeup Artist Program.* I expect Harvey and Sherrill to be the big stars producing the biggest retail sales in the history of Belk! Stephanie, I want you to work with the Account Executives to create the launch calendar, and Harvey, I need to talk to you privately."

In my deepest, sexiest, Barry White voice I say, "Okay, Rick." I think I sounded more like Bea Arthur."

We go outside on the balcony, me first, then I turn to face Rick. "Harvey, we need to fill out your new hire paper work for Revlon and discuss your salary. What kind of money are you looking for?"

"Huh?" I'm blank. I've never had this discussion. What should I say? If it's too much will he fire me before I've even started? *HELP!* I blurt out," $20,000."

Rick smiles "How about $ 23,000?"

"Okay Rick."

"Harvey, all new Revlon employees have to get a physical when they start and I've booked your physical for tomorrow at 9 am. Any questions you have, feel free to speak with Stephanie."

I shake his hand one more time for good measure. We step back in the room and my head is just spinning. *$20,000 dollars! I'm rich!* Stephanie told me later that I should have asked for 35 to get 30. Being screwed by Rick happened in a different way than I had originally imagined.

We join the others and start drinking to toast the new program. "Here's to the new team!" We are beyond drunk in less than an hour and Janet and Mark keep disappearing to the bathroom. In fact everyone but Sherrill and I are invited into the bathroom.

Sherrill looks toward the bathroom. "What's going on?"

"Sherrill, I think it's snowing in there, if you know what I mean."

The next morning, still hung-over from my first district meeting, I arrive at the corporate medical facility at 9 am. If they have to draw blood I bet it'll come up gin-positive! Little do I know that I will be screwed this morning for a second time by Revlon. After checking in at the reception and filling out my paperwork, I sit in the waiting area with all kinds of professionals. People in suits, truckers, nurses, etc.

"Glenn Helms?"

Ugh, my first name! I hate Glenn. My twin sister's name is Gwen. Glenn and Gwen? We love each other but as with all of my other sisters and my brother, we're not connected. We more or less see each other once a year at Christmas and sometimes Thanksgiving. I know this sounds strange, but I guess you could describe us as happily dysfunctional. Welcome to the Helms family.

I'm escorted to a private room where a nurse takes my blood pressure and temperature. As she leaves she tells me, "The Doctor will be with you momentarily."

Oh good! They have *Vogue* magazine's November issue early! November? Thanksgiving will be here before you know it, and as scary as it seems, Tim and Richard want me to invite Mother and Daddy over for dinner. I have to decide soon so that Tim can plan the menu. Grace and Mac visiting the Farrington's? What if Rebecca unexpectedly drops by for a quick Thanksgiving shampoo and holiday highlights? *Oh My God, I sound just like my mother. That's it! Oh, they're coming all right. Ladies and Gentlemen, it's time for the gayest Thanksgiving ever!*

The doctor comes in about 15 minutes later. He's 6'5" with a big square head that looks like it should belong to Herman Munster.

"Good morning, Glenn. So you're a traveling man for Revlon?"

"Yes sir, but I go by my middle name so please call me Harvey." Oh my God he's talking to me like I'm 15 years old! He continues to poke and prod my back and belly telling me to breathe in breathe out.

"That sure is a lot of responsibility for such a young man, Harvey."

"I guess so." Now he's talking to me like I'm five years old. "Harvey please stand up, turn and face the examining table, drop your shorts and bend over."

"What? *Why?*"

"I need to check your tail pipe."

"My what?"

"Your tail pipe. I need to poke my finger up there and feel around."

"*In my tail pipe!?*"

I reluctantly turn around and notice the doctor is putting a rubber glove on his right hand. I also notice that his fingers are fat like kosher dill pickles as he greases up his index finger with Vaseline.

The next thing I know I've woken up on the floor with a nurse bending over me with smelling salts. I immediately feel my head aching while this cherub-like nurse is smiling looking down at me. "Poor little darlin'. Bless your heart. You hit your head on the examining table on the way down. How are you feelin'?"

"How should I feel? I had a pickle shoved up my butt before passing out and hitting my head."

Doctor Frankenstein is looking down at me "I guess when you're not used to that you could be overcome, young man."

I look up at him from the floor, now with an ice pack the nurse has given me for my lump on my head. "Overcome? You have *really* big hands, you know, and next time I recommend that you let a guy know before you starting pointing that big fat finger of yours, Sir!"

I finish dressing and leave. God, I need to lay down, my head is killing me! At home I tell Tim and Richard the whole story expecting sympathy, but I should've known better. Every time I'm about to fall asleep, Tim and Richard keep coming in my room asking, "Do we need to check your tail pipe?" and laughing wildly. *Ha Ha you bitches.* Tim and Richard don't stop laughing for three days.

HARVEY'S DIARY:
NOVEMBER 10, 1985
"Dana is a man?"

"You can't be friends with a squirrel. A squirrel is just
a rat in a cuter outfit."
-SARAH JESSICA PARKER

As the new Belk Directors of Beauty, Sherrill and I are traveling every week to execute special events at a store near you. Staying in hotels and seeing new cities every day, with a company car and an expense account? I feel a new freedom and I'm starting to think that I *won't* be stuck here forever, as I originally feared. The flipside to this, though, is that our first special events are a slap in the face of beauty reality. Fortunately Sherrill and I are paired together for learning the event schedule. Some of our events produce incredible sales while others don't because certain beauty advisors can't book makeover appointments to save their lives. Sherrill is the Appointment Nazi and she gives these girls hell when they make excuses.

"Why haven't you booked any appointments Missy?" After some hemming and hawing the beauty advisors give her every excuse in the world. "I've been sick." "All my customers have already bought recently." "Business is slow." "I'm PMS-ing" "I hate Ultima II and want to quit." "I just broke up with my boyfriend." I even think that once they said, "My dog ate my appointment list." The absolute worst, however, are the beauty advisors who fill the appointment books with fake names, which is really naive because all we have to do is call two or three phone numbers listed to know they aren't real. I love to watch Sherrill deal with these slack beauty advisors, reapplying her lip gloss as she screams about the lack of appointments. Classic Sherrill.

Another possible cosmetic hiccup with our new positions is the fact that the New York office has deemed that we need yet another manager to help drive our business. This hiccup's name is Dana Lebrowski. Dana is a man?

The first time we lay eyes on Dana, Sherrill and I are doing an event at her former Eastland Mall store. Stephanie called, explaining that Dana would be moving to North Carolina from California to help build the Belk's business. She also said she and Rick would be giving Dana a tour of the stores and that we're invited to dinner immediately following our event. Now I know I haven't been in the business that long, but I'm starting to notice that the cosmetic industry has a revolving door of executives that makes it seem like they're in one position for five minutes and later they're either promoted or fired.

It's business as usual this day, until out of the corner of my eye I see a big, football-player type of guy—who looks like he could have fit in perfectly with the jocks at UNCG who wanted to kill my gay ass—approaching the counter. Enter Dana, stage right. A new homophobe in town and he has control over my career, watching my every move and unsmiling in the process. Sherrill keeps trying to catch my eye as she applies skin care to her makeover and her throat turns beet red as it always does when she's nervous, so I walk over to her pretending to ask for a blush brush and whisper "Sherrill, button your blouse! You're splotching up!"

I can see that Dana is sizing us up from head to toe with an expressionless stare. The funny thing is that we're not being introduced to Dana, maybe because Sherrill and I are with customers, and Stephanie is explaining to Rick the new merchandising strategy. Stephanie winks at me as I'm finishing up my makeover and explaining every step to the customer. I see Rick, Stephanie, and Dana huddled together whispering, then turning to leave with no introductions at all. Very odd! Perhaps we'll meet Dana later tonight at dinner starting at 6:30 at a steakhouse near the mall.

"What do you think, Harvey? Are we okay?"

"I don't know, Sherrill. Stephanie winked but that Dana man didn't look happy at all. Have you ever heard of the name Dana used for a man? Oh for God's sake, Sherrill, you better take a valium or at least let's buy you a scarf to hide your neck before we face Dana again!"

We arrive at the restaurant fifteen minutes early to get our bearings. "Sherrill we need some liquid courage in case things don't well, so let's have a martini at the bar first while we refresh our look!" I immediately pull out my Erno Laszlo Controlling Pressed Powder in medium for instant mattifying. I had to confess my Laszlo secret to Sherrill because we travel together five days a week, but surprisingly Sherrill has *also* been a secret Laszlo devotee, coveting his Phelityl Cream as her favorite moisturizer for months! I came to find out that Linda at Montaldo's had cast the same beauty spell over Sherrill. I'm so glad I could finally come out of the Laszlo closet to somebody!

"Sherrill, drink up!"

"I can't. Here, you finish it. Harvey, is Janet coming tonight?"

Slurping down the rest of her martini I mutter, "Don't know but she's probably shopping, wherever she is. I see Stephanie waving us to come with her. Okay, let's fix your scarf. How's my face?"

"You're matte. Wait, you have gin on your chin."

"Ready?"

It's hard to explain, but to paint a vivid picture: we're all circling the table like it's a showdown at the "OK Corral." Everyone is standing around the table just staring and posturing, ready to draw for the killing shot. Rick finally breaks the ice.

"Everyone, this is Dana Lebrowski." Out of nervousness I'm the first to say, "Hi Dana! I'm Harvey Helms and this is Sherrill Webb. "

He doesn't utter a word and I consider trying again, when Sherrill interrupts. "You don't look like you would work in cosmetics."

That finally gets a response out of him. "What does that mean? I've been working in cosmetics before you were born, Miss Webb."

Rick Jordan quickly jumps in. "Dana was a football player for the Washington Redskins and he's a big Polish man's man."

"Oh." Sherrill moves as far away from Dana as she can coming up behind me and grabbing my arm.

Stephanie saddles up beside me and whispers in my ear, "Harvey, Dana is married to Ultima II President Stanley Noland's sister Betsey. He's been working for Ultima II on the west coast, living in Long Beach, California."

"What's he doing here, Stephanie?"

"Good question."

We sit down to dinner with the continued awkward silence looming over our table. Rick, trying to ease some of the tension again, asks me, "How are the events working? I hear from Sherrill that some of our beauty advisors are having difficulty booking appointments." I start to speak about how great I think the events are going when Dana interrupts me.

"Harvey, you can go get another job at Elizabeth Arden tomorrow because you're the sloppiest makeup artist I've ever seen in my life. Who taught you to do makeup? And Sherrill, don't sit there with that smirk on your face, the same goes for you. The business sucks in Belk's, and things are going to change around here."

I look at Sherrill and whisper "*Pull your scarf up.*" Fortunately for me, I remember Sue telling me to toughen up! I look at this bully from California and very calmly say, "Mr. Lebrowski, is it? Elizabeth Arden is a very nice company, however, Sherrill and I have a very large following at Ultima II."

Luckily, fate intervenes to disrupt this recent unpleasantness; we hear some loud voices at the restaurant's reception desk. "Honey will you store my shopping bags? Now be careful they're fragile! What kind of foundation do you wear? Here's my card Sugar, so call me and I'll see what I can do! We're expected at dinner. Do you have a table for the Ultima II party?"

Yes, it's Janet, and she's on the arm of Mark Cooper. Rick stands and kisses Janet on the cheek and shakes Mark's hand. "Dana, this is Janet Russell and Mark Cooper."

Janet screams at the waiter, "Honey, can I have a martini, up, dirty, with two olives? So how's everybody tonight? Who are *you,* handsome?"

Stephanie cuts a look at Janet. "This is Dana Lebrowski, Janet. I told you about him."

"Oh! Hi, Honey! Welcome to North Carolina!"

No response from Dana.

Mark Cooper, with his 70's mustache and a very business-like voice says, "Dana, I think you'll find Belk a very productive account for Ultima II; I've spent months developing the business and people, including Miss Webb and Mr. Helms here." I dig my nails into Sherrill's thigh. *Mark is taking credit for all we've done when I've only been to one of his lousy beauty schools?*

Dana's face hasn't changed. "You don't talk very much do you Honey?" Janet asks after pulling out her pressed powder compact and lipstick for a touch-up.

Dana turns his attention back to me and we have a staring contest without blinking. He's not going to break me down. Sherrill's now digging *her* nails into *my* leg. Dana's tough guy face starts to slowly soften and this crazy laugh comes out of his mouth. "Harvey, I'm going to teach you a few things about makeup and life, boy!" *Boy?*

As this dreadful evening finally comes to an end, the girls and I give each other air kisses and say good night. Sherrill doesn't wait around and quickly excuses herself. Janet gives me a big drunk wet kiss on my forehead, grabbing my cheeks screaming *"Tutti! Tutti! Tutti!"* Mark walks out without a word while Stephanie whispers in my ear, "Dana's bark is worse than his bite. You two are still our stars." Rick pats me on the back and gives me his proverbial *Keep up the good work* look, as Dana shakes my hand. No, more like he *breaks* my hand. "Watch your back boy!" I look at him and think *Bring it, big man.*

HARVEY'S DIARY'
NOVEMBER 22, 1985
"I have a dream"

"Beauty is the only thing that cannot harm."
-OSCAR WILDE

It's almost Thanksgiving and I've been diagnosed with having head-splitting migraines. It makes so many things in my life make sense. The worst headaches I've ever experienced happened on the third Monday in January of this year. How do I remember that date so vividly? Well, I hate to do a rewind but you have to hear this crazy story! It begins as usual with Tim and I sitting at the bar in the kitchen.

"Tim, I think something is seriously wrong with me!"

"You're just starting to figure that out, Harvey?"

"Shut up, Tim. I'm waking up every day now with humongous gay headaches and this time it's not because of all the gin and tonics and dancing at The Odyssey to God-awful hours of the night! What's wrong with me? Do you think I could have a brain tumor from all the fragrances and cosmetic chemicals?"

"With all the shit you pile on your face every day, I wouldn't be surprised."

"Tim, don't speak about Erno Laszlo that way! It's gay blasphemy!"

"Whatever."

"Anyway, it might be my grueling schedule because I'm traveling six days a week. Or maybe it's the stress? Do you think it's the stress? You know at the end of very long days of doing events, I pick up my messages that are mostly from my mother and all her drama. You know... *Beep... Woman from the 8th floor... Beep... Huey and the underwear incident... Beep... Iris is smoking that Marathon again... Beep... Gary's back in jail.* All messages with a big exhale of smoke at the end, Tim. I'm exhausted. It's got to be the job plus Mother mania, right? Tell me it isn't anything more than that…

"Maybe, Harvey, you're coming to find out that the cosmetic industry works their artists into the ground with no mercy. You and Sherrill are doing about 40 makeovers a day, 6 days a week? You do the math! But on the bright gay side of the street, you guys are making names for yourselves as the artists that produce the most retail sales."

"Tim, when Sherrill and I work together at events, people ask if we're brother and sister, or husband and wife. Sherrill's like my sister, you know. We're inseparable and she keeps me sane."

"What about Dana? Maybe he's the cause of your imaginary brain tumor."

"If you don't stop making fun of me right now, I'm going to tell everyone that's not your natural hair color."

"It is too!"

"Tim, nobody's natural hair color is called Jet Grape."

"Anyway Harvey, you were speaking about Dana?"

"Well I knew the hair color reality check would change your tune. Anyway, as you know, Dana is ruling with an iron fist and we have these tedious touch-base calls with him every Monday morning. My call with Dana is always first at 9 a.m.; at about quarter to nine I place my cigarettes and coffee pot on the table because I never know how long or bloody the call will be. Dana's mood depends on how much he drank the night before. Hung over, he can be absolute hell. Actually Tim, sober he's no day at the beach, either. I always know when it's going to be a horrible call because he start's the conversation with "Mr. Helms. Just the person I want to talk to." He will proceed to rip me a new asshole even if my events are successful, finding *something* to bitch at me about.

"The other day while I'm on the phone with Monster Lebrowski, my call waiting starts going off like fireworks because Sherrill and Janet are calling to see what color his mood ring has turned. If it's black, I tell them *Fasten your seat belts!* You know that I love to fight with him; on our last call he screamed *You need to get another job!* but I fired back *Fine, Dana, I quit!* He always hangs up because he fires me every other week, but about an hour later after cussing me out, he'll call and say "*Meet me at TGI Fridays! We need a liquid lunch boy!*"

Tim looks at me skeptically and says, "You two just need to get a room."

"Tim that's extra gross! Listen, on our last touch-base, Dana said *Boy, you and Sherrill have been requested to attend the National Account Coordinator Conference in Atlanta Georgia next Monday.* He had the nerve to say *Don't you two embarrass me and stay out of trouble!* It felt like he gave me a kiss and then slapped me in the face. Atlanta, Tim? My headaches are getting worse and it feels like my head is going to explode."

Tim makes me a Long Island Ice Tea but it doesn't help alleviate my suffering. "Tim, what am I going to do about this important career trip to Atlanta?"

"I don't know, Harvey, but your face does look swollen. When's the last time you went to see a dentist?"

I hiss-"You know I hate the dentist!"

Tim starts feeling my face like some voodoo witch doctor. "It's your wisdom teeth and you're going to the dentist tomorrow. I'll call."

"No! I'm not going to the dentist!"

"Oh, you're going bitch, and if you don't I'll call Grace!"

"Okay, I'll go to the dentist, damn it!" I hate it when he uses my mother against me!

—Excuse me but "DANGER, GAY ROBINSON"; I have to interrupt my wisdom teeth story because Tim just walked in to say, "Be sure to call Grace to make sure they'll be here for Thanksgiving! I have to know how much dressing to make!" Yes, Grace Jr., I reply. Tim picks up a big knife and starts walking toward me. "Don't make me come over there!" Sorry about another story interruption! Try to keep up!—

So I now put my diary down, pick up the phone, and slowly dial, thinking about the

nightmare of my parents being here for
Thanksgiving.

"Hello?"

"Hi, Mother. Listen, do you and Daddy want
to come here for Thanksgiving dinner, and I'll
totally understand if you don't want to come
because your schedule is busy or something like
that."

"Why we'd love to, Harvey. You've never
invited your parents over so I'm glad to FINALLY
see where you live. It's not painted pink is it? Do
you have white carpet because I heard
homosexuals love white carpet."

"Mother, where did you hear that?"

"On the Phil Donohue show. Phil had these
two homosexuals on the other day and they said
they loved white, even had white carpet. Does Tim
want me to bring anything?"

"No, Mother. So I guess I'll see you and
Daddy on Thanksgiving?" Oh good! Back to my
headache drama!

Well, the black voodoo mistress turns out to
be right because my wisdom teeth are the culprits!
All four are impacted and have grown in
sideways. I decide to have them surgically
removed the Friday before I am to leave for
Atlanta on the following Monday because I can't

stand the pain anymore. Tim and Richard pick me up after the surgery but I'm in a painless haze thanks to my new friend vicodin.

"Harvey, you look like Alvin the chipmunk."

"Don't make me laugh, Tim, it hurts to open my mouth."

Safely back at home, Tim and Richard tuck me into the sofa in the living room and put in *The Wizard of Oz* video they gave me for Christmas. I was so high on vicodin that I watched *The Wizard of Oz* seventeen times. They said when the video would finish, I'd say *Play it again*. This has to be the reason I quote *The Wizard of Oz* so much, other than I'm like every other queen who loves this movie. I can recite every line from beginning to end and maybe someday it will come in handy.

When Monday morning arrives, Tim asks, "Are you sure you're ok to drive?"

"Yes Mother, what can go wrong? Atlanta is only four hours away from Charlotte and I've driven there before so I kind of know the way." I'm still on vicodin and I can't open my mouth to eat regular food so soup with a straw is the only thing on my menu. God, I'm so hungry but the beauty benefit is I'm so skinny from not eating. I must remember this next time right before bathing suit season arrives!

I'm not really good with directions but magically three vicodin's and four hours later, I somehow arrive into downtown Atlanta.

Two wrong turns and I don't know where the hell I am. Another wrong turn and I'm in a long line of cars. *God, the traffic is so bad here in Atlanta.* I start beeping my horn, rolling down my window screaming, "Come on! Hurry up! I'm going to be late! Don't you people know that Evangeline Sarafoglou, the National Director of Training for Ultima II from New York will be here tonight and I have to meet her for my career! What's wrong with you slow-ass Atlanta people?" *Oh, my teeth throb! Hmm, I think I'll pop another vicodin.*

I hear all these people applauding and for a brief moment I'm lifted out of my vicodin fog to realize that I'm in the procession for the Martin Luther King Day Parade. The only reason that I know this is because of a float with a banner proclaiming it in front of me, with a choir from the Ezekiel Baptist Church singing *I will put my trust in Jesus, Yes I will! OOHHH!* Some of the choir members are flipping me off! I can't get out of this parade because the side streets are blocked.

I don't know why, but at that moment my mind drifts into the illusion that everyone attending the parade is here to see me. How fabulous to be the queen of the parade! I roll down the window and do what any other beauty queen would do! I began a very ceremonious wave like the Queen of England, blowing endless kisses and thanking my subjects for their loyalty and devotion.

Several parade hours later, with my left arm sore from waving, I arrive at the Marriott, jumping right out of my car and leaving the motor running. I'm quickly ushered into dinner in a grand ballroom where I can barely say a word through a tight unopened mouth except, "Hello. I'm so sorry to be late."

Someone takes me by the arm and leads me to a seat where I sit by a woman who politely says "Hello. I'm Evangeline Sarafoglou. I'm so glad you made it Harvey. Excuse me, waiter? Can he please have a bowl of soup?" Evangeline hands me a straw and says "Enjoy."

I'm so embarrassed, not only because I'm beyond swollen, but I'm also flying high. Evangeline's a beautiful petite Greek woman with soulful brown eyes filled with compassion and kindness. She was so good to me that night I'll never forget it, or at least what I can remember due to my vicodin high. I don't remember the rest of the meeting but I definitely remember her. Oh, and by the way, Happy Post Martin Luther King Day everyone! Better late than never!

Okay, enough of that. Back to the Thanksgiving drama!

While I'm worrying about my mother and her *visit* this Thursday, the phone rings and it's Sherrill. "Harvey! I think you better sit down because you are not going to believe what I'm getting ready to tell you! Ready? Are you sure?"

"Yes, Sherrill, you're killing me! Spit it out!"

"Okay. Mark Cooper is getting a promotion to be the new National Training Manager in Dallas Texas working for Evangeline!"

"What? Sherrill, he was just promoted to Account Executive! How did Mark Cooper procure this prestigious National Training position when you know this group of trainers are so revered they practically have to die for you to get a chance at their jobs?"

"Well Harvey, I heard that Dana sort of arranged it because it's no secret that he hates Mark and honestly he's not that fond of Janet either. When Dana wants you out, you're out… Evangeline probably owes Dana a favor, who knows?"

"So Mark isn't replacing a National Trainer because Ultima II just added this new position especially for him?"

"I guess so, Harvey! I'm also hearing rumblings on the street about Stephanie, Janet, and Rick."

"What do you mean, Sherrill?" "Well, I'm noticing that Janet and Stephanie seem to be more and more unavailable. You know I love them, so when people ask *Where are they?* I lie and say *They're both really busy.* Something is definitely wrong, Sherrill, and I think it's only going to get worse. And speaking of worse, Sherrill, I have to get off the phone now because it's prep time for the gayest Thanksgiving ever with Grace and Mac! Wish me luck!"

HARVEY'S DIARY:
NOVEMBER 23, 1985
"There are only two bedrooms?"

"We had gay burglars the other night. They rearranged our furniture."
-ROBIN WILLIAMS

I wake up to the sound of pots and pans dropping. No, more like flying and slamming, as I sit up in bed hearing Tim yell "You damn turkey! I just need to tie your legs so stop sliding!" *God, what time is it?* As I look over to the clock I see it's 7:00 a.m. I hear a big thud and I jump out of bed and rush to the kitchen, surprised to see Tim trying to get a twenty-pound turkey back up on the counter.

"Tim, don't you know it's only seven in the morning?"

Tim shoots me a *Get out of my way* look. "Harvey, I'm trying to get this damn turkey in the oven because it's got to cook for at least six hours. I've been up since four a.m. getting the stuffing ready. Have you forgotten? Your parents are coming. No, the truth is your *mother* is coming and I don't want Grace judging me for my turkey."

"Well Tim, that's your suffering today 'cause you know how Southern women are. You will be judged by how juicy and succulent this turkey will be and I don't want to hear you complain when my mother says, *Tim, the turkey was good but how long did you cook it? Anytime I think my turkey will be as dry as this I baste it with gravy before serving. But your cranberry sauce is just delicious.* Sorry Tim, but you wanted her to come. So I wish you good luck with your turkey drama!"

With that, Tim grabs the turkey, shoves it in the oven and slams the door. "There, you damn turkey!"

Deciding that changing the subject might be best, I ask, "Where's Richard?"

"He's at Nadine's and will have an early brunch before he comes to have this dinner. I can't mess with his mother! Nadine can be evil as your mother! And Harvey, don't you go back to bed either, because you have to de-gay this house before your parents arrive! The Macy's parade will be on in a little bit so I'll make Mimosa's!"

"Well all right, 'cause you know I do love your Thanksgiving Day morning feast prep mimosa's. Let the official *Oh my God my mother is coming* de-gaying begin!"

I look around. "I guess I'll start by hiding the million porn magazines stashed everywhere around the house that you two, that I now dub *The King & Queen of Adult Gay Literature* have collected over the years."

"Queen, you know you look at it too!"

"Tim, my eyes may have caught a glance or two of naked gay technicolor men but it was only by accident while I was cleaning, I assure you."

"Queen, the forecast today is for thunderstorms so I'm not standing anywhere near you when God strikes you with lightening for that bold-face lie! Besides, if your daddy gets his hand on a Blue Boy and sees eight inches staring back at him I don't know what will happen. Do you think your mother will say *I know it's wrong for them to be looking at another man's penis Mac, but the boy in the picture does have good hygiene.*

"Wow Tim! Thanksgiving kudos for that spot on Grace imitation! And yeah, let's not have that happen. Maybe I better hide most of our videos too."

"Yes, all the porn, plus Victor/Victoria." At the same time Tim and I break into song *Oh baby won't you play me Le Jazz Hot, maybe? And don't ever let it end,* with Tim doing the Julie Andrew's big finish! "Yeah Harvey, that video plus The

184

Boys in the Band, Making Love, and the Richard Simmons exercise tapes. He's almost as bad as the porn, so let's not take any chances."

After two delicious refreshing mimosa's, as I'm cleaning, I start to have dark Grace thoughts. "Tim, I don't want to hurt your feelings, but what if Mother and Daddy don't show up today? I mean, you remember that weekend when we were new at UNCG and I brought you home to Charlotte for the first time without telling my parents that you're black? Remember how well that that went? My mother said to you *Well I think it's just fine that Harvey brought a colored boy home even if he didn't tell me beforehand. We'll just stay in the house this weekend with the drapes shut.* I wish all the old Southerners could just move on."

Tim looks at me lovingly. "Harvey, your mother means well and I've grown to love Grace. I actually think she's changed some, but let's face it. Your cousin Jesse Helms just beat Jim Hunt in the North Carolina Senate race so that automatically sets us back 100 years."

"Tim! W*hy* did you say that vile man's name on Thanksgiving? Homophobia will continue to be alive and well thanks to good ole Jesse!"

"Here, down this Mimosa, we'll get through it together like we always do." *One drink at a time, hmm? Drink #3.*

Around 3:00 Tim is feeling good about the feast he's created because the turkey is on time and it's juicy! He's finished cooking his collard greens, macaroni and cheese, dressing, string beans, sliced tomatoes, rolls, and a beautiful chocolate cake! Richard has also made his mother's famous Jello congealed salad with fruit and cool whip. My job is to make sure the bar is stocked and the table is beautifully set with fresh flowers in a cornucopia motif. Seasonal and appropriate. The house is so de-gayed that you'd think straight people live here.

Tim and I have applied Ultima II's Mineral Mask for a little deep pore cleaning while dancing to Tina Turner's *You better be good to me!* The doorbell rings and right on time it's Rebecca from upstairs.

"Why are your faces purple? Oh, you gays are always up to something."

"Rebecca, we're doing a pore cleaning before my parents get here for Thanksgiving dinner, if you must know. I thought you'd be out of town."

"I'm on my way out but I wanted to give you guys this Stuckey's pecan roll that someone gave me 'cause I thought y'all could use it for dessert today."

Tim looks skeptically at Rebecca and says, "Thanks." She then hands Tim a paper bag, "Tim, here are two vogue dress patterns and some lovely cream silk that will help you whip up two fabulous dresses for me by the time I get back Sunday, right? Thank you so much! Y'all have a happy Thanksgiving!"

Tim closes the door without saying a word.

"Tim, are you going to do that?"

"No, but I didn't want to get into it with her on Thanksgiving. She did give us a pecan roll. I know Stuckey's is tacky but I love a pecan roll."

Richard comes in from Nadine's yawning looking full and tired. "What time are your parents coming? I think I need a little nap!"

"4:30 I think but I haven't heard from Mother today. Maybe I better call." I try calling but there's no answer. Not a second after I hang up the phone rings.

I hear whispering: "Harvey?"

"Who is this?"

"It's your mother."

"Mother, I just tried calling you. Why are you whispering?"

"I don't want your father to hear. I started thinking today and I just need to know how many bedrooms y'all have?"

"What?"

"How many bedrooms do you have?"

"Why are you leaving Daddy? We have two bedrooms."

"Harvey, let me speak to Tim."

"Tim, my mother wants to speak to you." I hand the phone to Tim and decide I'm going to need a lot of gin. All Tim keeps saying is, "Yes Ma'am. Yes Ma'am. No Ma'am. I will." I go to grab the phone but Tim hangs it up.

The only gay bar open on Thanksgiving night is that other lesbian bar called Scorpio's. Once or twice a week, normally Wednesdays and Thursdays, Scorpio's welcomes gay men. Gays and lesbians together would seem natural but it's not, due to the fact that gay men and lesbians are so different. Lesbians meet and move in together the next day, unpacking a cooler full of snacks and a suitcase of plaid shirts. There are lipstick lesbians, but they're few and far between because lesbians seem to have more testosterone than any gay man I know. Anyway, despite our differences we're in the same fight for equality, and we try to get along. We're not always successful but we all keep trying. Why did I just explain all that? Well I thought you should know because Tim and Richard have dragged me to Scorpio's this Thanksgiving night so I won't go over and kill my mother.

"Who does my mother think she is to call at the last minute and tell *you* Tim, not *me,* her son, that they're not coming? I don't care if she apologized to you 1,000 times, Tim, it's just not right."

Richard came from the bar with a tray of drinks and tequila shots. "Drink this!" Richard hands us a shot and lifts up his glass. "Here's to only having two bedrooms!"

"Y'all, she wouldn't come because we only have two bedrooms? I can't it take anymore. I'm really done with trying to hide my life so that they can have some false sense of reality. If Grace can't accept this then I don't ever want to see her again and I mean it. I know I've said this a million times but I'm not calling her."

Five cocktails and four shots later I'm on the dance floor with Tim whooping it up to Chaka Khan's new hit *I feel for you… I think I love you!* Across the floor I think I see John but this guy I see is blond. "Tim is that John?"

189

"Yep." *Blond John? Who's he with? That's not Barrett. The guy he's with looks like he's twelve years old.*

"Harvey, today has been traumatic enough, so stay away from him."

"I love you, Tim, but I'm drunk and I still love John. I have to talk to him because deep down in his heart I know he still loves me."

Breaking away from Tim's clasping hands I find it hard to get through this crowd because the club is packed. I'm trying to get past a big group of militant lesbians to get to John, but every time I try to go right they move right. I try to go left and the same thing keeps happening.

Smashed and perturbed I finally scream "Get out of my way you butch dykes!"

I hear gasping but before I can react the biggest girl grabs me by my shirt collars and yells, "What did you call us you, little bitch?" Tim comes rushing over and literally picks me up and moves me out of the way. He pushes all the lesbians in one direction and they fall on each other like lesbian bowling! All the lights come up and security has me, Tim, Richard, and few lesbians cornered questioning us.

On the ride home Tim turns to look at me in the back seat saying "Did you really have to mess with six butch lesbians? They could have kicked your ass, and besides that, we'll be lucky if they let us back in Scorpio's next week! We only have two gay bars in Charlotte Harvey so we can't afford to piss anybody off! We could become gay outcasts."

"I know, Tim, but I was just trying to get to John and that gaggle of lesbians wouldn't get out of my way. I couldn't help it. John looked at me like I was crazy!"

"And your point *is* Harvey? John is a slut! How many times do I have to tell you that? I know you've had a bad day but get over it!"

"Well happy Thanksgiving to you too Tim!... Tim? Do you think there's any more of that Stuckey's pecan roll left at home?"

Tim sighs, "Yes, Princess, and after the day you've had you can finish it, as a reward for not killing your mother."

HARVEY'S DIARY:
JANUARY 29, 1986
"Fade to black"

"I had a lot of dates but I decided to stay home
and dye my eyebrows."
-ANDY WARHOL

1986. Christmas and New Year's came and went. I eventually called my mother on New Year's Eve and I told her that next year her attitude of protecting Daddy by not letting me be myself would not be acceptable, and if she was going to cancel coming to one of my dinner parties, she had best provide a twenty-four-hour notice like they do at fine salons. I told her I wasn't born to live the life that she thought I should live, especially at the holidays. Parents of gay children can be particularly sensitive around the holidays because it reminds them that their children "aren't normal." You know, "queer." She will just have to deal with it. I love my mother but I have dreams and aspirations that go beyond Charlotte, North Carolina, and the entire intolerant South. Don't get me wrong. The South is lovely. I adore every bit except for the prejudice, bullying, and ignorant death-threats.

Speaking of ignorance, John moved away to Greensboro right after Christmas so I don't have to see him out at the bars or parties anymore. His departure makes finally getting over him more of a reality. My question, though, is when you love someone and they leave, where does the love go? I wish it was as easy as chocolate cake. Once that piece is gone you know it's either going to your ass or love handles.

I'm reliving all this drama in my mind, looking out the window on a flight with Sherrill to Tuscon, Arizona, for our first Ultima II National Sales meeting. This morning before I left for the airport Tim said, "Go have a good time and for God's sake meet a cowboy and fall in love! You've been cranky for months. You need sex, Doris Day! Okay I said it! HARVEY, GO GET LAID!"

"Yes Ma'am!"

My mother's only advice was, " Don't drink the water or you'll get sick."

"Mother you're thinking of Mexico!"

"Isn't Arizona part of Mexico?" Thank God my mother's beautiful.

The meeting is being held at the fabulous Ventana Canyon Resort and Spa and yes, I called ahead to book some spa services that I've never experienced. The complete body salt rub? Hot stone massage? Galvanic current facial? *So excited.*

After landing, and while being driven in the courtesy shuttle to the resort, I'm amazed at the beauty of the desert. It's cold and gray back home but absolutely warm and sunny here. The mix of mountains and desert is just breathtaking. It's "high season" so all the snow birds are in the desert to escape the winter.

Standing in the lobby, waiting to check in, I start looking around to see if I recognize anybody. "Sherrill, do you see any people we know?"

"No," she says and shrugs her shoulders.

I faintly hear this clickety-clackety sound that seems strangely familiar. "Honey, don't scratch my Louis Vuitton luggage and stop dragging my fur on the floor!" It's Janet.

"Hi, Tutti! Did you check in? Well come on!" Janet literally pulls me and Sherrill to the front desk. "Hi, Honey, I'm Janet Russell and I'm checking in. Also Mr. Helms and Ms. Webb."

"Miss Russell, we can only check one person at a time."

"That's nice, Honey, and be sure to upgrade my room to the concierge level and their rooms, too. What kind of eyeshadow do you wear?"

The front desk woman looks mortified.

"You need Ultima II Eyeshadow Base so it won't crease like that." Reaching into her handbag, Janet says, "Your eye makeup is really a mess, so here, I'll give you mine." Janet is a critical yet generous soul.

After Janet's mini makeover of the check-in girl, we get our room keys. Janet is upgraded to a suite overlooking the pool, while Sherrill and I have to keep the rooms we're assigned to somewhere over near the golf course. We also have roommates, which will be interesting. As Sherrill and I head toward the elevators, we see Dana stomping toward us.

I whisper to Sherrill, "Sherrill, we can't be in trouble already, we just got here!"

Dana stops and points his big muscular finger at us. "Listen, if people start asking you to do events in their regions, you are to send them to me. Got it?!" He turns and sees someone he knows and yells, "Meet me in the bar! Ok you two, stay out of trouble!"

Before Sherrill and I get in the elevator, I stop the door from closing because I see a tall woman with hair like Cruella de Ville from Walt Disney's 1960's animated film, *101 Dalmatians.* You know, she's the one who wants the Dalmatian puppies to turn them into fur coats. This woman looks like a fashion model straight out of Erté's art-deco sketches. Mysterious and glamorous.

"Sherrill, do you think she's with Ultima II?"

"Wait," Sherrill says. "Look over there. Stanley! That's Stanley Noland, the President."

"Simone! Darling! How was your flight?" he asks her.

Her name is Simone? What a chic European name. "Oh my God, Harvey, look!" Sherrill and I watch as Stanley hands Simone a room key. We turn and look at each other. "Harvey, Janet told me crazy things and *bedfellows* happen at these meetings, so we better keep our eyes open and our mouths shut!" We nod our heads in agreement and shake hands.

Arriving at my room, I cautiously turn the door handle and politely say, "Hello?" No answer back. Good! Roommate hasn't arrived yet! I throw my bags down and quickly perform my Laszlo Ritual. I try to do my splashes as quickly as I can, which always makes the bathroom look like a swimming pool. I have to hide my Laszlo because Janet said, "Tutti, don't get caught at the meeting using any competitors products. You'll be fired on the spot!" Erno is now undercover.

I'm probably going to have a straight roommate so just like my mother used to say to me when I was little, *Harvey, you're different, so you need to dose your craziness out a little at a time so people can get used to you.* Terrible but true. Full-blown Harvey scares people at first but after they get to know me they think *That's just Harvey!* I open my meeting agenda and see I need to be by the pool for a meet and greet in 15 minutes! I jump into my new cute khaki walking shorts and Perry Ellis Linen shirt that I purchased especially for this trip. It's business casual yet chic, set off with a gorgeous new pair of Cole Haan loafers. Without socks of course! I look in the mirror and complete my resort look with new Wayfarer sunglasses from Ray-Ban. Look at me! I'm almost a Kennedy.

Down at the pool I see Janet drinking a martini, laughing with Mark Cooper. What's up with their relationship? They kind of seem like a couple but that can't be possible because I discovered that Mark is gay one night at The Odyssey while I was out dancing with Tim and Richard. I noticed him walk in with a gorgeous model-like creature and he immediately stopped dead in his tracks when he saw me. Without missing a beat, he walked over and barked, "I keep my business and private life separate so please remember that after tonight Mr. Helms." End of conversation. I spent the rest of that disco evening trying to avoid him.

Where's Sherrill? No Dana? No Rick or Stephanie? There must be about 50 people around the pool which makes me instantly feel nervous and awkward, but I know I need to network for the sake of my new budding career.

"Hi Tutti! Come over here."

Mark looks down his nose at me. "Harvey, you need to pay attention during this conference. This will be a great education for you—"

Janet interrupts, "Mark, Harvey is the top producing makeup artist in the company so I think he can teach these people a thing or two—"

"Janet, when I want your opinion I'll ask for it."

The awkward silence is broken by the woman who saved me with soup in Atlanta. "Harvey! So glad you made it."

"Hi Evangeline!"

Mark jumps in. "You know each other?"

"Yes Mark, I met Harvey at the Coordinators meeting. Harvey, congratulations on top sales! Is it okay if I borrow Harvey? I want him to meet the other Regional Managers. Mark, I'll see you later at the trainer's meeting."

Mark keeps his hawk eyes on us as we work our way around the pool. Everyone I'm introduced to say the exact same thing. "You're the Harvey from North Carolina? Where's Sherrill Webb? When can you two come to my market to do an event?" I see Dana and Sherrill across the pool and I look at him with a big fake smile. He looks back with his *You better be a "good boy"* face. After meeting so many new people, I'm exhausted, but I realize it's time for another costume change.

As I'm splashing in the shower, the phone rings. "Harvey, it's Sherrill. Should I wear the yellow Oscar or the blue Ralph? Big Aztec turquoise earrings or simple diamond studs?"

"Blue Ralph and Aztec turquoise but wear your nude beige pumps instead of the azure suede flats so you don't look too matchy-matchy. Sherrill, who's your roommate? Mine hasn't checked in yet."

"Her name is Freddie Swartz and you'll just have to see her to believe it. Let's meet in the lobby and go together in about ten minutes." Hanging up the phone I decide to wear a navy linen Alexander Julian suit with a pink dress shirt and another new pair of black Cole Haan loafers. A chic evening resort look that I found in GQ magazine. Ultima II doesn't make a men's fragrance so I decide to risk it and give myself a light misting of Christian Dior's Eau Savage. Another new purchase courtesy of my Laszlo Guru Linda from Montaldo's.

I arrive in the lobby first and decide to find out what's happened to my roommate. Standing behind the front desk is the woman on whom Janet performed her emergency makeover magic. "Hi. I'm Harvey Helms in 212. Has my roommate checked in yet?"

"Let me check. No, Mr. Helms, his flight is delayed and won't arrive until tomorrow morning."

"Thanks you. Oh, and your makeup looks very pretty this evening."

She says "Thank you," as she cocks her head and bats her eyes.

Entering the Ballroom, Sherrill and I see the new Ultima II advertising, exciting lights and displays. Cocktails are flowing and dinner's about to be served as Stanley Noland steps up to the podium and clinks his water glass. "Ladies and Gentlemen! I want to kick off this beautiful evening by introducing you to our Vice President of Marketing, who's responsible for all of the product innovation you will see over the next few days. Let's have a big round of applause for Simone Asherton!"

Cruella takes to the stage in a long black jersey knit number with a slit all the way up to there. (You know where there is, don't you?)

"Thanks Stanley! I would like everyone to know that despite the fact that our field sales team is under-performing, the products you will see tomorrow are going to make up for your mediocrity. The marketing is so great that the products will practically sell themselves!" It became so still and quiet in the ballroom that I could almost hear the coyotes up on Camelback mountain howling miles away.

Stanley intervenes quickly and starts applauding. "Thank you Simone for that inspirational message to start our dinner!" Everyone applauds and each table begins whispering about what just transpired. *Simone Asherton? Have to remember that, but now it's time for yummy prime rib with garlic mashed potatoes and crème brûlée for dessert.* Alcohol continues to flow nonstop. Did I say flow? It's more like a river that's getting ready to break the dam.

The after-dinner-party is in the Snake & Lizard lounge where Dana is on the dance floor with Sherrill, Stephanie, and Janet. Dana hates Janet, so I know he's totally wasted. Like all the straight bars I've been to, they're playing Huey Lewis' *Power of Love* from the movie *Back to the Future*. I like Huey Lewis and the News and I saw *Back to the Future* twice in the theater, but this song is very Hetero. I know they will end the night with that college frat song *Shout!* You know the one from the movie *Animal House*? *You know you make me want to… SHOUT!… Lift your hands up and.. .SHOUT! BLAH BLAH BLAH BLAH and SHOUT!* Everyone of course throws their arms up in the air on the word *SHOUT!*

The music is so loud you can't hear yourself speak. Dana keeps handing us shots of tequila which Sherrill secretly dumps in a cactus pot near our table. No dumping for me! I'm downing every one of them because I love the warm feeling of tequila that travels all the way down to my toes! On a break from dancing, Dana staggers over and whispers in my ear, "Boy, you look really good tonight so I may have to do something illegal to you later, heh heh!" My memory then fades to black.

I wake up the next morning on the floor of my room dressed only in my cute little bikini Garfield underwear that Tim and Richard gave me for Christmas. As I begrudgingly try to open my eyes, through my squinting, I see a strange man, who's shaking me and saying "Hi, I'm Bill, Your roommate? I just got in because my flight was cancelled yesterday. I'm from Ohio and we were hit with a freak winter blizzard."

With a raspy Lauren Bacall voice I say, "Hello Bill, I'm Harvey," feebly reaching up from the floor and shaking his hand.

"Uh, Harvey, you have dirt all over your face and we're to be downstairs in about fifteen minutes. I'll see you downstairs?" I wait for Bill to leave the room and limp to the bathroom and look in the mirror. *Oh! Not good.* I shower and skip Laszlo 'cause I'm so hung over and late. After quickly dressing, I buzz the elevator and think, *What happened last night? Oh my God, Bill, my roommate from the conservative Midwest, woke me up with dirt all over my face, on the floor, in my Garfield underwear.* I feel like I'm still drunk.

I quickly exit the elevator and I try to find Sherrill to see what she knows! As soon as I walk into the conference center I feel an arm grabbing mine and pulling me aside. "Hi Honey, how you feeling?"

I whisper, "Janet what happened last night?"

She tries to reply with a straight face. "Well Honey, you disappeared and were nowhere to be found. After about thirty minutes of searching, Tutti, we found you face down in the dirt near a cactus bead. You were mumbling something about Dana doing something illegal to you when we turned you over, so Sherrill and I dragged you to your room. And look, I broke a nail. Honey, you still have a little dirt in your ear and you're super-oily this morning. Here, use my powder. Do I need lip gloss?"

"God, Janet, my head hurts and no, your lips are fine." Then I see Sherrill, who looks as fresh a daisy because instead of drinking she got the cactus pots all liquored up.

I go into the meeting room and jump into the first available seat by someone I didn't know because the presentation had already begun. The marketing team is unveiling our latest miracle moisturizer called "Photo Aging Shield" which promises to be the industry's next big "It" product and the first to openly address Free Radical formation in the skin! The package design is beautiful but the woman sitting beside me under her breath says, "Looks a little like Estée Lauder." Actually it does look like Estée Lauder's "Eye Zone" eye gel.

On the break I see Dana, who looks like hell, and Stephanie, who looks like she's been crying. Janet is in the corner touching up her lip gloss and talking to Mark Cooper. The rest of the day, through bloodshot eyes and a pounding head, I'm beginning to understand the inner workings of the Ultima II New York corporate team. Marketing, Training, Operations, and Public Relations. Most noticeably one woman stands out. Yes! Simone Cruella Asherton.

Admittedly, she fascinates me. I'm so compelled to watch her; in fact, I literally can't take my eyes off her. She seems to be above it all, but most noticeably she's Stanley's favorite. Vice President of Marketing huh? I sit there thinking about my possibilities. New York's a place I've always wanted to live in, and if you can make it there, you can make it anywhere, or so the song goes. *Right, Liza? How will I get there? National Director of Beauty?* Speaking of that, Michael Cope isn't here. I remind myself to talk to Janet about that later!

By the end of the meeting, I feel like I'm dying, but fortunately it's time for the spa! I'm glad to check in with the spa receptionist so I can lie down!

"Mr. Helms, you will be having a deluxe salt rub and hot stone message this afternoon. Is that correct?"

"Yes!"

"Gerald will you set up in the gentleman's lounge. Enjoy your treatments."

"Good afternoon, Mr. Helms. My name is Gerald. Will you follow me please?"

"Gerald, I'll follow you anywhere if I get to lie down!"

"Too much fun last night?"

"I don't remember."

"Here we go, Mr. Helms. Here's your locker. Please remove all your clothing and put on this robe. Here's a safe if you'd like to store anything valuable while you're enjoying the spa. Toby will be here momentarily to escort you into the wet room for your salt rub treatment."

In the next moment I'm totally naked, getting rubbed down with salt and a thick hard brush by a man who is tough and strong and from the Czech Republic. My legs and arms are flying everywhere and salt is collecting in places that I never thought needed seasoning! Eventually Toby the Czech has me on a massage table and says to me in a thick accent, "Mr. Helms, no hot stone today, you need deep tissue massage. Scream if you need to!"

I limp out of the spa smooth, black and blue, feeling like I've been through a war, when I see Dana. "Come on boy, let's drink." This is where I learn the expression *The hair of the dog.* Two drinks and I miraculously feel better but still sore. Luckily Janet comes and saves me before Dana can order another round of drinks. "Honey, you better go take a nap before the dinner tonight." From this point forward I must have been in a walking blackout because the rest of my time here is very sketchy.

On the last morning, which is a rush of goodbye's, congratulations, and checking-out trying to get to the airport, I'm sitting in the courtesy shuttle holding a gold statue in my lap that says "Top makeup Artist." Mark Cooper is on the shuttle with sunglasses and looks like he's in no mood for conversation. He looks down at my award and quickly turns away to look out the window. I peer down at this little statue and know it means that Dana will become inundated with requests for Sherrill and I to travel to the big cities to do events. I see Sherrill coming out of the resort entrance carrying her statue, too. My very last memory of the Ventana Canyon resort is Janet screaming at the bellman while spritzing her favorite fragrance in his direction. On the plane home, I'm almost asleep when Sherrill nudges me and whispers, "Harvey, I love Garfield too!"

HARVEY'S DIARY:
APRIL 5, 1986
"Oh Romeo!"

The first thing I do in the morning is brush
my teeth and sharpen my tongue."
-DOROTHY PARKER

"GET BACK TO WORK! I made you two and I can break you too!"

"SHUT UP DANA! What do you want me to do?"

He's pissy because I've been booked to travel to other regions that now include a mix of Belk and, as Dana puts it, *The rest of the country that's "Not Belk"* events. Minneapolis, Dallas, Boston, Seattle, and finally New York City! The scene of my debut includes twenty makeup artists and myself executing a special event at Bloomingdale's 59th Street in the heart of Manhattan!

Entering through Bloomingdale's revolving door, I feel the electric energy and I'm amazed at the number of customers rushing down the aisle. It's nonstop! I have flashback of Belk's. *If I had this many customers, I could have had a million dollar counter!* The other thing I immediately notice is the number of men working behind the counters. Not only that but men wearing more makeup than any woman shopping here. All gay? No big deal. I wish some of those redneck boys who called me faggot at Belk's could see this! These queens would kick their asses! I feel liberated. On the way to Ultima II counter I'm also astounded by the size of the cosmetic bays here. Huge beauty shrines!

"Hi. My name is Harvey Helms and I'm so glad…"

"Who are you?" Betty the Ultima II beauty advisor gets right to the point.

"I'm Harvey. I'm one of the makeup artists?"

"Oh, well Harvey, find your station and get to work. We need sales and be sure to sell Procollagen Anti-Aging complex and Photo Aging Shield moisturizer to every customer."

"Oh no, Betty, is it? You don't understand. I'm a National makeup artist visiting from North Carolina and I'm not selling today."

"If you're doing makeup for Ultima II here today, you'll do your own skincare, foundation, and color makeover, then escort your customer to the counter and close your own sales. We will pull the product for you. Do you understand? See that line of customers that goes out the door? They're ready so go to your station. You have a 30 minute dinner break at 5:00. Good luck."

In the makeover area there are 20 tables lined up containing every product we make plus director's chairs out and ready for our waiting customers to sit in while they're being transformed. I spot a cute little brunette organizing her makeup table so I decide that I'll take the table next to her.

"Hi, I'm Harvey Helms."

"Connie Veneri. Where's that accent from?"

"North Carolina."

"Have you ever worked an event at Bloomingdale's before?"

"No."

"Okay, Harvey, well, let me explain how the event works. First the customer will begin with us for their expert skincare analysis and transforming makeover. How long does it take you to do a makeover?"

"About 30 minutes."

"Okay, well today you will be doing them in 15. After the makeover, you'll take them to the counter and close your sale. Hurry back, though, because the next customer will already be sitting in your chair. Your average unit sale needs to be

$250 a customer. All of our customers will then be escorted over to the camera to recite Shakespeare from *Romeo and Juliet*. You know, *Romeo, Romeo, wherefore art thou Romeo*? The grand prize is a walk on part on the daytime soap *Santa Barbara.* If they ask if you think they'll win, just say *yes* and move on. Got it?"

"Thanks Connie. I have to do all that in 15 minutes?"

"Yes, but faster than that if you can, so we don't get backed up." My first exposure to NYC selling is hardcore and cut-throat. It's definitely not as glamorous as I envisioned on the plane coming here. My first three makeovers only buy $30. I look at the other artists—is it just me, or are they as fast as lightening?—enjoying huge sales. *What's wrong with me?*

Connie steps over. "Harvey, you're talking too much. This isn't North Carolina, so get the makeup on and run to the counter. You're being too nice! You need to be more aggressive and make them buy."

I can hear Sue saying *You got what you wanted Harvey, so you better toughen up, you little Southern beauty queen!* Betty the beauty advisor comes up while I'm thinking. "Henry," she yells at me, "you can't just stand there day dreaming! Some of the customers are having difficulty understanding your Southern accent and you also need to get your sales up." I take a deep breath and try to move faster.

Before I know it, it's 5 o'clock. Thank God! Connie invites me to go on dinner break with her. "Come on. Let's get a slice across the street."

"A slice? "

"Pizza, Harvey!"

"Connie, I guess I look like a dizzy queen!"

Connie starts laughing. "You'll get used to it. By tomorrow it will seem like you're a native New Yorker!"

One of the artists, a fellow named Joseph who traveled here from Boston and is also getting a slice, overhears our conversation. "With that accent Connie? She's a Southern belle! *Ding! Dong!* Hi, I'm Joseph Pierotti from Boston."

"I'm Harvey from North Carolina."

"I know. The beauty advisors are complaining about how slow you are. Listen, I gotta get back or Betty will give me a black eye! Harvey, have you been out clubbing in New York before?"

"No, this is my first trip."

"Great! Meet me in the lobby of the hotel tonight at 10:00! We're going dancing to initiate this Southern belle!"

For the next four hours I slam out more makeovers in an unbelievably short amount of time. Every time I complete a makeover faster (and break my record!) Connie winks at me and gives me the thumbs-up while Joseph cries out "The belle is getting faster!" It's like training for a marathon, because I'm out of breath! As soon as I finish the makeup, it's hurry over to the counter to close the sale.

Betty is always hovering! "Come on, Henry, your next customer is sitting in your chair and be sure you spray everyone with a fragrance. Your fragrance sales are low today!"

"Betty, my name is *Harvey*. Harvey Helms. Please at least get that right!"

"Oh, you finally decided to grow a set of balls?" Betty gives me a cute wink and we burst out laughing. "Okay kid. You survived your first day!"

"Thanks Betty." I think I officially passed initiation.

Slowly walking the streets of NYC back to the hotel, I notice a number of cute guys on the street and some are even checking me out. *Take that John! I'll get a New York boyfriend and you'll be sorry!* Back at the Drake hotel, "The only Swiss hotel on Park Avenue" like they say on The Phil Donohue Show, I survey the lobby and see many interesting city people. I step into the hotel's lounge right off the lobby and order a gin and tonic to go, because I'm pooped!

After shutting the world out and appreciating the silence of my room, I strip naked and almost fall into the shower because I reek of Ultima II's Beautiful Nutrient Foundation and Loose Powder. I slowly lather up with my Erno Laszlo Hydra Therapy Cream bath soap, inhaling its aroma-therapeutic properties. Then while my skin's still warm and moist, I smooth on Dr. Laszlo's Hydra Therapy body cream in long relaxing strokes. Heavenly! Before placing my exhausted head down on a deliciously luxurious pillow, I think *Call Tim? No, my darling. Slip in between the sheets of your king-sized bed and take a fifteen minute disco nap, Harvey, because tonight, you're going out in NYC!!*

At ten o'clock on the dot I run into Joseph as I'm getting out of the elevator. He looks me up and down, head to toe, with a disapproving look. "Harvey, what the hell do you have on?"

"Ralph Lauren."

"Did you think you we're going dancing at a prep school tonight Missy? If you've been struck dumb due to all the chemicals we inhaled today, I'll remind you that we're on our way to a hot gay disco in the Village." Joseph has on expensive Italian designer black dress pants that are just tight enough to show he's packing, coordinated perfectly with a beautiful black silk shirt and chic black loafers with tassels. "Oh well, no time for you to change your schoolgirl drag, Harvey. Come on, or the line at the club will be so long we'll never get in!

We step outside and the doorman blows his whistle to hail a taxi. As we slide across the back seat of the taxi, Joseph slips the doorman two bucks and off we go on my first New York nighttime adventure! I'm looking out the window, awestruck as the taxi takes us down to The Village. I'm overwhelmed by the large number of people casually walking the streets this late at night. Not a soul in Charlotte would dare show their face downtown this late at night without a gun!

Joseph slides over to my side of the cab with a serious glance. "Now when we get in the club, Harvey, don't smile like some hick from North Carolina and please remember to keep your wallet in your front pocket. Pick-pockets, you know. Oh, and another thing! Don't ever leave your drink unattended 'cause somebody might slip you a mickey and the next morning you'll make the obituaries. But most importantly, if I go home with someone tonight, you're going to have to find your own way home, Little Bo Peep. Got it?"

The taxi pulls up to an alley behind a building without a sign in what to me looks like a dangerous part of town. As we stop, Joseph says "Ok, we're here Harvey, so open the door. " I sit there silently looking out the window as Joseph pays the fare. "We're here Harvey, get out!"

"Where exactly are we Joseph? There's no sign indicating that a club is around here somewhere, and I'm not so sure about this neighborhood, so let's go some other place."

The cabbie, becoming impatient, starts yelling at us in Chinese, followed by broken English screaming "You get out of my cab!"

Joseph is mortified as I scream, "NO!"

The cabbie leans over the back seat of the cab and screams in our faces, "You get out of this cab right now, you crazy fags!"

Without a moment to waste, Joseph reaches over me, opens the door, and with his legs and feet he shoves me out and I fall to the ground.

"Oh my God! You scuffed my Ralph Lauren deck shoes, Joseph!"

If looks could kill, I'd be dead. The cabbie is still screaming in Mandarin as he speeds away. It takes about two hours to get into this club. Let's just say that three hours later Joseph and I walk out the club wreaking of cigarettes and gin. "Joseph, it was so dark in there I couldn't see a thing. Men were grabbing me but I couldn't see what they looked like."

"Honey if men were grabbing you, you should be happy! Wow, you Southern virgin debutantes think everything is a barbecue! What will daddy think? Fiddle Dee Dee Scarlet!"

At this point Joseph screams *Taxi!* and it seems like minutes later that my alarm has gone off and I'm back doing the marathon makeovers! The next few days fly by like lightening and I have made two new friends that I know I'll love for a lifetime!

Luckily by the end of this life-changing week, I'd survived my first down town disco and mastered the New York beauty jungle thanks to Connie and Joseph! Betty wrapped her arms around me and smooched me with her big red lips, leaving an impression on my cheek. "Harvey, you're always welcome here at Bloomingdales

59th Street, but please work on that Southern accent!"

Romeo, Romeo. Where for art thou Romeo? With a New Jersey accent? I don't think that this is what Shakespeare had in mind. Landing in Charlotte I feel let down with the big city now calling my name. Fate will eventually land me in New York, however there is one fateful stop I must make first for a few years, so that I can experience more of life's hard beauty lessons.

HARVEY'S DIARY:
AUGUST 10, 1986
"Hooray for Harveywood!"

***"Certain shades of limelight can wreck a girl's
complexion."
-HOLLY GOLIGHTLY***

"Harvey, it's been month's since you been up north and I think you should forget all about New York and stay right here in North Carolina where you belong. Why, you could get up north and somebody might try to kill you! What does Tim say?"

"I don't know Mother, why don't you ask him? Tim! Pick up! Mother wants to talk to you!"

"Tim, don't you think Harvey should stay here and forget about New York?"

"Mrs. Helms, you know perfectly well that Harvey's your child and you can't order him to do anything! And if you do he'll turn around and do exactly the opposite."

"Thanks you two for all the love and support." I hang up.

Tim comes downstairs and sits across from me at the bar. "So what's the verdict?" I ask.

"Harvey, your mother loves you and she even said—now don't fall off the bar stool—*I bet if Harvey met a nice boy here he'd want to stay!*"

"Well she gets a C- for making efforts. Tim, I will miss you and Richard like crazy, but New York's where you have to end up to realize a successful career in the cosmetics industry."

"Well let's not worry about this until it actually happens."

The phone rings again. "Please let the answering machine get it. I've had enough of Mother today. You know I'm beyond exhausted because it's Saturday night and I'm not even going out!"

"Oh, Harvey, before you hear it, I changed the out-going greeting on the answering machine!"

"You've reached Tim, Richard and Harvey and no we're not in a three way so please give it a rest and leave a message."

Beep. "Harvey, what's up with that message? Anyway, it's Dana. A man named Ronald Perelman has succeeded with a hostile takeover of Revlon. I don't think you own stocks but, anyway, if the newspaper calls, you have no comment. Our business is struggling and this takeover is going to change everything, so I need you to meet me at The Marriott on Tyvola Road tomorrow at 8 a.m. I know it's Sunday but I can't wait. Your company car will be picked there." *Beep.*

"What? Tim? A three way? Really?"

"I can't help it Harvey, I'm sick to death of everyone thinking we're in a ménage a trois!"

"A what?"

"A three way, queen!"

"Well you have to change that message 'cause it's so unprofessional! God Tim, do you think I'm being fired? Well I guess my mother's wish will come true since my dreams of New York just went up in smoke." I spend the rest of the night pacing and wondering why Sherrill isn't answering her phone. What the hell is going on?

I arrive at the Marriott sleep-deprived and nervous as hell. I dreamed last night that I had to go back behind the Ultima II counter at Belk's and Alberto Scala was dancing around me, twirling his black cape screaming *Well, well, well! Look at what the cat has dragged in. I knew you'd come crawling back!* Patti and Debbie were dressed like little girls singing *I knew you wouldn't make it, I knew you wouldn't make it!* I woke up soaking wet in sweat and couldn't go back to sleep. That was around three in the morning.

Right off the lobby I see Janet sitting in the hotel restaurant fixing her eye makeup. "Janet, have you been crying? What's wrong?"

Before she can answer, Dana suddenly appears and barks, "Janet, hand Harvey your car keys."

Janet stands up and hands me the keys to her company car. "Tutti, I'm going back to my old position in Florida." Kissing me goodbye she whispers, "I'm going to miss you and be careful. Dana is on the war path."

Dana throws himself into the booth and takes a big swig of a Bloody Mary.

"Boy, our business is really tough and because of the takeover big cuts are being made! The New York office just let Rick Jordan go on Friday and I had to let Stephanie go this morning."

"What? Why?"

"Business sucks and cuts are being made. Welcome to the real world! You and Sherrill are okay for now but I can't protect you two this time. You better bust your ass boy if you want to keep your job."

I hand Dana my company car keys and try to find Janet's gray Ford Taurus in the gargantuan Marriott parking lot. *There it is!* How did I know? Well other than the fact that the key worked, the outside is covered with dents, and the inside carpet has permanent high heel indentions. The entire car smells like the mixture of about fifty fragrances, and I see a million used lip gloss tubes scattered all over the place. God, I'm going to miss Janet.

Monday morning, sitting with my cigarettes and coffee, waiting for what could be my final call from Dana, the phone rings. It's 8:30 so I'm thinking it's going to be Sherrill to discuss how to handle Dana today. Sherrill always calls early if she's extra nervous. She was away this weekend and didn't hear the news from Dana till last night. I was on the phone with her until midnight wondering if we'll be fired today.

"Morning, Sherrill!"

"Is Harvey Helms there?"

"This is Harvey Helms."

"Harvey, it's Evangeline in the New York office. Am I calling at a bad time?"

"No Evangeline. How are you? Are you okay? Dana told me about some of the changes coming because of the takeover."

"Well, there are definitely changes but some of them can create possibilities. So Harvey, the reason I'm calling is we're restructuring the training department. But first, I want to let you know that Michael Cope has left the company. I know you really admired him and he loves you too. It's just that his back can't take standing on marble floors doing forty makeovers a day any more. Don't be sad because this cloud has a silver lining! Michael's moving to Mexico to open an art gallery."

"That's great… but I'll really miss him."

"Harvey I also know you're close with Janet and she spoke with me about yesterday with Dana."

"Is Janet okay?"

"More than okay! I've promoted her to be the new National Trainer out of Chicago. She accepted this morning." I sigh a breath of relief since Janet's going to be okay.

"Harvey, you may not be aware that our West Coast business has continued to struggle for the last two years. New York management has decided to really shake it up out there with a whole new executive team. When I asked all the Regional Managers who they thought could turn training around in the west, your name came up several times. I need someone with presence who understands selling, and what it's really like to work behind a cosmetic counter. I also need someone who's a positive team player to help turn our retail partners around. It's pretty bloody, I won't lie to you.

"So, Mr. Harvey Helms, I'm calling to offer you a National Training position. If you accept, you will be based in Los Angeles, California. We're bringing in Sally Smith from Minnesota as the new Regional Manager. Have you met Sally?"

"I did a special event for her at Dayton's."

"Well, I think you two will be the dynamic duo! Sally will also have a new boss named Darren Rutherford, who's coming from outside the industry to take the west coast VP of Sales position." My mind starts to race! "Well, what do you think Harvey?"

I think *HOLLYWOOD* but simultaneously I consider Dana. He'll be beyond livid. "Evangeline, I'm shocked but I'm really excited and honored that you're offering me this position. Um, can I think about it and call you right back?"

"Of course, of course. I'll look forward to speaking with you very soon."

I know that I have to talk to Dana first because he'd kill me if I accepted the position before discussing it with him. I guess in my own strange way I love Dana. 9:00 AM comes and goes but around 9:45, when I am getting my nerve up to call Dana, the phone rings. After I pick up and say *Hello,* I hear "Mr. Helms, you're late, but you're just the person—"

I interrupt him. "Yeah, I know, just the person you want to beat up today! Before we start, I have to tell you, Dana, that Evangeline Sarafoglou just offered me a National Trainer's job in Los Angeles so I—"

"WHHHATTTT THE FFFFF—" Then the phone goes dead. I hang up the receiver and take a breath. The phone rings again and scares the shit out of me!

"God Harvey, just pick it up!" My inner voice seems to be having a nervous breakdown too!

I whisper, "Hello?" "

So, how's Dana this morning?"

"Sherrill, if I were you, I'd let your answering machine pick up when Dana calls. A ton of shit is going down so I'll have to call you back later!"

"Are you okay?"

"Oh yeah, I just have some things I need do to right now. I'll call you later." Sherrill knows something's up but I can't tell her the news. Dana doesn't call me later as he usually does for liquid lunch so I know that I'm totally in trouble with him, but *damn it*! I just got *promoted*! Not only that! *Hollywood*! I could be discovered!

I sit back in my chair and think, *Los Angeles? Not New York? Big risk. Big Reward? You've been waiting to get out of North Carolina and today the opportunity came knocking!* My heart aches a little because I'm going to miss Tim and Richard and I don't have the slightest clue about how I'll live without them. Where's my "Sue Vision" when I need one? I look up to the ceiling and prayerfully say "Sue, are you there?" No reply. I guess it's time for me to put on my imaginary push-up bra and make the big girl decision on my own. One shot of vodka and several cigarettes later I finally pick up the phone. "Evangeline, I've thought it over and I'm really honored that you want me for this position. I accept."

Later, I speak with Janet. "Did you hear, Janet?"

"Of course Honey, 'cause you know that Evangeline called me right after you accepted. How's Dana?"

"Mad and unavailable. Have you talked to Stephanie or Rick?"

"Not yet but I'm going to try them both tomorrow. Listen Tutti, screw Dana Lebrowski!

It's Los Angeles for God's sake and I'm coming to visit you to find a rich husband!"

"Any time, Gorgeous!"

"Harvey, can I ask you a question? Do you like Madonna? I want to know every reason why right now." We start laughing. "I miss Stephanie."

"Me too!" Janet's voice darkens. "Have you talked to Mark Cooper yet about all of this? You should probably call him." Janet's always weird with anything involving Mark Cooper.

"Well if you let me get off here, I'll call him now. Love you."

I light a cigarette as I dial and he picks up "Hi Mark, I–"

He quickly blurts out "Are you sure you want to leave a good thing in North Carolina Harvey? You're a star with Dana and he's probably mad as hell with you for betraying him today."

"Mark, I—"

"It's a big competitive world out there, especially Los Angeles. Are you sure you're really ready? You know, Harvey, you could be making the biggest mistake of your life and this move could totally ruin your career," I hear him take a drag off a cigarette and then he abruptly says "Oh, that's my call waiting, I have to go." *Click*. That's funny! I didn't hear a call waiting beep.

I light another cigarette, considering everything Mark just vomited my way. On the inhale, I realize that I'm smoking as much as my mother. *Call Tim and Richard? No, wait. Have I made a mistake? Can I do the job? I've accepted the job with Evangeline and there's no backing out now. She wouldn't have offered me the job if she didn't think I was ready, right?* I pour myself into a bottle of gin and drag myself into my room before Tim and Richard arrive home so I won't have to deal with this tonight. When I dreamed about being promoted, everyone was happy and proud of me in the dream…

One month later on this five hour flight from North Carolina, I am dreaming about everything that's happened ever since Evangeline offered me the job. The most recent unpleasantness was the tearful but truly supportive goodbye with Tim and Richard. *You better call us every day queen! We'll be out to visit after you get settled.*

The farewell with my mother was of course bittersweet. Other than *Don't get the AIDS,* she also said, "Your father's so upset about you moving, he went to bed early tonight."

"Mother, Daddy goes to bed early every night!"

"Well, tonight he went to bed extra early."

Dana gave in and met me for a drink, hitting me in the arm while saying, *Don't you forget who made you a star, boy!*

Sherrill surprised me with a Fendi briefcase and kept crying *What am I going to do without you?*

I suddenly feel someone tapping me on my shoulder. "Mr. Helms, Please bring your seat forward, we're getting ready to land in Los Angeles."

My first time at LAX and my eyes immediately start scanning the airport for movie stars. Walking from the skyway bridge into the gate area, it suddenly strikes me is that everyone is tan, beautiful, and in great shape. Their clothes are relaxed and the people move purposely but with a look of *I don't care* on their faces. I must seem white, Southern, and uptight.

In baggage claim, I hail a porter—*Oh My God, that is such an old-fashioned Southern word my mother would use... AHHH... Sky Cap, I mean*—to help me with all the bags. He's friendly till I give him his tip and he dumps me with my eight heavy suitcases at the rental car shuttle pickup. The shuttle pulls up and of course I need help with all these bags, but not one person offers any assistance. They watch me lift the bags like

I'm their favorite TV show or something. People must think that I look like Ma and Paw Kettle arriving with everything I own. It takes more than a moment to get all my bags on that little shuttle bus, so everyone looks exasperated with my luggage drama. I collapse into a seat and grab my Normalizer Shake It to touch up!

As the bus pulls away from the curb, I start thinking that I need a makeover! Go blonder? Join a gym? Shop for new chic laid-back clothes? Maybe I need to change my shade of Shake It from "Beige" to "Sun Tan"? Perhaps I'll begin this look overhaul after I'm back from New York. The trainer's meeting coming up next month is going to be huge, what with all the trainers from every Revlon brand descending on New York plus the changes in management since the takeover.

The most newsworthy changes are that Adrian Anderson has left Estée Lauder to join Revlon and reorganize our department store brands, and that Angela Lewis-Cartwright will be leaving her post as Chief Beauty Editor of Mirabella magazine to redesign and invigorate Ultima II. Yes! My makeover will commence right after this trip! I subtly glance up at everyone on the shuttle (unlike my mother who would blatantly stare at people, peering down her nose saying *Will you look at her!)* I realize that no one knows who I am and that I can be whoever I want to be, living here in LA! I can be the easy breezy cover-girl I've always wanted to be!

After successfully picking up my rental car and cramming all eight suitcases anywhere I can put them, I drive away from the airport, spotting a million signs for different highways to use. Excuse me, *Freeways*! The jerk at the rental car counter corrected me three times when he was explaining the directions. I could tell he was speaking extra slow so dumb ole Southern me could understand. I can't remember which exit to take now so I circle the airport three or four times. I don't like driving to begin with and this is totally scary merging with a million cars. I only have to leave the airport and go about five blocks but it takes 30 minutes! Welcome to driving in LA!

The bellman puts the key in the door to my suite where I'll live for the next three months and immediately asks, "Where should I put ALL of these bags?" I motion towards the bedroom and hand him a twenty. After he explains all the hotel amenities and departs, I open the French doors and step out on the balcony. The air here has a very clean smell that's very different from North Carolina. I know there's a lot of smog here but it still smells so clean to me! As excited as I am, I didn't expect to have this lonely pit in my stomach. I think to call Tim, but it's three hours later there and they're probably fast asleep. The excitement of getting here is quickly wearing off and so is the gin. I love Greta Garbo, but I don't want to be left alone.

HARVEY'S DIARY:
September 23, 1986
"The Princess and the pea"

*"I will buy any cream, cosmetic, or elixir
from
a woman with a European accent!"*
-ERMA BOMBECK

"How's L.A., Tutti? Any star sightings yet?"

"No, Janet. I haven't even left my hotel room this weekend 'cause I'm a little afraid to drive here. Are you ready for the New York training event?"

"I guess so, but I'm thinking that you, me, and Mark should pull our expense money together and rent a suite with three bedrooms at the Barbizon hotel in New York. Don't you think that would be a blast?"

"Are you sure, Janet? Did you ask Mark?"

"He won't care. So are you in?"

"I'm in! On a more interestingly life-changing subject, what do you think Angela Lewis-Cartwright will do to Ultima II?"

"Anything will be an improvement after the Photo Aging Shield disaster. Having the FDA force us to remove that from the counters was a total industry embarrassment. It's Adrian Anderson coming from Mystique Cosmetics that I'm more worried about, pulling all of our cosmetic brands together in one bay and having two measly days to learn all those products and unveil it at the Museum of Natural History to the press?"

"God, Janet I've missed you and can't wait to see you in New York! I'll call you when I land!"

"Kisses!!"

Monday morning while boarding the flight to New York, I'm again thinking about my blond transformation. Ash blond or cool-iced blond? All the cute boys at the airport this morning have bi-level haircuts with the bleached top and dark underlay that's so popular here in L.A. Maybe that's it! I'll let my hair grow out and then find a fabulous stylist in Beverly Hills to Hollywood up my hair! Maybe I need to introduce some black into my wardrobe? I'm starting to see tons of that, especially in New York. I'm becoming a jet setter just like the designer Donna Karan with her fabulous seven easy pieces for the woman on the go! I'll shop in NYC! Also, definitely need to hit a tanning bed, because Southern lily white skin is definitely out!

The Barbizon Hotel is one of those old New York legends that years ago I believe it was a hotel exclusively for women: in particular, for actresses or girls in between rich boyfriends. Probably a few closeted Lesbians hanging out there too. While checking in, the front desk receptionist informs me, "Mr. Helms, the other members of your party have already checked in."

The bellman opens the door with my bags.

"Tutti!!!"

"Janet!" We take a big long smoochie hug. "It's time for a cocktail!"

"Let me re-Laszlo and I'll be ready. Where's Mark?"

"Oh Honey, he's having drinks with some man that's new to the company named Darren Rutherford."

"Really?"

"Honey, have you met Darren Rutherford?"

"Not yet."

Janet, obviously trying to change the subject, coos, "I switched the shade of my foundation from Aurora Beige to Tuscan Beige. Can you tell the difference?"

From all over the United States, the National Trainers who work for the Revlon Department Store brands will descend on the Revlon corporate office this week. This huge undertaking was dreamed up by Adrian Anderson so as to place all of our brands in one huge cosmetic bay, due to our miserable sales performance as separate companies. His groundbreaking concept is called *The Head to Toe Beauty Stop,* containing six complete Revlon product lines and all the fragrances. We only have two days to learn all the lines' specific product knowledge and be able to teach it ourselves, culminating in a big press event at the Museum of Natural History. Every retailer in the U.S. will be at the museum for the unveiling. Janet's right. Sounds like mission impossible!

140 moisturizers. 65 foundations. 45 cleansers. 1500 shades of lip color. My junkie side is so excited that I want to jump out of my skin. As each tenured National Trainer presents their brand's products, I want to touch, feel, smell, and try everything! Cura Forte, Fango, and Crema Saponetta from Borghese? Supposed to contain miraculous properties from the Montecatini spa. Decongestant Cleansers from Germaine Monteil? Decongestion! My pores could use that transformation. Speaking of Germaine Monteil, the company that transferred Sue to Atlanta, I haven't heard from Sue. Not only that, but the phone number she gave me has been disconnected with no forwarding number? She better call me! Also custom blended powder from Charles of the Ritz? I bet Alberto Scala is sweating his ass off in rehab hearing the news that Revlon has acquired Charles of the Ritz! There's instant karma for you!

Some trainers who present are mesmerizing to me and I aspire to be like them. Others, though, are deadly dull and subsequently make up for that by becoming the scary Nazis of the makeup industry. After almost falling asleep from the last presentation, Steve from Lancaster Monaco Skincare is introduced and takes the stage. A bald, jovial man, equipped with a wickedly funny and sarcastic sense of humor, he begins his lecture with an expensive skincare line from Lancaster Monaco called Suractif! "Ladies and Gentlemen, before I educate you about Suractif Day cream, European skincare for the stars, I feel I must pass the tester around for you to experience because it's simply a wordless state."

We lift the gold plated petite spoon and delicately deposit a small amount of cream onto the back of our hands, after which we delicately smooth and massage the cream until it's absorbed. The room begins to reverberate with the *ooh's* and *ahh's*, like we're rubbing actual liquid gold into our skin.

I take a long, thoughtful inhale of the product on my hand and ask, "Steve? The fragrance in this cream is heavenly! From where does this scent originate?"

"Harvey, I'm so glad you asked." With the most solemn expression on his face, Steve proclaims: "Lancaster luxury skincare is produced in Monaco, adjacent to the palace of the Royal family. When we require more of this precious scent, we call the palace and her Royal Heiress, Princess Grace, driven in her royal limo, enters the factory. Assisted by royal nurses, she pees through white bread which is bottled for the production line." Steve picks up the jar and takes a big whiff and says "*HHHMMMM*." Silence, followed by hysterical laughed induced crying and choking. We can't get serious for an hour after that, which I should've enjoyed because the rest of afternoon is a total drag.

"Janet, I'm almost brain-dead and I can't hear about any more product information. I won't be able to remember all we've learned so far! Is it always like this?"

"Welcome to the glamourless world of the training department. We never have enough time to learn but are expected to do the horse and pony show at the drop of a hat. Just wait till we're at the Natural History museum. We'll do all the work and Management will take all the credit. Wait and see."

As I'm closing my training folder, a short, severe-looking woman with a jet-black bobbed haircut and severely over-drawn eyebrows, enters the room. "Will all the gentlemen please follow me!"

Thank God! Done with product! We now have to be fitted for the uniforms that we'll wear the night of the event. In a strange room the size of a closet, the woman I have now named Miss Severity, announces "You men have to wear these black blazers and charcoal trousers. You will bring a freshly starched white dress shirt the night of the event. Now pay attention, I did not say *off white* or *cream*. I said *white,* like, Snow White, which you'll wear with this striped tie. Do not under *any* circumstances replace this striped tie with another tie because you don't like it. Your personal taste is not important. Uniformity is critical. Please form a straight line to have your uniform chosen by size for alterations. I'm sure I have made myself clear and that there are no questions."

I hate the word *uniform* because it reminds me of high school when I had to wear brown polyester as a cashier at Burger King. The tailor is measuring and grabs me inappropriately. He smiles. Total pervert. Minutes later my skin's itching from all that polyester.

That night, all the trainers collapse at the dinner table, dead silent until several bottles of wine started arriving during the appetizer course. Ten bottles of wine later, it's so loud in the restaurant you can barely hear yourself speak. As I stand up to go smoke outside, I pass the cocktail lounge and see Mark Cooper speaking with a man whom I haven't seen before. As I'm standing there trying to eavesdrop, Steve from Lancaster startles me. "Can I bum a cigarette, Handsome?"

"Sure. Steve, who's that with Mark?"

Steve looks surprised. "Baby, don't you know your own boss? That's Darren Rutherford, the new VP of Sales in the west? Come on, Sweetness, let's smoke. Say, do you have a boyfriend?" Later walking back to the table, I notice that Mark and Darren have disappeared. Strange? I haven't even met Darren yet and Mark has seen him twice?

Next morning bright and early the training begins with more Cosmetic history followed by even more product instruction. I don't know how I'm going to possibly keep all this information straight! After eight more grueling hours of training, our learning misery comes to an end. As I'm leaving the training room, I accidentally drop all my training folders and paper goes flying everywhere. *Damn it! I just organized these by brand.*

As I'm bent over on the floor, trying to gather them up, I see an expensive pair of Gucci loafers. As my eyes travel up I see that it's Darren Rutherford, so I pull myself up off the floor while I put a smile on my face and confidently extend my hand. "Hi Darren, I'm so glad to finally meet you! I'm Harvey Helms, your new National Trainer on the west coast."

No response. He doesn't smile or attempt to shake my hand. "Harvey, I never approved you to be the west coast trainer." I watch him as he gets on the elevator and I stand there staring as the doors close.

I can feel myself shaking, trying not to cry. What should I do? I call Evangeline and her answering machine picks up. "Hi Evangeline. This is Harvey—your west coast trainer, I think? I just met Darren Rutherford, well, I kind of met him.

Anyway, call me. Oh, by the way, do I still have a job?"

Leaving the Revlon building, I jump into a taxi and scream "The Barbizon Hotel please," like I'd seen in the movies. No more waiting to cry in the cab. I cry all the way to the hotel, across the lobby, into the elevator, and finally in Janet's arms. "Can you believe this Janet? DARREN RUTHERFORD DIDN'T APPROVE ME! Who does he think he is? We work for Evangeline and besides that all my clothes are in L.A.! Do I have a job? Why hasn't Evangeline called me? Do you think she knows? Do I have a job? JANET SAY SOMETHING!"

"Honey, sit down. I have something to tell you."

Right at that moment Mark Cooper walks through the door. "Janet," I blurt out, "maybe Mark knows, I saw him speaking with Darren at dinner the other night. Mark, do you know—"

Janet interrupts me and stands up to face Mark. "Either you tell the kid yourself, or I'm going to."

Mark lights a cigarette as he walks to his room and closes the door. Janet screams "*YOU ASSHOLE*!" She takes a deep breath and lowers her voice a little. "Okay Harvey, you're not going to like any of this but here it goes. Yes, you saw Mark talking to Darren Rutherford but what you *don't* know is that Mark has been coveting the training position in L.A. Evangeline said *No way*, so Mr. Cooper has been poisoning Darren Rutherford, telling him that you're too young and inexperienced to handle such a big territory. I'm sorry, Tutti, but I didn't have the heart to tell you. God, Harvey, I'm so sorry."

Janet pulls a Virginia Slim cigarette out of her purse. I walk over to the window to look at the New York skyline. "Janet, you should've told me."

"Honey, do you want a drink?"

"No."

In my bathroom, I look in the mirror. I've been crying for hours and my eyes look like crap, and the stress of betrayal is showing in my face.

Later I lie on the bed, looking up at the ceiling. The real world's slapped me in the face again. This situation is too important for any actions that are rash or impulsive. If I listen to those thoughts, I'll be tossing Mark off the roof of the Barbizon and hiding all of Janet's cosmetics so she'll have a nervous breakdown. After an hour of soul-searching, I devise a plan. *Wait until Mark and Janet leave the hotel tomorrow morning then get to Evangeline. Right after that, give Mr. Stone-*

face Darren Rutherford a reason for his blue eyes to bulge out of his head. Harvey, you're not leaving Los Angeles because you haven't even gotten your hair done yet!

I look in the mirror and call upon my other angel of beauty! *Okay Dr. Laszlo, work your magic!* I lie down again and rehearse in my mind tomorrow's script of survival. I laugh to myself, as I never would've guessed that I'd appreciate all that heinous time with Anorexic Blue Eyeshadow Debbie and Patti Garrison. Will it pay off now? Tomorrow is going to be like the MGM 1939 movie *The Women*, when Norma Shearer looks at the camera and says to her Mother, *I've had two years to grow nails Mother,* as she dramatically raises her hands with nails facing the camera and screams *Jungle Red!* Or in my case, REVLON RED!

HARVEY'S DIARY:
SEPTEMBER 26, 1986
"Harvey Golightly"

"Thankfully, beauty is easier to remove than apply, and a swipe of demaquillage in the right direction, and you are you once again."
-MARGARET CHO

It's 6 a.m. and since the Sandman hasn't made a visit, I finally decide to get up and go for a walk. I throw on a black sweat suit I'd bought from Bloomingdales—it's so comfortable, with a modern sensibility. Dragging myself aimlessly through the streets of New York, I decide to go where one of the most famous women went when she needed inspiration during her trials and tribulations. But first I need to grab breakfast. I stop for a bagel with a smear and coffee with milk and sugar. A few blocks later I arrive in front of one of the most expensive windows in the world. I'm Harvey Golightly! Just like Audrey Hepburn in the movie, I'm standing in front of that famous window at Tiffany's on the corner of 5th Ave. and 57th Street.

As I'm mulling over my first professional corporate betrayal by someone who's close to me,

I marvel at the most beautiful yellow diamonds I've ever seen in my life. I watch *Dynasty* every week, for God's sake. I even threw a party the night Alexis and Krystal beat the crap out of each other! It was also the first time I heard the actual word *bitch* on TV. What would Alexis do? I have to work with Mark and I've got to figure out how to handle this. *Stay calm, Harvey. Let's see what the day brings.*

All National trainers are meeting at the National History Museum at10 a.m. to merchandise the cosmetic cases with product and point of sale literature. Right past the rotunda, I see our area buzzing with complete pandemonium. People are yelling *"Where are the eyeshadow duets?" "No, that case is for moisturizers not masks!"* There are boxes piled everywhere stacked almost to the museum's high ceilings.

Mark and Janet are working on our skincare cases and I decide this isn't the appropriate time for a confrontation. My inner voice keeps whispering *Wait for the right moment*. It's taking all the inner strength I have to not go over there and smack Mark upside his big, mustached, arrogant head! Meanwhile every 15 minutes someone yells *"The Press and retailers will be entering at 7. Please finish what you're doing and move on to your next project!"*

After the presentation, we'll be off to the grand dinner in the Bill Blass designed Whale Room, followed by a fabulous musical show with celebrity Peter Allen. As I'm merchandising an Ultima II color case, I'm thinking about where I'll be sitting at dinner. A trainer's table in the back of the dining room? Angela Lewis-Cartwright has entered the museum for the first time, surmising what needs to be completed. I recognize her from all the magazine articles I've read about her. Blonde, model thin, and wearing these incredible Chanel hoop earrings with the double C's. Noticeably though, she doesn't have on one drop of makeup.

She examines the Ultima II cases we've just merchandised and puts her hands on her hips. "NO, NO, NO! This merchandising says *Loving hands at home!"*

I stand up from behind the case and ask, "Loving hands at home?"

Angela points her laser stare at me. "Who are you?"

"I'm Harvey Helms, your west coast national trainer."

She raised her brow slightly, which I took to be her way of saying hello. "My name is Angela Lewis-Cartwright and I'm the new President of Ultima II. You may call me Mrs. Cartwright. *Loving hands at home* means, young man, that this merchandising looks unprofessional. Do it over immediately and make it prettier, cleaner and more modern. Do more of something that's not what you've already attempted."

"Yes, Mrs. Cartwright." It takes about two hours to re-merchandise this one case to her satisfaction.

Tonight at the gala, Ultima II will be unveiling a new product called *Color Shots*, which is a direct rip-off of Guerlain's Meteorites. Little balls of color that, when activated by a brush, turn into one luscious shade with light-reflecting properties. Angela's vision is that these big fake color balls, made to look like the Color Shots, will be swirling inside one of the display cases for effect. Instead it looks and sounds like colored basketballs are jumping back and forth in the case, getting ready to crack the glass. We can't get it to work and the look of disappointment on Mrs. Cartwright's face paints the whole picture. *Loving hands at home.* Through the PA system we hear

"It's almost 7. Please go change into your uniforms."

I'm looking at the floor surmising the loving hands at home situation when Miss Severity hands me my uniform. Trousers fit! Check! Jacket? Oh no! The sleeves are way too long. I turn to Miss Severity "My jacket doesn't fit!"

"Pity. Why are you telling me now? It's minutes to show time so you'll have to work with it."

I glance at the other guys and mine is the only uniform that doesn't fit. Did Mark switch? No! Did He? UHH! As I'm walking out of the wardrobe closet telling myself, *Don't worry, no one will notice,* I run right into someone. As I look up to say "Oh, I'm sorry," I see Adrian Anderson looking down at me. This is my first time meeting him since he's come from Mystique Cosmetics to fix our brands. First Mrs. Cartwright and now Adrian. My cosmetic karma is showing!

"Your uniform doesn't fit. Here! You will hold this walkie-talkie that controls the models to keep your sleeves up. Do not under any circumstances put your arms down while the press is in the room! Do you understand? We must look perfect for the *Head to Toe Beauty Stop!*" Adrian doesn't wait for my response and off he goes.

What an asshole. Of course he doesn't care because *he's* wearing an expensively tailored tuxedo.

It's finally 7:00. Enter the Press and the heads of every important retailer in the United States. The National Trainers are behind the cases acting as if they're the new beauty consultants in The Head To Toe Beauty Shop. I must admit we do look good, but my biggest problem, other than wanting to scratch because of this polyester uniform, is walking around for an hour as my arms throb, telling models to "Go here" and "Go there."

Adrian speaks, everyone applauds, and then they're off to dinner. At first my arms don't want to go down because they're frozen like the Tin Man in the Wizard of Oz before Dorothy and the Scarecrow use the oil can. When the last guest leaves the room, we scream and applaud! We're exhausted but now it's time for dinner and the show!

As we begin to leave, someone screams, "HEY! Where are you going? You have to dismantle these cases! "

No way! Janet looks at me. "I told you this would suck Honey! But Harvey, I'm not missing the dinner and show. I bought a dress at Bloomingdales' that's to die for and I'm showing it

252

off tonight! Watch this!" Janet tips a shelf toward a box and shoves the product with a flick of her wrist, which takes all of about five seconds. Everybody looks up and starts imitating Janet's demolition method. Needless to say, we have everything dismantled in a record time of fifteen minutes!

"Honey, how's my makeup?"

"Flawless!"

"Harvey, are you really mad at me beyond repair?"

"Janet, let's talk later, okay?" Peter Allen's taking a big bow, signaling that the show is ending. As we stand on the balcony overlooking the dining room, I can't get over the marvelous job Bill Blass did with the decor. I see Dana and he's laughing and drinking with a table-full of Belk executives. As I'm thinking about descending the long steps the to the dining room floor, I feel a tap on my shoulder. Evangeline comes up behind me and whispers in my ear, "Harvey, don't worry about Darren Rutherford. I told him that he didn't need my approval to hire Account Executives, and I don't need his approval to hire trainers. You'll be ok. I know you'll do great things! Try to get a glass of wine!" I look at all the people around me, who by now are drunk, and decide *I'm out of here.*

Back at the Barbizon, I take off all the scratchy, ill-fitting polyester, and order a cheeseburger. I'm emotionally drained. I call my mother and when she picks up I say, "Mother, I miss you. There are so many mean people in the world."

For once she keeps it simple. "Harvey, people will show you who they are but you have to be there to see it. I raised you to be a tough-as-nails beauty queen so I know you'll be fine. Don't you worry. Keep flashing those beautiful dimples God gave you. I love you." How is it that sometimes only your mother can make you feel better? Even my crazy Mother!

Sitting naked in my bed eating a cheese burger while Janet and Mark are probably out getting bombed somewhere, I'm glad this hellish week is almost over. Tomorrow is my last day in New York and Mark, Janet, and I have to do makeovers at Macy's Herald Square. I'll be working side by side with Benedict Arnold and his lip gloss accomplice. God, I can't wait to get back to L.A. to start my new life. Have to handle Mark first at the store , then Mr. Darren Rutherford before I get on the plane. I decide to sleep in Lancaster Suractif night cream so Princess Graces' pee can work her magic on my tired, disillusioned face.

I'm up the next morning, packing my stuff, and dressing quickly. I check out and hand my bag to the concierge to be stored until it's time to go to the airport. I want to get to the store, do my makeovers, straighten out Mark and Darren, then go get on my plane and start drinking gin and tonics. I walk into Macy's Herald Square. Are all of these people in a bad mood or is it me projecting my foul mood on them? Have I become Hector Projector?

I find the Ultima II counter and see Mark and Janet out front of the counter trying to give makeovers, standing there with two artists whom I've never met. I introduce myself to the counter manager Susan. "What's our sales goal today Susan?"

"$4,000, but with these two new artists sent from Mrs. Cartwright, I don't think we'll make it."

The two mystery artists speak without introducing themselves. "We've been hired by Angela Lewis-Cartwright from Mirabella magazine. We're here today to show you and the customers that makeup should be natural-looking. We're definitely not pushy sales people, so you need to learn from us."

This is the icing on the cake of my week, Mrs. Cartwright. I decide that silence is is beat for right now and go stand beside Mark and Janet. Mark looks at me and in his normal condescending tone starts lecturing. "Harvey I think as you get older and become more professional—"

So much for silence! "Mark, Shut up! I'm doing the talking this time! Don't you ever treat me this way again! I'm the new trainer in Los Angeles, not you. Okay? And another thing! At my very first beauty school you gave me used product in my gift! You ... *you... used-product-giver!* And that wasn't very nice!" (That sounded way more professional in my head when I was practicing.)

Mark glares at me and steams off the floor in a huff. Janet says, "Good for you, Honey, and don't worry, he won't be back."

"Well, we haven't sold one thing today Janet, so it's time to pull some customers. These Cartwright goofballs from Mirabella can't sell anything."

"Tutti, do I need lip gloss?"

"Yes. Hey, thanks for being my friend, but next time warn me before my career is almost ruined. Oh and Janet, can you tell me every reason why you love Madonna right now?" I know Janet loves me, so it's not hard to forgive and forget.

I pull a woman off the aisle for a makeover and look over at the two artists from Mirabella. The beauty advisors behind the counter just keep rolling their eyes at these two. It's definitely going to be interesting working for this Angela Lewis-Cartwright because it seems that she doesn't even like makeup. She personally doesn't wear any, and these two don't want to sell any! I finish my makeover and close the sale. $600.00. I look at the Mirabella artist. "If you two aren't going to sell anything, you won't last. If I were you, I wouldn't quit your day jobs at Mirabella."

Sitting in the bar at JFK waiting for my plane, I fall in love with the typical strangers you meet over drinks, revealing things you'd never tell anyone you know! After paying your tab you say goodbye never to see them again. Tonight I've been in the bar for quite a while because we're delayed due to weather in the middle of the country. Right on cue there's Bulging Eyes Darren Rutherford. I guess he's on his way back to the west coast as well. I look at him and this time I don't look away. I'm not going to move. I'm so disgusted with the week and full of gin that I just don't care anymore. Darren finally makes the first move and gets up to take the seat next to me in the bar.

"Quite a week, wasn't it Harvey?"

"Yes, it's been quite a week. Listen, Darren, I'm your trainer for the west coast and I know it's been an awkward beginning but I'm looking forward to working with you and Sally Smith. We're all there to turn the business around."

He looks transfixed like he's casting some voodoo spell on me. He finally speaks. "Harvey, I'm holding a west coast meeting in Newport Beach next month for the entire team to meet each other, and of course you must be there as our National Trainer. I'm bringing in some outside consultants to help us team build. I'll be in touch with the specifics. Have a safe flight."

Music to my ears! *"Ladies and Gentlemen, we will now be boarding the flight to Los Angeles, California."* I'm going home and somehow *home* feels right. After landing and getting all my bags, I catch the shuttle bus to the hotel and go straight to bed. As I lay there I think about where I'll live. West Hollywood? Brentwood? Santa Monica? Maybe Melrose Place, because I hear there's going to be a new TV show about Melrose Avenue. First stop though? The Antennae Salon! Step one in *Harvey gets a Hollywood makeover.*

HARVEY'S DIARY:
OCTOBER 28, 1986
"Hollywood Way"

"Only good girls keep diaries. Bad girls don't have time!"
-TALLULAH BANKHEAD

"Okay Lolita! How blonde are you? With Jean Harlow being a ten, Marilyn Monroe an eight, and Farrah Fawcett being a one with highlights, where do you fall?"

"I'm like a four, Tim, which is June Allyson from her MGM musical days, sort of light ash with a medium brown underlay."

"Next question, 'cause you barely call me so I have to get all the pertinent info while I have you on the phone. You're mother always thinks I'm lying when she calls asking *Have you heard from our Harvey, Tim*?"

"God, Tim, you do such an amazing imitation of my mother that it scares me. And what are you talking about, I call you all the time!"

"Whatever, queen! Have you found an apartment?"

"No I haven't. I'm totally exhausted from traveling and all this current betrayal drama, you know."

"Oh yeah, I know you! You'll be happier once you have a real home. Where are you thinking about living?"

"Well, I've thought about living in West Hollywood, because my hair colorist, tanning salon, and facial guru are all right there. I also drove over Laurel Canyon Boulevard into the valley looking and it seems calmer, yet it's accessible to the craziness and fun in West LA. What do you think?"

"Just get an apartment so your mother will get off my back! Richard sends hugs and kisses. Oh and P.S. Rebecca from upstairs came down to see if you could do her makeup for the Junior League Gala. We didn't tell her you had moved and said *He's not here.* That ding bat will never know the difference. Kisses! Now get up and go! Love you."

After driving around on too many freeways, I end up in the valley looking up and down streets for several hours, hunting for apartments. I turn off a street called Hollywood Way and I think about how that will sound. *I'm Harvey Helms from Hollywood Way!* Love it. I find a really cute apartment complex, coral stucco with teal accents, complete with gym and pool in Touluca Lake. The little chic city adjacent to Burbank. I remember "Lovely Downtown Burbank" from that 1960's show called *Laugh-In*. The apartment is on the same street as the Warner Brothers Ranch studio where they film the TV show *Growing Pains*. Alan Thicke who plays Mike Seaver's dad is so handsome! I feel close to the stars. Maybe I'll get my own TV Show!

With Tim's advice, I move into a studio apartment pretty quickly the next week because all I have is eight suitcases of clothes. Ikea won't open their first west coast store (in Burbank no less!) for another four years, but I'm sure I'll find something cute and affordable. Nothing elaborate, but very cute. Futon bed and little black love seat withcoordinating black coffee table.

There are many young, adorable actors and models who live in my complex. We lay out by the pool, drink, and talk about their acting auditions and who they have to sleep with to get the part. They love that I work for Revlon because, according to Sue, "Beauty is the closest thing to having an acting career." The first few times I fly out to facilitate beauty schools, I fly back in and forget how to get to my apartment.

Everything's so new but I guess the real reason is I should be called *Driving Miss Crazy!*

My first beauty schools in the west are difficult. Sally Smith and I have been sent west to "clean up" the business so every school is eight hours of beauty advisor hell, complaining about everything. *"Where's my Account Executive? I never see her!" "I'm out of stock! Is the Revlon factory that slow?" "Why did Ultima II discontinue Couture lip color in Coral Charmeuse?" "My customers are complaining that they ruined the formula when they changed the packaging of Fresh Blotting Lotion!"*

Just *blah blah bitch, blah blah bitch* all day long. I call Evangeline at the end of every day and ask, "Will this ever get better? These people whine through my entire training presentation!"

Evangeline patiently listens to me, and at the end of the every nervous breakdown call, she ends by saying, "Harvey, it will get better. Keep doing what you're doing!"

Sally has it equally difficult having to deal with the problems in our Retail Accounts. But we're both hard workers and not afraid to roll our sleeves up!

When I'm not facilitating schools, I visit stores and do makeovers. I begin to have the reputation of someone who can really help beauty advisors develop their businesses. After all, I've paid my dues working behind the Ultima II counter in Belk's. If there's a beauty advisor who is discouraged, I recant my tales of Anorexic Blue Eyeshadow Debbie, Patti Garrison, and Alberto Scala. Every time I bring up Tammy Faye, they ask, "Did you really do that to her?" Poor Tammy Faye!

The Friday before Darren Rutherford's District meeting, I receive a message on my answering machine to call Evangeline in New York. I dial the phone and I hear Evangeline's voice. Her *Hello* doesn't sound like her usual upbeat self.

"Evangeline? Is everything okay?"

"Harvey, we have a little problem."

"It's not Darren Rutherford or Mark Cooper again, is it?"

"No. Harvey, many times in life it's hard for people to accept something new, or well, someone different."

"Okay Evangeline, I've heard that a million times in my life so far, and I know what's coming, so just go ahead and spit it out. And don't be afraid you're going to hurt my feelings. I can handle it."

"Well, the problem is that your Nebraska Account Executive Anne Nielsen doesn't want you to do her schools because she thinks you're too *flamboyant* for her market."

"So Evangeline, let me get this straight. The translation for your lady-like way of saying *flamboyant* is: Anne doesn't want a big nellie queen from North Carolina teaching her schools. Is that right?"

She tries not to giggle at my impersonation and then asks, "What do you want me to do, Harvey?"

"Not a thing. I'm the National Trainer and I have plenty of experience handling homophobic bullies! I'll call her right now."

Before I ring Anne, I decide to relax and breathe. I light a cigarette and think *I've never been to Nebraska but isn't that close to Denver where Alexis, Krystal and Blake Carrington from Dynasty live for God's sake! I thought it would be gay friendly. Okay Harvey! Big cleansing breath! That's right. Let all this nastiness just flow right through you.* I learned this Buddha-like de-stressing breathing technique lying by the pool with an actress one afternoon. I calmly pick up the phone. "Anne, it's Harvey Helms. The National

Trainer for the west coast. Am I catching you at a bad time? How are you today?"

"Oh! Hi Harvey. I wasn't expecting to hear from you." She sounds nervous and shocked that I called.

"Yes, I just spoke with Evangeline Sarafoglou moments ago, Anne, and since we don't know each other yet, I'll get right to the point. I'm calling to let you know that if you want training schools this season, I'll be facilitating them. If you don't want me, then you won't be having any schools. It's up to you, but looking at your sales numbers I think you may want to have me come and train your beauty advisors. I started behind the counter and I know how to sell."

Silence. She stutters and dances around the issue. "Well Harvey, I never... I didn't mean to... It's just that we never had a man..."

"Well, Gail, I went through this discrimination in the South, so it's not new to me. But one thing you should know about me is that I won't back down if someone's prejudice is trying to hold me back."

"Well, Harvey, I guess then I'll see you in Nebraska." *Click!*

Screw the breathing. I know I was a total bitch but I don't want to be the poster child for gay bashing anymore!

"Nature gives you the face you have at twenty;
it's up to
you to merit the face you have at fifty.
-COCO CHANEL

"Mac! Our son is alive!"

"Mother, that's melodramatic, even for you. I'll have you know that *I've* been really busy but *you'll* be glad to know that homophobia is alive and well in Denver, Colorado. This woman named Gail thinks I'm too big a fag to do her schools!"

"What? Don't say that horrible word, can't you just say *sissy* or *queer*? Give me that woman's number."

"No, Mother. Listen, things are good but this new job is crazy. I love you and will call you soon so we can catch up 'cause right now I have to drive all the way down to Newport Beach for a sales meeting!"

"You're always rushing me off the phone because you have to get to work. Well all right then. I'll tell your father that you just don't have time for us right now!"

"Mother! Daddy could care less."

"I've got to go Harvey. Somebody's at the door. Probably someone one wanting to know if I ever had son and if he will ever visit us again."

"Mother!"

Click. Sissy or queer? She thinks that's a nicer way of saying fag? Interesting. No time to think about Mother's recent unpleasantness. Have to pack!

Darren Rutherford's District meeting is being held at the Ritz Carlton in Newport Beach, near Fashion Island, where, according to the same actress who taught me the breathing exercises, it's a mecca for fabulous shopping. I must have shopping time! I've lost more weight and now that I'm down to a 30 inch waist, so I'm desperate for cute shorts and new chic dress pants. Arriving at the hotel is no small feat for me because I have to take the 101 to the 710 to the 405. (Those are all freeways, if you don't live here.) Crazy! When I arrive there is an agenda waiting for me as I check in. Dinner will be outside, at 5:00.

After getting settled in my room, I brush some Terra Cotta bronzer from Guerlain through my T-zone for a fresh sunny look, and slip into a Perry Ellis multicolored linen shirt with walking shorts and Cole Haan loafers without socks. I know it's a repeat of my Sales Meeting look, but definitely worth a second viewing. Very fresh. Looking in the mirror I see the new hair and tan look is working. Now all I need is prospective husbands to line up to date me! Newport has to be full of nice men! Right? Is it time to take a chance on men again? *No broken heart this time, please;* I look up to the ceiling, putting my new husband menu request in God's direction.

I step out of the elevator and see a sign with directions to the Ultima II barbecue outside by the pool. As I walk to the outdoor promenade, I see everyone gathered at the dinner tables with a Ritz Carlton chef basting one of the biggest hogs I've ever seen! Barbecue is in every Southerner's essence and my mother always turns *Gone With the Wind* off right at the end of the Twelve Oaks barbecue. You know, right before that recent unpleasantness of the Civil War begins? I call that barbecue denial. It's rampant in the South.

I see Darren's big bulging eyes staring at everyone. Why doesn't he blink? Then he spies me and waves. "Harvey! Down here! I'm so glad you could make it. Look everyone, here's your new Trainer Harvey Helms."

Hello Harvey in unison from Lisa, Cathy, Zandra, Merrill, Pat, and so many others. Anne

Nielsen from Nebraska is conveniently absent because her child is ill. These are the Account Executives from the west coast territories, and I will soon be facilitating their training schools. Jean "Jeanie" Hayes, the ex-National Trainer in California, is here too. She decided to be an Account Coordinator and step down for a while because of family issues. This is also the reason I was given a chance to be a National Trainer at my young age. I am so glad to see her. I love having the support of another trainer and kindred spirit.

Dinner is a total meet and greet. Lisa, one of the May Company Account Executives, obviously has been chosen to get all my pertinent info, asking questions like a machine gun. *"So, Harvey, are you married? Where are you from? Are you divorced? What's your favorite Ultima II lip color? Do you think collagen really works?"* On and on. As she and I are talking, Darren clinks his glass a few times and gives a toast.

"Here's to the new team and a warm welcome to Harvey and Sally. My hope is that this team building will pull us closer together and make the west coast #1!"

After dinner, I pull Jeanie away from the group so we can "talk." "Jeanie, do you know Anne Nielsen?"

She rolls her eyes. "You don't have to say a word. She's a nightmare. You'll win her over just by giving her Coca Cola. She's addicted to it."

"Good to know. Listen, I'm not clear what these meetings are about, either. The agenda says the facilitators are from a company called Transformational Technologies. Have you ever heard of them?"

" I have, but under another name. *E.S.T.*" She looks around to see if anyone's eavesdropping. "Darren has brought in consultants from Transformational Technologies to help improve our communication process, or at least that's what his public dialogue is."

Public dialogue? Hmm... E.S.T.? "Jeanie, don't you think Darren is, well, creepy?"

"You mean the stare? I know. I have a feeling that some brainwashing may take place here tomorrow. We better stick close together."

"Jeanie, what is E.S.T.?" Out of the corner of my eye I see everyone's walking toward Jeanie so I just let that go. "Good night everyone! See you bright and early tomorrow morning."

Walking back to my room, I think, *Brainwashing?*

The next morning I wake and see it's an hour before the Diabolical Darren Show. I look out the

271

window of my room. Life is bizarre, but what a view. California is so beautiful and I live here now. Oh pinch me, I must be dreaming! I put on Ralph Lauren beige everything with chocolate crocodile loafers. Ralph with crocodile is always appropriate, you know.

At the door of the meeting room, Darren and his two female consultants are standing and greeting everyone. Strangely, yet not surprisingly, these two women have that same creepy stare. They speak slowly and hold onto my hand a little longer than I am comfortable with. Both women say in unison, "Good Morning... How... are... you?" Their hands are so cold and clammy.

"Fine, thank you." And I pull my hands away. I spy a chair empty beside Jeanie and rush toward it. Jeanie looks at me, grabs my hands and says, "Good... morning... Harvey... How... are... you? Did I blink?" I lightly slap her hand away.

"Listen, I called a friend last night and they told me that Transformational Technologies is based in Werner Erhard's company E.S.T., so I was right!"

"What? Who?"

"Werner Erhard! That Guru who brainwashes people! Haven't you ever heard of Scientology? Dr. Ron L. Hubbard?"

"No, but it sounds evil and really boring."

Jeanie looks at me without blinking and in a zombie like voice says, *"Anything that causes human beings not to blink, can't be good for you!"*

"Jeannie, stop making me laugh."

"Harvey, these women are going to try to brainwash us, and get us to do exactly what Darren Rutherford wants!"

"Jeanie, I'm from North Carolina. I know about Jesus, and sometimes we speak about Satan, but honestly, I've never heard of anything like this before!"

The creepy tone for the rest of the day is set by these two women who are definitely cosmic ball busters. They speak without interruption, and if you do interrupt you're reprimanded. Not fun. They just keep talking and I don't understand a word they're saying. It's *blah blah blah* and then they say *blah blah blah* and whenever you want something, you have to say *I would like to make a request.* For example, *"I would like to make a request to go to the rest room please."* Jeannie whispers to me, "I'd like to make a request, too. Will you two zombie bitches shut the hell up please?"

Hours and hours of talking proceeds, and it also seems that we don't get to eat. I whisper to

Jeanie, "I'm starving! Do you think they're trying to starve us too! It's already 2:00 and we haven't had lunch yet!" These two women are really focusing most of their attention on Sally Smith. They ask her question after question until they break her down and she cries like a baby. "Those witches made Sally cry Jeannie!"

"Harvey, I guess with her being the manager under Darren, they want her hypnotized immediately."

On the way back to my room that night to drink champagne with Jeanie, she says, "If we don't look them straight in the eyes tomorrow, I think we can avoid being put under their spell." Jeannie and I shake hands and do a double pinkie swear! We'll pretend to go along so tomorrow when we practice the *I would like to make a request" blah blah blah, so* these zombie bitches won't know that we're on to them. It's business as usual the next morning with the two zombies talking until they're blue in the face again. Everyone looks confused. But at 5:00 it's finally over.

"Jeannie, do you think they left subliminal messages or post-hypnotic implications?"

"I hope not, but call me if you end up on stage somewhere with your pants down or some other strange thing like sleep walking or liking Darren!"

Ironically, exactly one month to the day after the meeting and all that crap I took off him in New York, Jeanie calls me saying, "You're not going to believe it, Harvey, but Darren Rutherford has left the company and no one is saying anything. He's just gone!"

"Well Jeannie, the cosmetic executive revolving door continues to spin here at Revlon, but this is the fastest yet!"

Weeks later, Sally Smith tells me that Darren owns an ice cream shop in Hawaii. Go figure. Maybe E.S.T. has come up with some chemical to put into ice cream to change the masses. When I see someone with that *No Blink Stare,* I wonder.

HARVEY'S DIARY
NOVEMBER 10, 1986
"The return of Cruella"

"A woman's perfume tells more about her than her handwriting".
-CHRISTIAN DIOR

"Simone Asherton, VP of Marketing."

"Hello Simone. We didn't officially meet at the sales meeting in Arizona but I'm Harvey Helms and I just got a message to call you?"

"Did you? Oh yes, I remember you! You won a little makeup award that night with Sissy Webster."

"You mean Sherrill Webb?"

"Yes, that's her. Anyway Harvey, Evangeline Sarafoglou has been let go as of this morning, and before she left she told me you'd be a good training resource until a new Director can be found." *What? Evangeline's one of Mrs. Cartwright's first casualties?* I could tell that night at the Natural History Museum that Angela didn't care for Evangeline. She wants new, young, and modern. I guess Evangeline was too *Loving hands at Home*. I loved her and will always be grateful for everything she did for me.

"So, Harvey, obviously since the new Head to Toe Beauty Stop concept isn't performing up to par, and given the recent absence of a head of training, I'm in need of help with new product launches that will require instructional programs. First and foremost I want Mrs. Cartwright to host an internal Telethon that will be broadcasted to all stores, through meetings we set up using AT&T. The telethon will be called *Megadose* after our new night cream, Megadose All Night Moisturizer. We don't have a moment to spare, so you're coming to New York for a month to help pull this together Your airline reservations have already been made for you to fly out today at 9."

"At 9 a.m. this morning? It's 7:00 here already, Simone."

"Is that a problem?"

"No. I guess it's not. "*Gee, thanks Cruella, for all the advanced notice.* Only a half an hour to pack and I was going to get my roots touched up today, but screw that! LAX here I come.

I arrive in New York after a three hour delay due to bad weather at JFK. I grab my bags, a taxi, and then I check into the Barbizon. As soon as I walk in to the lobby, I get a sinking feeling in my gut. I haven't been here since the Mark Cooper and Darren Rutherford betrayal, complete with the ill-fitting polyester uniform, during the launch at the Museum of Natural History. I would've stayed at another hotel but Simone's secretary negotiated a good rate for my month's stay. *Maybe I'll have better luck this time?*

As the bellman opens the door to my room, I know this has to be a mistake, because this room is literally the size of a closet. I can sit on the bed and touch every piece of furniture in the room at the same time. If my suitcase is open, I can't open the bathroom door. And speaking of the bathroom, not only is there not enough shelf space for the products in my Laszlo Ritual, there is barely enough space for the new and improved skinny me! *Where's the phone?*

"Simone Asherton's office please."

"Hi. It's Harvey Helms. Is she there!"

"Oh hi, Harvey, I'm Jeanine Recckio, Simone's assistant! I can't wait to meet you! Hang on, I'll put you through!"

"Simone Asherton."

"Simone, it's Harvey. I hate to complain but my room is literally the size of a closet and I—"

"Where are you? Aren't you supposed to be here already working?"

"No Simone, I just spoke with you this morning and I start tomorrow."

"Oh, I thought it was today. Harvey, in the future, please remember that I'm not your travel agent nor am I a hotel manager so I couldn't possibly help you with your room dilemma. You need to speak with Jeanine. Please remember that she's the assistant and I'm the Vice President. Be here at 8 a.m. sharp tomorrow morning because you have a lot of work to do in a very short time. As a courtesy, you can bring me a coffee with two sugars and nonfat milk first thing."

Oh my God! I guess I must look like a waitress at a diner! It's just like Alberto Scala at Belk's telling me how he takes his coffee! I redial the number and Jeanine is very helpful having the hotel move me to another room. I decide to visit the hotel lounge and have a cocktail, ordering a refreshing Beefeater and tonic while sliding back into the yummy leather cocktail chair. The pianist is finishing up the song *New York*. "*If you can make it there, you can make it anywhere. It's up to you, New York...* (big finish!)... *New Yooooork!*"

Yeah, sing it sister!

I oversleep. Exasperated, I literally end up running over to the Revlon building at 625 Madison Avenue. Hailing a taxi at 8 in the morning is murder, so I finally gave up! As I arrive at the security desk, panting and winded, I blurt out: "I'm Harvey Helms and I'm here to see Simone Asherton."

The receptionist, Jackie, nods her head. "I know, because Jeanine Recckio has called every minute for the last *twenty* minutes asking if you've arrived. Mr. Helms, here's your electronic pass to click you in and out of locked doors. Watch me as I demonstrate. After you go through the door, Ms. Asherton's office is left, down the hall, and to the right."

A brisk walk with a forced smile and I'm at Simone's office. I see the name plaque *Jeanine Recckio* but she's not at her desk. Simone's office door is cracked open, so I lightly knock. I hear "Jeanine, where is Harvey with my coffee?"

At that moment, a woman who looks just like Snow White, with shiny black hair and glorious alabaster complexion, places a coffee in my hand and says "He's right here, Simone! He's been out here waiting patiently for you to get started!" I turn and mouth the words *Thank You* as I walk in to her office. Jeanine is a treasure!

I'm immediately overwhelmed by the amount of 18th century fake French furniture crammed into this office, so I decide that channeling my mother will be the best approach. "What a lovely office you have Simone, and where ever did you get all this lovely French furniture?"

She takes a big sip of her coffee. "France." I take a seat in front of her as she begins bringing me up to speed about this training assignment. "Harvey, first I have to tell you that since Mrs. Cartwright has arrived at Ultima II, she isn't impressed with anyone in the field. Sales *or* Training." Simone adjusts herself in her King Louis chair. She's 6 foot 1 so it's like watching a giraffe switch positions, throwing one skinny leg over the other.

"Yes, Simone, I've heard that." I lie so she'll think I'm in the know!

"This is your golden opportunity, Harvey, to change that. This Megadose Telethon is the biggest training program that we will produce this year, so it must be flawless! You and I will work together day and night until the script is polished and ready to present to our beauty advisors live across the nation."

"Live? Oh Simone, I'd hoped it would be recorded because so many things can go wrong with live performances!"

Simone stands up to pour herself a glass of water, revealing one of the shortest skirts I've ever seen. She sits back down and the Giraffe has to get settled again. "Soooo, *live* will be great! Let's start!"

Stanley Noland pops his head in the door "Are we on for lunch?" Then he stops, surprised to see me. "Harvey! Welcome to New York!"

"Thanks Stanley!"

"Simone? Lunch? The Pierre at noon?" Just like the room key pass at the sales meeting. Must remember to tell Sherrill.

I spend the next month sitting in Simone's office, surrounded by fake French furniture and writing the script for the Megadose Telethon. Mrs. Cartwright, who never welcomed me or anything, pops her head in occasionally to see how it's going. Simone, on the other hand, works me to the bone till very late at night. Now, you should know that when I'm ultra stressed, occasionally my gums start to bleed! I was diagnosed with periodontal ulcerative gingivitis in my late teens so instead of getting ulcers in my stomach, I have microscopic ulcers in my gums. They're not visible to the naked eye and I haven't had an attack like this since UNCG.

One night while Simone is whining "*Why can't you make these changes faster,*" and yelling "*Jeanine, I need pretzels!*" my gums start to bleed profusely. Jeanine appears with pretzels.

"Harvey do you need anything?"

"Yes he does, he needs to make the changes faster!"

I look at Jeanine, "I'm fine, honey."

Tonight the Giraffe cannot get comfortable in her chair and I'm getting ready to just jump out my skin. She's moving around and chomping on these gargantuan hard pretzels with crumbs flying everywhere. Looking up she nonchalantly says "Harvey, your mouth is bleeding." Simone hands me a tissue and without skipping a beat says, "Now, this next part of the script needs to be edited one more time." I didn't know that Hell would be furnished with French furniture. I stuffed the tissues into my bleeding gums and kept writing.

Frustrated and exhausted, I leave the Revlon building around 11:30 pm. *Barbizon? No! The Town House*—a gentlemen's bar on the upper east side that Joseph from Boston recommended for a drink and possible new husband sightings. As I walk in I see the queens who are probably here every night because they stand beside the piano waiting for their turn to be Patti LuPone and sing Evita's *Don't Cry for me Argentina*! Of course there are Sugar daddies galore looking for their boy toys and vice versa…

On my third strong gin and tonic I spot a handsome man who looks Jewish or Italian. I can't tell. He saunters over and bellies up to the bar next to me. "Hi. My name is Jackson. What's your name?"

"Harvey"

"Well, you're awfully cute, Harvey."

"You think so? Thanks. So Jackson, what do you do?"

"You mean for work or what I'm into sexually?" I give him a raised eyebrow. He clears his throat nervously. "I'm a lawyer." He's looking at me with his big brown eyes like I'm naked.

"Jackson it's nice to meet you but I'm on my way out. I have an early day tomorrow."

He looks disappointed. "Can I have your number at least?" I smile and nod yes. I stumble back to the Barbizon knowing I have another long day with Cruella.

Days pass and gum bleeding is now a daily occurrence. My biggest fear with our script is that these corporate executives will totally suck on camera. It'll be teleprompted, but if you have the personality of a cold wash rag it doesn't matter how good the writing is because it will look like they're reading whole thing. Surprisingly Simone looks at me and says, "Well, I think we've done all we can do. You're bleeding again." I grab a tissue. Just when I think I can take a breath, Simone drops the H bomb. "Harvey this afternoon, I've made a hair appointment for you at Mr. Jonathan's Hair Salon. Mrs. Cartwright has decided that before you're on camera for the Telethon, your hair color must be addressed."

"*Addressed*, Simone?"

"Well Mrs. Cartwright thinks, well, let's just say, that you are a little too *L.A. blonde*, and I agree. Mrs. Cartwright spoke with Mr. Jonathan himself this morning and told him that she'd would like you to be... a brunette."

In the cab ride over to the salon I'm just shell-shocked. *Brunette? I don't want to be brunette!* The cab stops and I look up to the salon on the second floor. As I walk up to the receptionist, I say, "I'm Harvey Helms."

She gives me an expressionless look and pushes the intercom. "He's here."

Out step six people and the obvious leader orders, "Come with us." Cinderella's step sisters lead me to a private room and sit me in a chair facing a mirror.

"Well, I like being blonde and..." It's like I'm not even there. They pull and prod every hair follicle, saying things like, *"Who colored this?"*

285

"I'm surprised it's not breaking off!" "That L.A. bleach is faster and harder, you know." "I guess he thinks he's Heather Locklear." Then all six became silent, standing at attention because the handsome and charming Mr. Jonathan has entered the room. "Harvey, Angela has requested that I make you a brunette, closer to your natural hair color for the upcoming broadcast. Don't worry, you're in good hands."

Two hours later I'm once again standing in front of the expressionless receptionist. "That will be $450.00 please."

"Do you take American Express?"

I'm a poor brunette again, crying in the cab all the back to the Barbizon.

As I'm lying on my bed fighting the urge to go to the drugstore and pick up Revlon's Frost and Tip kit to add some highlights to this desperately dull brown hair, Jackson calls. "Hey Baby! Can you meet me at the Townhouse in an hour?"

He does have big sexy brown eyes and seems a little on the naughty side, but there's something that's not quite right. I can't put my finger on it. Maybe he's straight? I wonder if he's one of those closeted married men who cheats with men on the side? But after this week from hell with Simone, I need some fun. "Sure,

Jackson. I'll meet you at the Town House but let's say two hours from now, ok? I have something I need to do first." Let's just say for $7.99, I am back to being California Blonde in a matter of 30 minutes.

The day of the Telethon dawns and things are intense. I feel better though because I had sex with Jackson this weekend. He's very assertive and I just couldn't say no looking into those brown eyes. Well, that plus all the alcohol we drank. I'll call Tim with the good news after this Telethon is over! I arrive at AT&T and walk into the studio where the telethon will be broadcasted, seeing Simone coaching all the executives about where to stand and when their cue is etc.

As I look left I see the makeup room and maybe some peace of mind because I know that other beauty junkies are probably in there. As I enter I see Mrs. Cartwright sitting in the chair, telling the makeup artist "Not too much, now. I hate it when people are too made-up." The artist goes to apply a little more eyeliner and she grabs her hand "That's enough eye liner, Dear." Then with a fake voice she looks at the artist and says "Very nice." Mrs. Cartwright has on absolutely no makeup. The artist spins the chair around and as Angela's getting up she spies me, with my blonde hair. "Harvey, was Louis sick? I must call and make sure he's okay! You're so… blond. Do you know where Simone is?"

"She's outside rehearsing people." As Mrs. Cartwright is leaving, I sit in the artist's chair and say, "Pile it on! I like lots of makeup!"

We're live in 3... 2... then the director just swings his finger silently telling us *action*. Two and a half painful, horrible, stiff, unfunny, line-forgetting, clumsy, career-ruining hours... and then it's over.

Simone is like a black widow spider looking to kill me with her venom. I hear her telling a group of executives, *"Well Harvey's never written a script before. Live and Learn."* I hear Mrs. Cartwright say to the Director, "When this is edited, please place visuals over Harvey's shots so it'll hide that dreadful hair."

Back at the hotel I look at my hair and decide I need an immediate appointment at the Antennae salon to dump stronger and faster California bleach to alleviate the brassiness. After grabbing a taxi, I meet Jackson at the Townhouse.

"Hey Blondie!" he says.

"Hey," I say kind of glumly.

Jackson takes his finger and pulls my chin up so that I'll look at him. "Bad day?"

"Career ruining," I say.

"You need a drink. No, several drinks I think," as he leads me over to sit at the bar.

"Jackson, I'm just sick about this horrible Telethon experience and Simone's blaming the entire calamity on me. Do you think this has killed my career?" I take Jackson through every painstaking moment of the broadcast and he's trying not to laugh. "I'm so glad you find my suffering amusing, you asshole!"

"Harvey, I have a brilliant idea! Why don't you quit your job? I can put you in a nice apartment on 5th Avenue and you won't have to work. I'll take care of everything and you can take care of me." *What?* Now for a moment, being taken care of does sound inviting, especially after the month I've had. Fifth Avenue? The fabulous shopping? The parties? My mother would definitely call me a Rip (Grace's polite Southern word for whore)! I'd be closer to Tim and Richard, though, living on the east coast—and they could fly up on the weekends!

Then I think of my dream. *Meet Harvey Helms. National Director of Beauty.* "Jackson I may not be at the top, and I may be losing my job thanks to Cruella, but I'm no quitter. And I guess more than anything, I'm not a whore. It's definitely an interesting offer, but I don't want to give up my career and I definitely don't want to be considered a boy toy. I'm kind of insulted that you would think of me this way."

I thought Jackson would just say *Fine, I understand*. But of course there's more to this story. My bad day isn't possibly over. "Harvey, I haven't told you the exact truth about myself." *Here it comes*, I think! *He's married?* No. Listen to this.

"Harvey, I'm not a lawyer. I'm a Federal Court Judge for the state of Connecticut. My real name is Jackson Polistano. The Honorable Jackson Polistano." I begin thinking about possibly being exposed in the National Enquirer.

"Jackson! The Star magazine could be going through my trash as we speak! God, I hope that they don't print any pictures of me as a brunette! Jackson, you waited till *now* to tell me? This could have been scandalous for me too! Revlon is one of the largest cosmetic companies in the world."

"Listen Harvey, I have to keep a low profile for my political career. It's just the way it is. You'll get used to it."

"I will get used to it?"

For the first time in my life I realize that I'm surrounded by total control freaks. "No thank you, your Honor. I object." I stand up and throw a twenty dollar bill on the table and walk out of the Townhouse with my dignity intact. Having Cruella make me the scapegoat, *the brunette incident* as it will be known going forward, and the closeted judge who just wants me to be a pretty unemployed whore waiting at home naked, ready to give him a blow job and hand him a martini and the New York Times, is just the icing on my cake of a week. *No! Thank you very much!* Walking back to my hotel I decide I'm going back to L.A., where people are normal.

The next morning as I'm packing, Jeanine Recckio calls. "Hi Harvey! Simone wanted me to let you know that you will be coming back to New York right after New Years to help develop more training."

"What? Really Jeanine? God, I thought I'd be fired this morning."

"Are you kidding? Things are always like this here at our little beauty asylum."

"Thanks Jeanine. Hey, listen, next time can you book me at the Drake hotel? I think the Barbizon is bad luck!"

I hear her giggle. "Sure, Honey! See you soon and Happy New Year!" I wonder what happened...

As soon as I get off the plane at LAX I want to kiss the ground, but no time for that now because it's straight to the Antennae salon, with stylists who have the fastest bleach in the west, and an understanding of the importance of being blonde.

HARVEY'S DIARY:
DECEMBER 24, 1986
"Christmas Crazy"

**When I eventually met Mr. Right, I had no idea that
his first name would be "Always."
-RITA RUDNER**

"Mother! Robert Mapplethorpe's photography is *art*! It's on the erotic side, but it's definitely art. What's worse Mother is you taking that idiot's side!"

"Harvey, you know that I cannot stand Jesse Helms, but these pictures of naked men doing things? Did you see the one, well I can barely talk about it, where the one man sticks his... I don't know if I can say it... fist and part of his arm up another man's"—Grace's voice drops to a whisper— "butt hole? I've never seen anything like that in my life! These pictures are a sin, Harvey... but I must say, these people in his pictures have lovely skin." My mother. Always a negative with a positive.

"Is that how you live with yourself?"

"Harvey, please let me remind you that you are speaking to your mother on the evening before our Lord and Savior's blessed birth! Since you moved to L.A., I think you've lost your mind and you've definitely lost your manners."

"Mother, Jesse Helms hates everybody except old, white, Southern people. If he had his way, I'd be dead for being gay and Tim would have to go pick cotton for being black and afterwards be killed for being gay."

"God, please forgive my son speaking like this before Your Son's birthday tomorrow!"

"Merry Christmas to you too, Mother.

"So there you have it Tim, the blow by blow Christmas unpleasantness this evening at the Helms household. Is Richard still at his Mother's?"

"Yes. You know he is because Nadine's almost as bad as Grace! Harvey every year you always say before going over to your family's house on Christmas Eve, *It's going to be better this year Tim. Wait and see!* And every year you always come back sad and disappointed."

"Why can't I have a family like the Brady Bunch?"

"When your mother is Scarlett O'Hara and your father is Bugsy Siegel, what do you expect? Did you get some nice presents at least?"

"Well, Mother and Daddy gave us money and that's good because trying to stay blond, getting weekly facials, and going to clubs costs more in L.A. than in Charlotte. I also got a 12 oz. bottle of cologne called Bravura."

"What?"

"Don't ask. A name like Bravura and the fact that the bottle is 12 ounces should tell you all you need to know. Let's see, I also got an IZOD shirt, but it's an extra-large."

"Look Skinny Minnie, just because you're down to 29 inches in your waist doesn't mean you can make fun of the big girls!"

"Tim, I've *never* been extra-large. Even when I lived here I was a medium. Straight people think that a man is supposed to wear an extra-large."

"How's the rest of your family?"

"Iris was high and Gary's probably in jail because he wasn't there and everyone else was just in the Christmas spirit. Anyway, I'm glad to be home with you and Richard. Where's Aunt Tillie's punch?"

"Here, drink up! I love me some Aunt Tillie's punch! It burns all the way down to your toes. Speaking of burning, what did Grace think about the new L.A. you? Did she call you a rip?"

"She might as well have. First she says, *Harvey, did you have to go that blond? If God wanted you to be a blond you would have been born one.* And I was like, *Really Mother? You're a redhead and I doubt that your drapes match the carpet if you know what I mean.* Then she asks me to turn around so I do a quick twirl and she says *You're too thin and it makes you seem prissier than you already are, if that's possible.*"

Tim chokes on his extra strong Aunt Tillie's Punch. "What did you say back?"

"I said, *Mother, if you don't knock this off, I'm going to go upstairs into your closet right now, and come back down wearing your last year's Christmas Eve Hostess pajamas. Remember how Daddy hated that look? Well just imagine if he sees me in it. And Grace, don't think I won't.* That shut her up, Tim. After which she's all *Merry Christmas everybody. We're all just having the loveliest time tonight, aren't we?*"

"What does your father do while all this is going on?"

"He drinks beer and cracks open chestnuts. Tonight before I left, he guzzled 12 beers. He did say Merry Christmas though, this year, and I guess that's an improvement. Gosh Tim! What time is it?

Where's Richard? I'm ready to drive around and see all the Christmas-crazy decorations!"

Richard finally arrives back at midnight and we take our traditional ride to see every house overdone in lights, tinsel, and a number of manger scenes. Everybody is judged by how many lights, reindeer, and Santa's elves they have and, of course, how cute their baby Jesus is. You'll hear things like *I think their baby Jesus is the cutest, but they need a little more snow around Frosty* or *Her three kings are the most festive but judging by the lack of Christmas lights, I'd say they ran out of money. Bless their hearts.*

We end our traditional yearly ride driving through PTL to see their Christmas Extravaganza, crafted with the most impressive amount of decorations that you know cost an absolute fortune. "Jim and Tammy Faye have outdone themselves this year! It's definitely a Christmas queen's dream!"

"I know, Richard, but tonight at the annual *Helms Hellish Christmas Jubilee,* Mother said it's disgraceful with them begging for money every day on TV and then spending it on this extravaganza with everybody starving over in Africa."

Tim whips around to look at me in the backseat. "Harvey, your mother doesn't even know where Africa is."

"I'll tell her you said so."

"Do that and a fresh lump of coal will be waiting in your stocking instead of all the cuteness Santa might be bringing tonight!"

"Tim, you're just like Grace, using Santa against me you Grinch!"

"Shut up Harvey! You're little Susie Lou Who from way down in Whoville!"

"Oh yeah? Well big deal and everything 'cause you stole the last can of Who Hash!"

Richard turns to both of us. "You two better stop being mean because Santa's watching!"

Tim takes a swig of punch. "Oh really Richard? Well then you're the little dog the Grinch turns into a reindeer so you better drive this sleigh, bitch, and get us home!"

The line of cars to get through PTL is a mile long, so I'm glad Tim brought the big flask full of punch. As we finally arrive at the end of the show, complete with the Three Wise Men on camels waving and screaming "*Merry Christmas Everyone!*" Tim proposes a toast. *Here's to Tammy Faye! May she finally find mascara that won't run!* Back at home, we open gifts, drink champagne, and eat breakfast pizza in front of the fireplace. Johnny Mathis' *Christmas* is playing as I give Tim and Richard all new dishes with dramatic blue glass drinking goblets, and they give me beautiful new sportswear in size small!

On the second bottle of champagne, Richard decides to get all serious. "Harvey, are you happy? I mean you look great but are you happy in L.A.?"

"Well, I like living in California and my job is exciting, although I think Simone Asherton may be the death of me. I'm going back for more punishment after New Year's. I guess I'm happy, but I must admit I'm lonely without you two. Maybe I'll make some friends out there this year? I just work all the time, that's all."

"Okay, but if you're not happy, you know you can come back home whenever you want."

Tim gives Richard a *get over it* look. "Queen, I know you had a bad experience with that Federal Court Judge, but I think you need to start dating in L.A. So get on that as soon as you get back. Understand? 1987 will be the year Harvey meets Mr. Right."

The three of us stand up to toast and hug but it's interrupted by a knock at the door. Tim quotes Rosalind Russell from the movie *Auntie Mame*: "If it's Santa, tell him we've already had it."

Richard opens the door and no one's there. "Hey, here's a box. Harvey it's for you." In the box is a fruit cake and a card that reads, *"Merry Christmas to the gays downstairs. Harvey! Tim finally told me that you moved but you'd be home for the holidays, so I need you to do my makeup for the Daughter's of the Confederacy New Year's Eve Ball & Cotillion. Come up around 7:00 on the 31st. I'm wearing a big white formal gown with hoop skirt and matching parasol. Thank you so much. XO, Rebecca."* God it's really good to be home.

HARVEY'S DIARY:
JANUARY 4, 1987
"Barely There"

"The best thing is to look natural, but it takes more makeup to look natural."
-CALVIN KLEIN

Looking out the window of the plane, I'm wondering what Cruella has in mind for torture this time. Luckily, this trip, I'm prepared for any stress she'll throw at me because while I was in Charlotte for Christmas, I went to my old dentist and she prescribed a magic elixir called Peridex. *No gum bleeding stress for me, Cruella! Bring it on!* The bad news is that Peridex can yellow your teeth. Very Un-L.A.!

Almost as bad as the thought of having yellow teeth is that Simone's fabulous assistant, Jeanine Recckio, has left Revlon to go to work at a new brand called Prescriptives from Estée Lauder. It's rumored to be Lauder's new company with latest-greatest formulas and, if that's not enough, they'll also be doing custom blended foundation and powder at the counter! Estée Lauder always does things first class. From a department store perspective, Revlon can produce industry changing ideas and formulas first, but they somehow get all twisted up and quite honestly the products turn out looking sort of ghetto. Once I was attending a meeting where Revlon was launching a new fragrance called—get this—"Downtown Girl." The Marketing Director took the stage in front of all those chic magazine editors and said, Downtown Girl. She's everything uptown isn't." Enough said. My parting gift from Jeanine is being booked at the Drake Hotel on Park Avenue, which is so much better than that bad-luck-causing Barbizon.

When I enter Revlon, the security receptionist Jackie recognizes me. "Welcome back, Harvey! Maybe this trip will be better than the last? " As I open the door with my security clicker on the 6th floor, I hear a mix of crying, screaming, and moaning. Who is that? Paramedics abruptly push past me and head toward Adrian Anderson's office. Within seconds I see his assistant Jan climbing out from under her desk with a handle bottle of vodka with red lipstick all over the top of the bottle's opening. She's scream-crying, *"I hate all of you. I work so hard but you only care about yourselves, you bitches! And he's the head bastard who treats me like crap!"*

A paramedic jabs her with a syringe of something and down she goes. Adrian Anderson, who I surmise is the Bastard who treats Jan like crap, is standing in the doorway of his office, just shaking his head. Another one bites the dust. When the gurney rolled past I could see the red lipstick smeared all over her mouth. I thought, *Hmmm? Cherries in the Snow? That's one of my favorite Revlon lipstick shades! Well, off to Belleview mental ward with her.* This trip might not be as good as I thought and just like Margo Channing from the 1950's Bette Davis movie *All About Eve*, I said to myself *Fasten your seat belt, Harvey, Looks like it's going to be a bumpy ride!*

Around the corner is Angela Lewis-Cartwright's office. I see her assistant Susan, typing as fast as she can, juggling the phone and faxing at the same time. She has this slow, effected, Southern way of speaking. I *think* it's Southern, but it's hard to know. She's a nice girl and seems to be able to handle all of Angela's personal and professional requests, including the two adopted children and their daily activities, her Ken-doll-like husband who isn't employed or has some job in title only, plus all the craziness around here. Angela's life looks just like *A Fabulous Day in the Life of [...]* expose for Life magazine. I think she adopted children instead of having them so that she could choose what they looked like. She obviously did that with her husband, because he's younger and gorgeous, but not as smart as Mrs. Cartwright. Her mantra is *"Presentation is everything—or at least, it's 90 % of the battle."*

I turn left to find Simone's office and see no one sitting in Jeanine's old chair. Sad. Love Jeanine. There's an envelope on Simone's office door with my name on it. I quickly snatch it and sit down in Jeanine's old chair. It's definitely Cruella's over-the-top gold French stationary. I can't believe what I'm reading:

Harvey,

I know that you've just arrived in New York but I must let you know that I'm ill. I've developed Chronic Fatigue Syndrome so I'll be taking a leave of absence and I'm not sure how long I'll be out. In the meantime, I'd like you to fill in for me. Adrian Anderson has hired a new Director of Training named Vicki White and she's starting in about three weeks.

I hope to be back as soon as I can, and in the meantime, you may use my office while you're here. Please DO NOT place any glasses that will leave a ring mark on my desk without a coaster.

Regards,
Simone

Back down the hall, I'm waving the note at James Shultz, who is our fabulous Creative Director. "What the hell is Chronic Fatigue Syndrome James and who is Vicki White?"

He grabs the letter out of my hands. "Oh! CFS? That's that new disease that makes you tired all the time for no reason. In Simone's case though, it's probably from screwing Stanley Noland every day and being a total bitch all at the same time. Adrian just hired Ms. White and… I have a suspicion that they know each other in a biblical way, if you get my drift. "

"James, I get Chronic Fatigue just thinking about Simone! I'll deal with Vicki White in three weeks when she gets here. We'll have already started the training season so there's not much she can do."

"Don't worry about Simone, Harvey. I don't think she'll be back. Adrian doesn't care for Simone or Stanley. "

The rest of the day, I sit in Simone's office making calls. "Hi Mother. Guess where I'm calling you from?"

"Oh I don't know, some secret homosexual place you're not supposed to talk about?"

"No Mother, I'm at the corporate office of Revlon in New York!"

"Well isn't that nice you could go to New York since you could only spend about five minutes with us here at Christmas. Your father brings it up every day!"

"He does not, Mother!"

"I know he's thinking it!"

"Mother, I'll come back home soon for a visit soon, I promise." This is a bold faced lie I tell because I just want to skip all the long distance guilt.

"Well all right, I don't want to bother you while you're at work; besides, this phone call will probably cost you a fortune."

"Mother, the Depression is over and, besides, Revlon pays for it!"

"Oh Harvey, before we hang up, did I tell you that the woman from the 8th floor hasn't called here in a month? Do you think she's dead?"

"I've got to go Mother." Hanging up, I hope she's dead because that would mean the end of hearing about *that woman from the 8th Floor*!

The next morning starts off with a coffee and bagel on my way to the office. As I click through the security door I can see associates walking toward the conference room. James Shultz comes up beside me and nudges my shoulder. "Are you ready to see Angela's secret project? The Barely There Collection?"

Intrigued, I am just about to ask James to tell me more when the security door clicks and Angela comes walking in. She has a slight limp, which she must be ignoring since she's wearing six-inch leopard print heels. She's spewing some story to her assistant Susan about falling. "Susan, I was walking and all of a sudden I fell! I *fell, Susan! I fell!"*

Susan, with her slow, affected speech pattern keeps saying "I'm sorry, Mrs. Cartwright. I'm sorry, Mrs. Cartwright. "

A crowd has gathered listening to her story. "The worst part Susan, the worst part was not falling. The worst part is that while I was lying on the ground, a woman in Manolo Blahnik's told me I was too old to be wearing these shoes!"

I see James Shultz making a face out of the corner of my eye and inside I'm thinking, *Don't laugh, Harvey!* I bite my lip so hard I think I draw blood. I decide in that moment, though, that if James can call Mrs. Cartwright *Angela*, then I can too!

Angela passes me without a *Good Morning* or a *Didn't I have your hair color fixed?* as we're being ushered into our conference room. The room, by the way, has been completely transformed by James: decorated in black and ivory and on the walls are the most beautiful face shots I've ever seen. They're natural yet very dramatic, showing the skin you've always wanted to have without makeup, but in reality wearing a makeup so natural it's like your skin is totally bare. Almost naked.

Hours later, I'm on the phone with Sherrill and Janet, dishing the Barely There news!

"Well, Harvey, This is new and revolutionary for its time, but I think it's going to be a pain in the ass to train."

"Why, Janet?"

"Tutti, our beauty advisors *love* color, and now we have to tell them they can only wear beige and brown? And whenever there's hint of anything new or if change is in the wind, you know they love to complain and say it will never work. Harvey I'm not talking about N.Y.C. or L.A., S.F., or even Chicago—but up till now it's been all about color, shimmer, and sparkle. It's a beautiful collection but I bet some of the beauty schools are going to be hellish! Sherrill what do you think?"

"Janet, you and Harvey know that in the South they won't even want to say the word *bare* because it's like saying the word *naked*. I asked Betty in Tennessee and she said *God will strike me down with lightening if I say that word to my customers!* You guys also know that they won't say *naked*, they'll pronounce it "*neckid*", which in the South means you have no clothes on and you're up to no good!"

We all burst out laughing. "Harv, have you met our new boss Vicki White yet?"

"No, but I'll be filling in till she's here, which might be a couple of weeks. Our training season will have started by the time she gets here; besides, James Shultz has our training materials ready and I'll set up a conference call to walk everyone through the info in the next few days. Sherrill, How's Dana?"

"Exactly the same."

"Janet, how's Mark? He's got to love that I'm filling in as his boss for a minute! Tell him hello, won't you?"

"I think I'll skip that for now Tutti!"

"Okay you guys, we'll speak later this week! Bye!"

I sit back in Simone's over-sized French chair. *I could like having an office here*. With no Simone stepping on my last gay nerve, I decide it's time to take Tim's advice, so it's off to the Townhouse to hunt for perspective husbands. 1987.The year of Mr. Right. Right?

HARVEY'S DIARY:
MARCH 17, 1987
"After another sip of iced tea"

"I'm crazy for trying, and crazy for crying,
and I'm crazy for loving you."
-PATSY CLINE

It's been a few months and so much has
happened that I haven't had time to write in my
diary! Time to catch up! Let's see, where did I
leave off? Ah yes, Mr. Right!

As I walk into the Townhouse that evening, an incredibly handsome man with dark hair, green eyes. and sculpted face comes straight up to me and says, "Hi! I'm John Buchin."

Well, he had me at *hi.* Since then, it's definitely been a whirlwind romance. Here is the "Tea & Back story:" John just ended a job as a feature reporter on Fox's Good Day New York Show. You know the people who report on the news or morning talk shows—who aren't the hosts like Regis and Kathie Lee, but the reporters who do special stories and comedy pieces? John won an Emmy while he was at CBS because of his brilliant comic timing and extraordinary segments. His firing from CBS made the Village Voice because he's so opinionated and mouthy. He's also currently an unemployed, nice Jewish boy from New York. Oh, and by the way, I'm in love and if you're counting, this is John #2.

John loves animation, especially vintage Warner Brother's Bugs Bunny, Daffy Duck, MGM's Droopy, and anything Disney. He dreams of being an Imagineer at the Walt Disney Company where the crazy creative's, locked behind Disney's gate's, think up the unimaginable for Disney movies, TV shows, and theme parks. John is six years my senior but he still brings out the child in me. We make up crazy character voices when we speak to each other and then fall over with laughter. When we're in public people stare at us like we're crazy. I guess we are.

On my last night in New York, he invites me to a party to meet some of his friends, but first we stop for dinner at a gay restaurant on the upper east side called Mayfair. As soon as we walk in off the street I feel blind because it's very dark, but as my eyes start to adjust I see a room filled with senior gay men. Translation? A bunch of queens standing around a piano—and of course belting out show tunes! *Sing it Judy*!

John seems very serious and quiet in comparison to this gay and merry atmosphere.

After our first round of drinks arrive, John sighs and takes a big gulp of his cocktail. "Harvey, I want to tell you some things that you should know about me."

" Well, John I have some things that you should know about me... like my Southern prejudiced family and the fact that you'll probably be their first Jewish person and—"

"Harvey, I have cancer. Lymphoma." John is looking me straight in the eyes as I down my cocktail and start to tear up.

"Cancer? Oh my God!" I start crying and he grabs my hand.

"Harvey, it's in remission and I don't know if it will ever come back," he continued as he knocked on the table for good luck.

I flag down the waiter. "Hey, will you bring us several double gin and tonics please? I'm really feeling stressed—I mean thirsty."

Right after the waiter serves our many drinks and house salads, he pulls out his pepper mill. "Would either of you like fresh ground pepper?"

John takes a big bite of his salad and I think he's going to say *Yes* to the pepper, instead he says, "Harvey, I only have one testicle." The waiter makes a quick about face and runs to the serving station.

What should I say? *Oh John, I'm sorry? It doesn't matter! Do you wear special underwear? Can I have another gin and tonic please?* Somehow we make it through dinner. I'm drunk and exhausted from crying, but I still feel pretty because I have on my Calvin Klein navy pinstripe suit with a vivid blue and white striped dress shirt and fabulous yellow paisley Perry Ellis tie. I really jacked my hair up on top like George Michael. As we end dinner, John looks at his watch and gently touches my face. "My love, we have to go, or we'll be late for Willie's party."

We take a taxi to a high-rise building where the party is being held 40 floors up in a penthouse. As we walk in John immediately introduces me to his good friend Willie, after which he disappears into the crowd to mingle. As I'm walking around smiling, pretending that I know everybody, I see that there must be at least 100 people here that I don't know. Their laughter and chatter makes me feel awkward and the longer John's away the madder I'm getting. I'm rebelliously drinking white wine like its water. Temper plus alcohol equals not pretty. I spot John. *There he is. Who's he talking to?*

In a slurry fashion, I more or less spit my words at him. "John, I need to see you on the balcony immediately." I think *Take that Alexis Colby Carrington.* I turn and walk out on the balcony, peering over the railing to reaffirm that we're definitely 40 floors off the ground. "John, I can't believe you brought me to this party and left me alone where I know absolutely no one and---"

Before I could finish my Dynasty re-enactment, John grabs me by the throat with both hands. I sputter out "I can't breathe" but he doesn't stop trying to strangle me. I can see him yelling but I can't hear anything because he has me bent over the balcony. It slowly dawns on me that he's trying to kill me. I'm going to die, 40 floors up, in Manhattan.

Suddenly, John's hands release me and the air rushes back into my lungs as a very strong set of hands begins pulling me up from the ledge. Thank God for miracles. John's friend Willie stepped in on us before I became the 11 o'clock news lead story.

Numb from the shock, or perhaps from embarrassment of the big red hand marks on my throat, John and I leave the party together and head straight for the elevator. Together! As the doors close on us, I'm not sure what to feel. At dinner I was sad because of his cancer and I felt this incredible love for him. Now standing here, I feel numb with a sore neck, having been almost thrown off a building and everything.

John starts laughing and I sort of laugh along nervously, not knowing what to think or say. My inner voice is saying *Harvey, he's crazy! Run away from him right now! You are dating Dr. Jekyll and Mr. Hyde!* My feet won't move and I can't produce one rational thought. *Doesn't it matter that he tried to kill me? Do I want love this badly?* If anyone's counting again, this is Harvey murder attempt #2.

After a silent cab ride we go back to John's apartment and somehow end up in his bed. It's incredibly beautiful and loving until he starts crying, telling me he was raped by this other feature reporter who does segments about travel. *God what a night. Cancer? One ball? Strangulation and almost being tossed off a high rise? A tale of forced sex?* Part of me thinks that this is as bad as it will ever get. *How could it get worse? Is the Universe giving me all the bad stuff up front all in one night after which I'll have a smooth life complete with love?*

Back in L.A., I rationally understand that I've only known John for a few weeks and his behavior up to this point has been crazy, maybe even deadly, but I can't stand the thought of being away from him. *Can you say obsessed? Do you think it's hormonal?* John lent me his audition reel on video before I left New York and I can't stop watching it. I put it in the VCR and just keep rewinding it to see his face. I don't care about anything else.

I take the red eye every Friday night from LAX to JFK so that I can see John for a day and a half. One morning while lying in bed, John pulls me close to him. "Harvey, I can't find work and I'm sick of New York. What do you think about me moving to Los Angeles to be with you?"

"Well, you definitely would have more possibilities for TV and you could check out being a Disney Imagineer. No more red eye flights would be nice for me too... so I say *yes*!"

As I'm cleaning for John's arrival, I have the TV on for background noise and in my distracted consciousness I hear the phrase *"Jim and Tammy Faye Baker are in a scandal that PTL will not recover from!"*

What? My Tammy Faye? Jim Baker had an affair with a woman named Jessica Hahn and is also accused of embezzling money from PTL! Tammy Faye has to be livid about the other women and all the crying Jim made her do so all those senior citizens would donate their monthly Social Security checks! I immediately stop cleaning and have a holy moment of silence out of love and respect for Tammy Faye.

Something in the back of my head keeps saying *If you call Tim and Richard to speak about this PTL fiasco, you'll also have to ask them if you're doing the right thing with John moving here! Harvey just keep cleaning and you can call them after John moves in because he's already shipped his stuff from New York and he'll be here any minute.*

The door buzzes and my heart starts racing. *John's here!* I push the button. *I can't wait to see him!* I hear his footsteps. *We're going to be so happy now!* I hear a knock. *Yay! He's finally here!* I open the door. We stand there and look at each other. John has a miserable, angry look on his face that I might as well get accustomed to seeing.

"Harvey, I'm hungry. The damn airline didn't serve anything but peanuts, and I sat beside this asshole who wouldn't shut up! What do you have to eat?" John starts sniffing the air. "I forgot to ask if you have a cat. I'm allergic to cats."

No. "Hello my love. So, glad to be here?"

John pulls out an inhaler and takes a big breath in.

"John, you have asthma too?" I know in this moment that this cross country move has been a big mistake but I can't turn back now. I'm not going to call my mother about any of this because she will triumphantly say *"Harvey, I told you when you were eleven years old that you were never going to be happy being gay."* Was Mother right? So far gay hasn't turned out to be so successful in the love department. But I will deal with my mother another time... or, as she's says when she wants to change the subject, *"After I have another sip of Iced Tea."*

HARVEY'S DIARY:
JUNE 5, 1987
"The revolving door continues..."

"Everyone coming out of a perfume store is smelling the back of their hand!"
-JONATHAN CARROLL

I'm standing outside the employee entrance of JC Penney in Dallas Texas, thinking and smoking a cigarette. I've been too depressed to even write this in my diary but maybe doing so will make me feel better. I'm gazing up at the sky thinking about the day I've just had. *How did I get here? Let's see.* Well first of all, the Barely There Collection was a huge hit, but Revlon couldn't keep up with demand because the factory stayed out of stock, so our new hit became our biggest nightmare. Our sales took a big dive and customers were absolutely livid. Ron Perelman wants profits so his solution is to open up our distribution. JC Penney? I can't imagine Angela Lewis-Cartwright and JC Penney being mentioned in the same sentence. Ultima II is in better Department stores and this is definitely going to be a step down.

I called Sherrill the night before, right after I had checked into my hotel in Dallas. *"Sherrill, I think we've hit an all-time low."* She sighed and just said, *"You know it. Call me and let me know how it goes!"*

Like it or not, the beauty queens who work with upscale department and specialty stores like Bloomingdales and Saks can be terribly judgmental about brands carried in the lesser environments like drug stores or JC Penney. Who even knew that JC Penney had a cosmetic department? I was quite honestly a little embarrassed when I first heard the news from Sally, so I didn't tell any of my friends about it. Today I have to train a hand full of beauty advisors who will be the first to present this Ultima II bay concept to our corporate executives.

As I walk in I am bombarded with the JC Penney smell. This probably sounds strange but all places have a certain smell, if you're aware of it. The JC Penney smell is a mix of polyester and dried flower arrangements with a hint of Matrix Biologie hair care. The people are friendly enough but everything feels strange. It's like when you go into a dollar store and from far away the products look like name brands but once you get up close you realize that it's a totally different story. Here too; it looks like a department store but up close I recognize very few of their brands.

The fact is, though, that JC Penney is financially sound and making profits. They want to elevate the product mix in their stores; so, enter Ultima II. Obviously, we must be desperate as well or else I wouldn't be here. JC Penney also wants to open Elizabeth Arden, but that's a no-go. It's probably for the best because Miss Arden would roll over in her grave. They now have Ultima II which is probably no problem for Charles Revson in his grave because he would've sold his own mother for a bit more cash.

I end up training four new, inexperienced girls who want to break into cosmetics so they can leave for the big city. Not unlike a gay boy from the South we all know who viewed cosmetics as his escape route from Charlotte, North Carolina. I decide to forget that I am in JC Penney's and concentrate on these four little birds who need to learn how to fly. What a flashback... just like Sue taught me when I knew absolutely nothing!

I pour my heart and soul into these girls. One of the girls says, "I was so nervous to meet you! Why are you being so nice to us?"

I look into her innocent face and respond: "Because someone was nice to me once on my very first day in cosmetics. Don't get me wrong, though, the cosmetic industry is not for the faint of heart. It's a business and you have to sell to survive. Don't ever forget it."

I think I speak the truth when I say that training and development is the heart of any corporation in every industry. We're the facilitators, people fixers, trouble shooters, special event producers, sales conference setter uppers, and all around jacks of all trades who will do anything when asked. Charles Revson said *Creative's are like paper towels. Use them up and throw them away.* Janet was absolutely right! T&D is always overworked, treated like crap, underestimated, and ultimately just a stepping stone to something else. It attracts an interesting group of people, including myself.

The payoff however, is in taking fresh faces with their looks of awe and inspiration and turning them into cosmetic experts. Unfortunately, some people in training and development don't belong here. As part of this recent Ultima II unpleasantness, the training department has had two such interesting people in the last three months come and go as the Directors of Training. Vicki White, who was hired by Adrian Anderson; and Sam Caldera, who replaced her after she left.

Oh, and James Shultz was right. Simone never returned. I wonder what they did with all that French furniture?

So here's the revolving door update. Vicki White is a backwards girl from somewhere in the Midwest who slept with Adrian Anderson to get where she is. Vicki began her career as a beauty advisor for the now defunct *true* cosmetics where she freely admits that she was a terrible beauty advisor. When she first came to critique our schools, she'd stand up in front of the room to show us how it's done. Her best presentation skill is that she would just get louder and louder to keep your attention. And just when you thought she was going to stop, her voice became even louder. Sally and the Account Executives would look at me like *is she for real?* Then Vicki would say, "Okay Harvey, it's your turn. Present just as I did, varying your voice."

What a mess. Her lack of training skills wasn't her downfall, though. She quickly lost favor with Angela because of Adrian. One day I asked Angela a question about the business and her reply to me was, *"Harvey, why don't you ask your boss? She's sleeping with my boss so she knows more than I do."* I guess sleeping with Adrian gave Vicki enough experience to accept a marketing job from the Maybelline corporation right after that. Obviously Adrian was back with Mystique Cosmetic's after screwing us up with the Head to Toe Beauty Stop concept. As with other people situations in my life, one bad Witch gets immediately replaced with another.

Sam Caldera: Boss number 2. This one makes Mark Cooper look like Santa Claus! Sam arrived immediately after Vicki as an easy fit because in his past he was the Director of Training for Ritz when it was owned by Squib Drugs. It was said that he was a master makeup artist for CBS for years and that he'd done makeup for all the greats. Think Bette Davis. Judy Garland. Maybe he did. If that wasn't true, then he's guilty of gay blasphemy to lie about Judy!

Sam was a big jovial guy with a thunderous laugh, and a head so large that it was like a balloon float in the Macy's Thanksgiving Day Parade. Once in New York after an emergency JCP meeting, we went to a gay bar down in the village. I thought it was harmless enough but Sam was really putting them away that night. I didn't drink that much, which was rare for me, as you know. He grabbed me, tried to kiss me, and I felt like the parade float was trying to engulf me. I slapped Sam so hard in the face that I think his foundation and cheek color flew right off of him!

A few weeks later while in Arizona teaching a beauty school, I received a message to call Sally and she was furious! "Harvey, Sam was lying to Stanley Noland saying that you had not set up the hotel direct bill as you were supposed to and that you can't take direction. I overheard him telling Stanley that you need to be fired, so I burst in and said *That's a lie Sam! I just spoke with Harvey and everything is in place as it should be!*" If you're still counting, that was Cosmetic Betrayal #2. Stanley had no choice but to fire Sam. Unfortunately, I know I'll think about Sam's big float head every Thanksgiving when I watch the Macy's Day Parade.

So here I am. Standing outside another employee entrance just like Belk's, wondering if I can make it in cosmetics. What has my life become, with two crazy bosses later, JC Penney and John Buchin. Where's all the glamour gone?

HARVEY'S DIARY:
AUGUST 15, 1987
"Mr. Pillow"

"There's no cosmetic for beauty like happiness."
-MARIA MITCHELL

"I can't find work, Harvey, don't you understand? And I hate California because everyone's so fake and stupid! Their museums are a joke!"

Yes, ladies and gentlemen, I'm back in L.A., and John is becoming more miserable and—to be honest—more disturbingly crazy as the days pass. He's crazy. Not crazy. He's crazy again. Not crazy again. He hides in his office or comes out to confront me about how his life is in the toilet. He looks at me with those big wild eyes while he picks *Mr. Pillow.*

"John, what's with this pillow thing?"

"I think moving here was a big mistake, so why do you care? You're never here. You're always off being Mr. Successful, aren't you?" This pillow he carries around is like a teddy bear and he picks at it with his fingers.

"Hey, I know things are difficult right now, but they'll get better."

"How would you know? The only thing you truly love are your cosmetics. Definitely more than you love me because our bathroom is a shrine to the beauty industry. I hope you and Erno Laszlo will be very happy together! You have a real sickness."

Me? Sick? He's plucking away at the corner of the pillow and I'm the one who's sick? I'm not surprised that nobody will hire him! He's tried so many outlandish things to grab people's attention and get his foot in the door for an interview. Probably the strangest is his recent "brilliant" idea, making this big cardboard ear attached to a red radio-flyer kid's wagon. He wants to work in radio and thought this would attract attention to get him an interview. We rolled it into this radio station and all the receptionist said was *"Deliveries can't be made through this door. Use the loading dock."* John put on his fake TV anchor voice and said, *"Really Honey? Not for me?"* He wouldn't let up and I started to sweat. The receptionist finally replied, *"Ok, you can leave it here. I'll make sure he gets it."* You know where that ear ended up.

When I come home after a grueling week of beauty schools, John's eyes are always bloodshot and he's lying on the sofa stroking Mr. Pillow, staring crazily into space. It's like I'm not even in the room. There's no dealing with him when he gets like this! When John announces that his mother Jean is coming to visit for two weeks, I'm hoping she'll relieve some of the pressure.

Yeah, right. She barely says anything to me other than *Why are you making my son so unhappy? Have you considered converting to Judaism?* This is Jean Buchin in a nutshell, and yes, I do mean *nut*! She's a therapist who specializes in helping people quit smoking but she can't quit herself. The apple doesn't fall far from the tree or, in this case, the insane asylum.

Watching these two go at it is absolute torture because John openly despises his mother. There's something about Jewish culture that makes the family stick together even though they are close to blowing each other's brains out. It takes me a week to get him to calm down from her visit. Jean will call and he starts boiling up and pacing the floor back and forth and then there's that crazy look again. *This is immediately followed with an explosive tantrum.* I never know what's going to happen. One night he went into our bathroom and broke all my skin care bottles with the grand finale of breaking the porcelain toilet bowl.

I might say something innocently and he's off to the races. The scariest thing happened one day in the car. I said, "Why do we always have to listen to talk radio, John? Put on some music, Honey."

"You want music, Harvey? If we can't listen to talk, we won't listen to anything." With his bare hands, John literally ripped the radio as well as the dashboard off the car. Afterwards, he sat there breathing heavily like a werewolf who'd just turned back into a man after eating an entire village. I sat there silent and didn't dare move because I now knew what he was capable of. I guess i always knew deep inside after almost being pushed off a sky scraper when we first met. John went into his office that night and never came out. I sat in the living room shaking with fear. My only remaining thought was: *I have to get out of this because John will probably end up killing me.*

Oh Tim please rescue me! I can't pick up the phone because my pride is standing in the way. The humiliation is paralyzing because I told everyone how much John and I were in love and didn't listen when anyone said *You barely know him. Are you sure he should move to L.A.?* They were right.

I guess I'm as bad as all those things I've said I've hated about being Southern. Just like

Mother, I'm pretending things are all right to avoid being disgraced. I can't, or the real truth is, I *won't,* call my mother, although she could definitely understand loving a crazy person. Now it's become my dirty little secret.

The saving grace is the massive amount of travel to launch Ultima II with JC Penney that will possibly give me perspective on what to do with John. The launch training will take an entire month and a half to execute. This training is a huge undertaking and will require two training teams. One East: Sherrill Webb and Connie Venen; and one West: Jeremy, Daniel, Donna, and I to train everyone across the United States. We call our team *The Dream Team* and the East *The PMS Team* because we hear they're fighting every day during the tour. I knew when I met Connie at my first New York event with Bloomingdales that she and Sherrill would be like sisters. They definitely fight like sisters.

We're flying from city to city without going home, spending part of the weekend in the next city that we'll be training in the upcoming week. This keeps me away from John. Part of me is relieved but another part of me is so worried. He's never happy when I call him.

"Hi John."

"Hi Harvey."

"I just want to see how you are."

"I'm still unemployed, hating California, and missing New York. Anything else you want to know?"

I keep imagining that when I return everything will be broken and John will have hung himself while managing to hang on to that pillow. Unfortunately the old adage *time flies when you're having fun* is totally true. This tour has been beyond fabulous with no mishaps and I've been waiting for the shoe to drop... but the universe has other plans. It deems that at the end of the tour, in a small town in Louisiana, will be where the high heel will plunge. Somehow, even though it's east of the Mississippi, it's part of our schedule with the Southwest locations. The corporate office has done a great job up to this point in booking good hotels, what with the number of trainings we had to accomplish in a short period of time. That is... until now.

As Donna, Jeremy, Daniel, and I descend down the escalator into baggage claim, we spot the driver who will shuttle us to the hotel. The only reason we suspect he is our driver is because he's holding a sign with my name on it. He's beyond skinny and has on a wife beater with torn up jeans. He looks like he's about 60 years old. We walk over to him and say, "Well we're here!"

When he opens his mouth to say, "Hey, my name is Gus," we see that he has very few teeth and that the ones he has are extremely stained and hanging on for dear life. My intuition tells me that he has a very kind heart and probably thinks we're from another planet. When I reach to pull one of my bags off the conveyor belt he says "Don't you worry, you point out your bags and I'll get them!" Of course the four beauty queens have so much luggage and if you combine our skincare alone it must weigh about 500 pounds.

We watch Gus wheeze (which I suspect is a smoker's cough) as he places our overstuffed bags on four carts. He never complains but you can tell he's never dealt with anyone like us before. As we step to the curve Gus says, "There she is." He's pointing to our shuttle van to the hotel. Did I say shuttle? The van is more like a storage vehicle with one seat. Did he deliver groceries before he picked us up? Donna sits in the seat and the boys sit on the floor. Jeremy says "This is the height of luxury!" To visualize this you need to understand our team. We're beauty divas used to high-touch and high-service. Where's our bottled water and complimentary Travel and Leisure magazine for the ride? Jeremy, Daniel, Donna, and I keep looking at each other wondering if the van ever had any shocks because the road is full of pot holes. Gus starts singing some country song from another era and lights a cigarette.

When we arrive at the hotel, Gus wheezes, "Y'all go on in. I'll get your bags. And don't y'all mind the smell, we had us a little flood last month."

As we enter we all stop dead in our tracks. The smell of mildew is overpowering; they must have laid new carpet over old wet carpet during that recent flood unpleasantness. We slowly move toward the front desk, spotting "the staff"—or, to be more specific, a woman who is about 100 years old, staring at us like we we're Yankee spies who've invaded the South during the Civil war. "Hey. Welcome. Are y'all the Revloners?" This is definitely redneck country so she probably has a six gage shotgun under the counter. The three flaming homos and fabulous New York brunette aren't going to give Confederate Grandma any beauty queen attitude.

Thinking of my mother yet again I say, "Why yes, even though it reeks of mildew in here, we're so glad to be at your lovely hotel." Sometimes channeling a little candy-coated evil can't hurt. *Thanks Mother.* As Granny's checking us in, I look out the side window and I think I see the KKK having lunch at the Denny's next door. I'm scared of them but I must admit that I love a "Moon Over My Hammy."

After thirty minutes of fumbling to check us in Confederate Grandma says, "There's your boxes, sitting over there, that arrived for your training. Enjoy your stay." Stacked almost to the ceiling are about 100 boxes delivered to the hotel from New York for our training sessions. We spied the boxes as we entered the lobby and I knew they had to be ours. She then looks at us and points up. "The training rooms are on the second floor. You'll have to use the steps 'cause our elevator is temporarily out of order."

We look at each other then have a stare-off competition with Grandma. *100 boxes up what steps?* I hear whistling and out of the corner of my eye I see Gus. "Here's your bags!" You know what happened next. Gus wheezed up and down those steps a million times. I felt guilty but I was already having such a horrible oil breakthrough from all the Southern humidity. Poor Gus!

I open the door to my room and the smell in the lobby was delightful compared to *this* lovely aroma. Everything in the room looks retro… but not in a good way. I'm deciding to keep my socks on so that my bare feet won't have contact with the nasty shag carpet, when the phone rings.

It's Jeremy. "So, how many cockroaches do you have in your room?"

I say, "Let's get a drink."

Donna calls next. "My room has a twin bed."

I say, "Let's get a drink."

Daniel is probably too mortified to call so I call him. "Let's get a drink!" When we'd first walked in I noticed a little crazy bar attached to the hotel.

I'd prefer to do a Laszlo refresh but I can't do my splashes for lack of a sink stopper. A swipe of Controlling Pressed Powder will have to do. I see that my cohorts have re-powdered and apply a fresh coat of lips and hair lacquer. Beauty queens always put their best face forward no matter what the venue!

We walk into the bar and all the good ole boys are just whooping it up. As I spot an empty table, there's a deafening hush, and then audible whispers begin to emerge. One of the rednecks belches and says "Will you look at that?" This incredibly tall, big-bosomed woman saddles up to our table with her order pad and pencil in ear. "Y'all ain't from here, are ya? Our drink special tonight is Pabst Blue Ribbon. That's only till seven. After that, your beers will jump to $2.00. I'd order extra right now if I were you. What will it be?"

Jeremy looks at her and says, "I'd like to have a dirty martini, up, made with Smirnoff vodka, accessorized with olives and onions please. And do you have any of those yummy cheese crisps like they serve at the Ritz Carlton? I love those."

I glare at Jeremy. "Are you kidding me? Honey, is all that sunny bleach in your hair affecting your brain?"

Across the bar I hear, *"Is there a pansy parade in town boys?"* followed by a round of guffaws and backslapping. As soon as Jeremy opens his mouth, I know that a bouquet of flowers is going to fall out. And if that's not enough, when Jeremy gestures it's like the singer Patti Page from the 1950s when she sings *How Much Is That Doggie In The Window?*

I quickly whisper "Y'all, this is queen-killing country. And Donna, they're not so fond of Yankees either. I'm Southern, I should know!" I *should* have known better than bringing these three in here.

I look at everyone and shake my head, continuing to whisper. "Let's have one drink and get out of here before we make the local news! Three gay boys and one Yankee brunette found dead behind the Piggly Wiggly! News at 11!" Luckily that night, the only things we receive are dirty looks and some muttered name calling. We drink and leave.

I wake up the next morning, watching cockroaches chase each other across the ceiling. I can't even do my Laszlo splashes because the sink stopper is still missing so I start thinking about John and what to do. *Should I just break up and send John back east?* I get dressed and proceed downstairs to start the training. As I descend the staircase, I see a large group of beauty advisors huddling in the lobby. The fake smiles on their faces can't hide the fact that they're horrified. Most have flown in for this training and will be here almost four days. If they think the lobby is bad, wait until they check into their rooms! I see Donna coming down the stairs with a forced smile on her face as well, for the benefit of the beauty advisors. She whispers, "A ghost appeared in my room last night and he said, *Wanna dance little darlin'*?"

Throughout the training, everyone is complaining about everything, but especially about the food. I think the cook in this hotel believes *If you can't fry it, it ain't worth eatin'!* Every morsel of food is double fried with lard in one of those portable Fry Daddy's from K-Mart. You know, the fryer that's responsible for burning down half of the trailer parks in America? Even the string beans are fried and probably out of a can, too. While sitting at lunch, I see this man serving the food and I think I recognize him. He turns around and it's Gus, the king of multi-tasking in this joint.

During the training sessions, the audio visual equipment is a nightmare. Donna and I are facilitating skincare in one room while Jeremy and Daniel are teaching makeup application in the other. I rotate back and forth as the leader to make sure everything is working and to observe these beauty advisors. I walk in Jeremy and Daniel's room and fortunately the video is working. I see Daniel but not Jeremy. The room is dark and everyone is focused on the video. I am about to ask Daniel, *"Where's Jeremy?"* when the video screen fades to black. The room is dark and dead silent until I hear a loud moan.

"Jeremy?"

"Uh huh?"

"Where are you?"

"Under the table."

"Are you okay?"

"Uh uh… Harvey, I have a cramp and decided to lie under the table and I'm sorry but my foot kicked the cord of the video off the socket."

"Will you plug it back in?"

"Yes."

"Thanks, Jeremy."

"You're welcome, Harvey".

The last night after the beauty advisors left to catch their planes, we decide to make another appearance at the redneck bar in the hotel. We are so tired and so over it, we don't care anymore. Our want for alcohol dissipates any fear about being lynched by these good ole boys. As we walk in nobody turns to look at us because everybody in the bar is shitfaced! Larry, Bubba, Merlene, everybody!

We don't care! Bring it on! We let loose of all the steam from this training event. Donna looks at me and says, "It's time these Southern boys were taught to dance by a full-fledged Yankee." Before I can grab her she grabs a cowboy on the dance floor. What did that ghost do to our mild-mannered Donna?

Jeremy says, "Come on girls, if Donna can do it, we can too! Let's do the Hustle." *Oh my God! The Hustle!* I love doing the Hustle. Jeremy put his money in the juke box and almost instantly I hear *OOOOOOO... OOOOO... OOOOOOOOH... Do It! Do the hustle!* Jeremy runs to the middle of the dance floor and a few seconds later he's teaching everybody the Hustle! Somehow it just happened and nothing mattered to anyone in the room. At the end of the night the good ole boys tell us, "You queers ain't so bad after all!" Even though the way they say it is derogatory, I suppose it is the thought that counts. I muse to myself, *That's the nicest thing any straight redneck has ever said to me.*

The next morning, we're beyond hung-over so we drink beer for breakfast after we board the flight. We're on a small prop plane to Dallas where we'll separate to get on our home flights. The beauty advisors had surprised us with big teddy bears in our sleeping rooms to say *thank you* for the training, so imagine four hung-over beauty junkies holding huge teddy bears and crying. We can't stop sobbing because this is our last trip together.

I am also really sad on the way home because, while yes we had a blast and we'll truly miss each other, I also know I am going home to the situation with Dr. Jeckyll and Mr. Hyde, which has to change and I know it. I thought I'd have time to maybe get my nerve up to call Tim and Richard to discuss what to do, but as I put my key into our front door of our apartment, John pulls the door open, waiting for me with that crazy look while of course stroking Mr. Pillow. One look at my teddy bear and he grabs it, ripping the head off. I stand there in that moment wishing I was back in Louisiana dancing with the Klu Klux Klan.

"The problem with beauty is that it's like being born rich and getting poorer."
-JOAN COLLINS

"911, What's your emergency?"

"Well Ma'am, my boyfriend has gone crazy and he's torn the head off my teddy bear!"

"He did what, Ma'am?"

"I'm not a Ma'am, I'm a Sir."

"Oh, I'm sorry. You still have a teddy bear? Well never mind, but that's not really an emergency."

"Oh," I said, "Well he's also totally gone crazy and wrecked our apartment and I think he wants to kill me."

After a brief silence she says, "That's definitely an emergency!"

The police and ambulance comes to cart John off to a mental hospital. Mother popped into my mind for a moment and said *"He's going to have an affair with some man on the 8th floor!"* Oh my God? Have I been in a relationship with my father? The sad look of despair on John's face will probably be burned into my memory for the rest of my life.

After they leave, I looked around at the war zone John has created. Everything is broken, or at least cracked in two. Surveying the mess, I know what I have to do. I pull a bottle of Beefeater gin out of the freezer and drink straight from the bottle. After a few swigs I compose myself and call John's mother Jean. "Well Harvey, what do you want me to do? He's your problem now, isn't he?" *No wonder John is the way he is.* In the phonebook I look up mental health professionals and find someone who can help John.

To make a long story short John is diagnosed with bi-polar manic depression, whatever that means. I think it means he's crazy and depressed at the same time. That would explain the last year or maybe his whole life. It doesn't matter how bad things were, because in the end I still feel sorry for him. *Should I have done something differently?* So much guilt! *Maybe I'm Jewish without knowing it?* The doctor tries to explain to me that John's problem is a flaw in chemistry not character. I just can't wrap my brain around it because so much has happened. *I still love him? Maybe I'm sick too? It's over.*

The next morning as I wake, the phone rings and I think it's going to be the mental hospital telling me to come get John because he's breaking everything in sight, but I hear a familiar voice that makes me sob.

"Are you alright? Richard and I haven't heard from you and that can only mean one thing. When did you break up with John #2?"

"Well Tim, one 911 emergency call later and John is now in a mental hospital with some crazy disease. I'm packing his stuff so there will be no reminders of how weak and stupid I've been. Tim? Do you think I'm crazy too?" More tears keep falling as I hang on to the phone.

"Yes queen, you are crazy but your life is not over! The Harvey I know will go buy some new skin care and start over! And next time, and I know there will be a next time, you better call me or I will cut you. I love you."

When I call Mother, all she says is, "Crazy, I understand! Don't tell anyone else what's happened to you, do you understand me, son? We have our Helms name to keep up, you know." The Helms name? Between Daddy and Jesse, I don't know who Mother thinks she's fooling?

I'm sick of crazy and crying so let's fast-forward and after six months of getting used to being without John, I'm out partying every night, meeting men to dull the pain, but all they want is a one night stand. They always say *I'll call you,* but they never do. My life now consists of traveling to teach beauty schools then coming home to my empty apartment, followed by a trip to the bars to drink the pain away. In the back of mind I'm thinking, *I'll be an old maid if I don't get married soon! Or since it's not legal, at least a commitment ceremony! Won't cousin Jesse just love that!*

My gay biological clock is ticking! No, not a baby thing; more like an *I'm getting old and no man will look at me* thing. It's just the same as how straight men treat aging women. Well, kind of. A quick explanation. In the gay world, some of us want the husband, the house, the cars, the kids, the pets, the country club, and yearly trips to Hawaii, Arizona/Palm Springs Spa/Golf combo, and Africa, just like straight people. It's really no different from one point of view. We also ask *Why didn't you pay the electric bill* and, my least favorite, *What do you want for dinner* and *I'm tired, don't touch me! I want to go to sleep!* I fall into this gay category that we call Doris Day. Good boy finds husband, stays loyal, and lives happily ever after in fabulous 5th Avenue apartment with doorman. There are many other subsets of gay culture, like Bears, Leather, etc. It's kind of the same but they wear different costumes and do sexual things you see in porn movies or at the circus.

Anyway, where is the man of my dreams? My last ex-boyfriend is in the loony bin. I'm tired of crazy people. *Where's Prince Charming? Time is running out! Come on, Universe! I believe in a higher being, that looks sort of like Judy Garland, who will conspire to help me if I try! Well I've tried Judy! Give me a sign! Where's my over the rainbow?*

I guess on some level I've always wondered what's really over the rainbow, with my fascination for the Wizard of Oz and not just because I watched it seventeen times during my wisdom teeth incident. I do love Judy eternally, but it's more than that. It's sort of like what her daughter Liza Minnelli said in the 1979 movie *Arthur* with the late Dudley Moore. She always felt there was something special, like the moon was always following her. I don't feel that way about the moon but I believe something is going on. Not in an organized religious way, but in some other spiritual realm you can access if you just believe. I guess my problem is that I don't have a pair of Ruby Slippers.

When I was five years old, my family would go to the Presbyterian Church occasionally, depending on Mother's mood. I loved Sunday school because the room we were in was bright and sunny. They also gave us fresh orange juice and a room full of games and toys to play with. Our Sunday school teacher looked just like Marlo Thomas from the TV show *That Girl* (TV show from late 60s-early 70s where Marlo plays aspiring young actress Anne Marie, living in New York trying to get work. Dated Donald Holinger, played by actor Ted Bessell, for nine years with no sex. Look for reruns on hulu!) She was perky and hilariously funny. When this Sunday school teacher spoke about Jesus, he was loving, kind and wanted to help us.

Then I turned six and forgive the expression but all hell broke loose. It was Sunday as usual and my mother escorted me to my normal Sunday school room. They said, "Oh no, Harvey's six now, he has to go upstairs to the first grade class." As we were climbing the stairs, I looked back longingly at the happy children having fun. When we finally reached the right room I saw dark mahogany walls with heavy dark green velvet drapes that were barely opened. The desks and chairs were lined up so precisely. My new teacher approached us and said, "Please take a seat. You're late. Little boys who are late get paddled." This woman was very tall and super skinny with varicose veins that were apparent even through her opaque beige stockings. She had a tight poodle perm brushed out ever so slightly to create that helmet head look. She had on a navy dress with a white blouse buttoned all the way up and not one drop of makeup to cover the dark circles under her eyes. I also remember that she had dull, gray, dingy teeth.

As she went to the chalk board, she made a list of things we shouldn't do or else we would go to a place called Hell, meet a man named Satan, and burn in a lake of fire forever. I thought that sounded really gross. How did she know that? Had she been there? Is that where she got that hairdo? Being the good little piece of candy-coated evil that I was, I listened attentively until the end of the class. My mother met me at the door and said, "Well, Harvey? Did you learn about Jesus today?"

"Yes Mother, I did, but if what she says is true, Daddy's in big trouble. Mother, I want to go back to the other room next week."

"You can't, because big boys go to this class."

"Well then, I won't be coming back here."

Mother looked at me and shrugged her shoulders. She looked at the Sunday school teacher and said, "Well, Harvey didn't like your class, so he won't be back, but that's a lovely dress you're wearing." Something in me knows there's something higher in the Universe—so I do agree with the teacher in that—but *my* path wasn't going to include Satan and a bad hairdo and ugly house dress.

I know the Universe will send me signs about what's next in my life!

Sign #1 came early one Tuesday morning. The phone rings and I hear, "Harvey, Mrs. Cartwright would like to speak with you. Will you hold?"

"Oh hi, Susan. Sure." I haven't heard from or seen Angela in months. She hates being associated with JC Penney and has been keeping a low profile. Stanley Noland is back in power and keeping close watch on Angela.

"Hello, Harvey? I won't make this long. You have to be the Director of Beauty and I need you here in three weeks. It would take months to find another candidate and I don't have time. Congratulations."

I am about to say *"Wow,"* but I realize the phone is dead on the other end.

Director of Beauty. Look at me, Michael Cope! I'm promoted to the position I always wanted from almost the very beginning at Belk's... but as usual, it's not the way I dreamed it. *Too difficult to quickly find other candidates?* Angela doesn't want me because she couldn't pick me out the way she did with her kids and husband. I'm one of the best in the industry and she just made me feel like I'm the K-Mart Blue Light Special. *"Hello, Director of Beauty on special, aisle three."* Finally though, New York! It's taken more time than I expected but the moment has finally arrived. The sad part is that I adore the weather in California. Should I leave L.A.? For the most part I've loved it here because I became the person I wanted to be. Maybe I should turn down Mrs. Cartwright's less than gracious offer?

Sign #2 comes in really early, around 4:30 in the morning. I'm having the strangest dream that Anorexic Blue Eyeshadow Debbie is Angela's new assistant and she's yelling at me when Simone comes up screaming about being tired and wondering who left the water marks on her French desk. James Shultz is wearing bright purple eyeshadow saying, *You'll never make me wear neutrals! Never!*

351

What a nightmare! As I stumble out of bed and turn on the light to go to the bathroom, I suddenly feel the house make this odd slow motion shift back and forth. My heart instantly climbs into my nose. *Earthquake*!

I jam myself into the door frame just like they tell you to on TV. *It's not stopping.* I keep screaming. *It's not stopping! It's so violent! Is this the end of my life?* I hear everything flying out of the cabinets and breaking. It's like the building is being shaken up and down by the Universe. It finally stops. Dead silence. My heart is racing a million miles a minute and then I realize that I'm smelling smoke and gas. *Smoke and gas, this can't be good.* I think I should go into the kitchen and see if the Scotch bottle has broken. *Find shoes first so you don't get cut by all the broken glass Harvey!* Two big swigs of scotch, and right on time Earthquake # 2 hits. Earthquakes always come in twos. Seconds later the bottle of scotch is empty. I look up to the ceiling and say *Okay, I get it! It's time to go!*

After that, my exit from L.A. happens pretty quickly. The movers come and pack everything and put it on the truck for New York. I board the plane and after taking off I look at all the lights that go on for miles and miles, remembering the very first time I flew to L.A. from North Carolina. I sip my gin and tonic, and cry as I apply a smidge of Prescriptives Flight Cream to re-hydrate my skin in this awful airplane cabin recycled air. As I'm smoothing it into my skin in an upward motion, I realize that L.A. has changed my life. Or rather, *I've* changed my life and LA gave me the freedom to be who I really am. At any rate, I've definitely come a long way since the UNCG days and I owe California a big debt of gay reinvention gratitude.

I feel a little bit chilly so I wrap one of those little blue blankets around me. Then reality hits me and I really start crying because I realize that all of my winter clothes are packed in boxes in the moving van that won't arrive in New York for a month. Coincidentally, New York is experiencing the worst winter blizzard in the history of the city. Maybe I'll start a new trend of tank tops in the winter? *Well, if I can make it there, I can...* Well, you know the rest.

HARVEY'S DIARY:
NOVEMBER 1, 1987
"Shop till you drop!"

"People who say money can't buy happiness
don't know where to shop!"
-LOVEY HOWELL
[Gilligan's Island]

I arrived in New York months ago but I think it's time for another little beauty break, to speak about a subject that's near and dear to my heart. Shopping! N.Y.C. is an island that's really a small, tall, shopping mall. You forget it's an island when you are standing in the middle of 5th Avenue or at Lincoln Center on the Upper West side. It's the smallest big city ever, where you can literally shop vertically from one end of the island to the other, as well as horizontally from side to side. It's a mall that has everything. Consider this a beauty junkie mini-shopping tour from my perspective.

Bergdorf Goodman

The N.Y.C. version of Neiman Marcus on steroids and hands down my favorite shopping destination! It has the best of everything in the world, including the latest well-edited fashion collections, made easily accessible because you're assisted by delightful sales associates. I hate to call them *sales associates* because they truly understand high-touch clients and deliver consistently with real smiles on their faces.

Lower Level Beauty is a delicious smorgasbord that includes everything from the tried and true to what's hot and new. Every brand is displayed demurely without those monstrous cosmetic bays and dreaded fragrance spritzers. Knowledgeable beauty experts behind every counter who understand every line in the department. They don't just sell one line, so you receive the best of the best from everyone, depending on your skincare or color cosmetic concern. Have I made it sound like cosmetic heaven? Well it is.

After being refreshed on the lower level, go for lunch on the seventh floor and have the Gotham salad with extra Thousand Island dressing. If there's a long line in the women's store for lunch and you're in a hurry, pop quickly across the street to the men's store and push the elevator button to the top floor. The cafe is in the back and serves the same fabulous salad. It's two seconds away and you can quickly pop back to the women's store to shop for shoes, immediately following lunch on the same floor. How convenient! No visit is complete without a trip to the home store on the top floor with yummy linens and the decorative arts. The visual staff is genius and I've ripped off their ideas several times when planning my own dinner parties.

Bloomingdales 59th Street

This store is unique as well for its shopping experience. There's no other Bloomingdales like *this* Bloomingdales. I've been to locations in other cities but it's not the same. This N.Y.C. Bloomingdales definitely embodies the electric energy of New York, that's why Donna Karan chose it to launch her DKNY fragrances—because it has that special energy.

The cosmetic department on the main floor is big and well lit. It's called "The B Way," lined with an iconic black and white checkered floor. This store definitely masters the special event or circus side of cosmetics. This is not your quiet, attentive experience. It's your *Wow! I need that product!* experience. Full of actors and actresses who know what they're talking about, peddling their creams and magic potions. It's like the hit Broadway show of cosmetics and there's always a good makeup artist available whether you need a quick touch-up or the complete overhaul! You simply ask and your wish is granted. This circus normally has special promotions or great free gifts every day. I love coming here when I'm depressed, bored, or if I just happen to be walking on 3rd or Lexington Avenue.

Barney's New York

Like Bloomingdales, this is another store that only works in New York. It's fabulous but you'll never understand why, so don't even try! Barney's is in its own category and it's hard to explain to people who've never shopped here but I'll try. Barney's is like that hip, chic, different friend, relative or acquaintance that you don't understand but admire and wonder how they do the things they do. You may never wear what they wear, but you love it on them. You would have never put it together the way they have but you love it for some unknown reason. You walk in and immediately you're in this state of fascination and wonder. It's not loud or showy, but it's not quiet and attentive either. Don't be afraid, my pretties! It's just Barney's New York.

The cosmetic department has its own unique sense of merchandising that makes tried and true older brands look new and fresh so you may not recognize them. The beauty advisors are helpful... to a point. They know their stuff and eagerly help you, but they are like holograms, having a *now you see them, now you don't* quality. You experience great service without even realizing it. Don't try to understand it. Enjoy it. They have eclectic brands that are a beauty junkie's dream. Brands you've never seen or even heard of. Creme de la Mer would look like Jergens lotion in this store.

Barney's is always a great place to grab lunch at its chic bistro Fred's, but get there early because it's always packed. Great food and the best view of the latest plastic surgery procedures in New York. If I'm making this sound like a Twilight zone episode, I'm not meaning too. You'll have to go there and experience it for yourself. Buy the things you love while you're there because fashion and beauty are merciless creatures in this store. They change quickly and you won't be able to get them again. You'll walk into Barney's and say to yourself *Didn't I get this here?*

Henri Bendel

This is another New-York-only store. I call it *The little store that you always think is bigger than it is*. Two floors of fabulous stuff plus a great cafe to have a chic something to drink or nosh. Lots of great skincare and makeup brands with lots of makeup and skincare people doing lots of things. Just like reading this commentary though, shopping is over before you know it. You know you must go in, but it only takes a New York minute.

Saks 5th Avenue

The one and only. Every cosmetic and skincare brand available today. The cosmetic department is a war zone so you have to be in the mood to navigate and say no a thousand times before you get to the elevators in the back. Tourists flock here that's why this store is really known for its phone ordering and delivery service. All the locals occasionally shop here but would rather have the expert staff call and send! It's always crazy. Always.

The men's department on the seventh floor is the best mix of young modern gay designer clothes in the size *I haven't had a carbohydrate since 1983 XXS.* Huge selection of all the *it* shoes. It's like being in a disco when you shop here because you can find a quick date for Friday night if you need one. You can also dine at the Rainbow room, have a Dean & Deluca coffee, see Saturday Night live, as well as Matt, Anne, and Al all right across the street! It's an honored and revered New York institution!

These stores are all within walking distance of each other. Easy beauty junkie emergency navigating!

For example: let's say you need to replace your Natura Bisse Stabilizing Gel Cream and you're at Bergdorf' Goodman. Oh no, they are out of stock?! You don't want to wait for them to get it from another store do you? No! You can go to Saks or call and have it waiting within minutes. What about that Bobbi Brown Eye Brightener that's been repackaged and Bloomingdales doesn't have it yet? Do you want to wait? No! You can run four blocks to Bergdorf Goodman to purchase it before the other junkies get their hands on it. This is a beauty junkie's dream shopping situation because you have lots of great eating places to choose from in case you get hungry during your beauty journey. It doesn't get better than that!

*"Beauty may be skin deep but ugly goes clean
down to the bone!"*
-REDD FOXX

"We would just like to say that you, Angela Lewis-Cartwright, have changed the cosmetic industry forever and we know that you will do great things wherever you land! This is definitely Revlon's loss today and we will miss you."

I'm standing by Jeanine Recckio, Simone's old assistant, who's left Prescriptives and is now working in marketing for Ultima II, because obviously the Lauder Corporation has a revolving door of its own.

Jeanine whips her head around and whispers in my ear, "Yeah I'm definitely going to miss her stealing panty hose out of my office, that evil bitch!"

"Don't make me laugh because Madame is still in the room and will probably make me change my hair color one last time as a parting gift!"

"Harvey you know that she's probably dying because there are paper plates and plastic forks on her goodbye sweets table!" Jeanine pulls me by my collar into a quiet corner of the room. "I'm leaving too, and don't say anything!"

"But you just got here again!"

"I know, but the handwriting's on the wall and please don't tell anyone!"

As I look around the room I realize that Angela's almost the last of an era, what with the departures of Stanley Noland, Dana Lebrowski, Janet Russell, Mark Cooper, and—well, almost everyone I started with except me, Sherrill, and Sally. I guess Jeanine's departure really is the end of an era.

Angela is made for luxury, and just the fact that she had to produce cosmetics for the JC Penney customer speaks volumes about her karma. She treats everyone like servants but she was born to make products for the people whom she treats like servants! It probably says something about my karma too, being her indentured servant? We fought daily over product direction that would ultimately drive our business.

You remember how Angela told me *Presentation is 90 % of the battle*? Well, she's right; however, the product also has to resonate with the clientele and as just Connie once told me *"This is a business and you have to sell all the product you can."* Angela was never kind to me or encouraging because she considered me to be beneath her. Well, myself and almost everyone else who walked on the earth, except for maybe Adrian Anderson and Stanley Noland.

I always wonder why people change when they get to the top. That since of entitlement and the *better than thou* attitude always leaves me yearning for the richer side of humanity. If she had created the Barely There Collection at the Lauder corporation, she wouldn't be having this goodbye party! She'd still be an elitist but her path would have been secure. The beginning of her end began when I first arrived in New York and it was becoming clear to me that the Revlon's Department Store days might be numbered.

Fresh off the plane in New York from L.A., Revlon places me in luxurious corporate housing at The Sutton on East 56th, with wonderful, twenty-four-hour maid service, Concierge, Butler, and Health Club. I thought it was crazy to have to use a realtor to find an apartment but I learned that this is how it works in New York, so I decided to take my time. The funniest thing at the office is that I've inherited Simone Asherton's antique

French desk! Can you believe it! While getting settled, I remove the drawer from that desk because it was sticking and I find one of Simone's Neiman Marcus charge card statements with a sticky note attached telling Jeanine Recckio to be sure to pay it. Classic!

It's been a downhill slide since I first got off the plane in zero degrees weather with no winter clothes. As we launched JC Penney, every reputable department store in the country literally threw us out overnight to send a message to any other cosmetic brands considering taking this route to increase their distribution. Now Ultima II will only be available in JC Penney, and Revlon has no choice but to open in as many drugstores as possible to make up for all the distribution we've lost. Ultima II was once one of the top three cosmetic companies and now it's winded down to a ghetto drugstore brand. No offense, but once you've been a department store girl it's hard to date down. What's the old adage? *The only thing worse than not having money is having a lot of it and then losing it*? Amen, sister! Can you say *Revlon with Anorexic Blue Eyeshadow Debbie?* Talk about karma! Selling in drugstores? I'm the Revlon girl again! *"Can I interest you in a lip*

color from Ultima II while you're shopping for
your tampons and cat food?"

As Andrea exits, enter Nina White, the new
VP of marketing who Ron Perelman brought over
from L'oréal . Love at first sight, because she just
gets me and she's definitely a kindred beauty
junkie! As Director of Beauty, I'm working with
the magazine editors and making television
appearances. People in the industry want to know
what I think and I'm having chic lunches with
interesting people who make New York the great
city it is! I'm lucky enough to be involved with
certain Revlon cover models during this magical
time. My favorite? Ultima II spokes model Kim
Delaney from the hit TV show *NYPD Blue*.

I have my press kit shot with her in her
Beverly Hills home by a famous photographer
who agrees to photograph me to get pictures of
Kim. She normally has the corkscrew curly New
Jersey hair for the show but that day I give her a
chic straight look. The photographer has us sitting
on two stools side by side and he keeps saying to
me, "Get closer to Kim, Harvey. Get closer to
Kim. Get closer to Kim."

I finally say, "If I get any closer to Kim, I
will *be* Kim."

Kim looks at me and whispers, "This man is a prick so just do as I say and keep looking up at my forehead."

I hear the photographer screaming, "Perfect! Beautiful. That's a wrap."

Thank God!

Kim and I share a PR person who comes from Tampax, named Donna Shapiro. A tall, fit, gorgeous blonde who's gracious in a no-nonsense kind of way. One day, when I am giving myself a little makeover using a trainer from the New York Sports Club to get in shape for my media/appearances tour, Donna says, "Harvey, you should know that exercise may not fix everything, so here's a nice list of plastic surgeons whom you may want to consider."

"Thank you, Donna…"

She immediately has Kim and I media-trained by the same man who coached President Richard Nixon. The media trainer was difficult but he had to be, so that Kim and I would bring our *A-game* during interviews. For instance, I know I might be asked on TV: *"Does Collagen really penetrate the skin?"* Kim might be asked *"Are you and Jimmy Schmidt really sleeping together?"* God, I wish I would get asked that question! Whenever Kim's name comes up, fans always say

I loved her as Jenny on All My Children. I totally understand because I loved her as Jenny too!

I finally find my new home on Riverside Drive after months of searching. Beautiful tree-lined street that reminds me of Europe. Revlon helped me find a realtor whose name, of all things, is Harvey! No kidding! After seeing about fifty apartments, Harvey said, "Harvey, what about up near Harlem?"

We journey out there together. As the taxi is turning left from Broadway on to Riverside I see Columbia University. It's a great area but I've never been to Harlem. We pull up to the corner of Riverside and 119 Street, and I see the exquisite Concord Hall that was built during the great architectural time of the Vanderbilt's and Astor's, at the turn of the century. As we walk up the stairs, the building super recognizes Harvey the realtor and says, "Hey! You didn't call first so you're not getting no keys today!" He then struts off and slams a door behind him. Standing beside him is a little doorman whose name is Charles, who coincidentally looks just like Charlie Chaplin. Seeing the tears in my eyes and quickly looking over his shoulder, he turns back and softly says, "Come with me."

We get off the elevator and I see a beautiful big green door labeled F in gold. As we slowly open the door, I see a thirty-foot hallway with molding that is made for fine oil paintings. Lord Joseph Duveen, the great art dealer of the early 20th century for Mellon, Kress, and Henry Clay Frick would've screamed to fill these walls with Rembrandt and Vermeer. As I walk down the hall in awe, to the left I see a large bathroom, and then a large bedroom, and then another large bedroom. As we turn the corner I see another twenty-five foot hallway that eventually takes you down to the serving area, and then I spot the third bedroom, and a little further down is a spacious kitchen.

If you walk on and go left instead of straight, you find yourself in a beautiful formal living room with a decorative fireplace and five windows with a view of the Hudson River. Off the living room, through glass pocket doors, is a formal dining room with yet another decorative fireplace and river views. From the dining room, I see Harvey the realtor standing there, looking at me. After one more panoramic look around, I say, "Harvey, get me this apartment."

Miraculously fast, the next week, Harvey hands Harvey the keys to his new home.

Maybe now with all the wicked witches gone, the fabulous New York apartment, and the job that I always dreamed of, life will move smoothly so I can find the man of my dreams? Right?

"I would rather lose an earring than be caught
dead without makeup!"
-LANA TURNER

"*Christmas time is here... Happiness and cheer... Time for all that children call their favorite time of year*! Tim, you know *A Charlie Brown Christmas* is my all-time favorite!"

"I know, Harvey, but that's because you're Charlie Brown's little sister Sally who says *All I want is my fair share, what's coming to me.* That is you to a T, Harvey Helms!"

"Tim, my holiday suggestion for you is to not get your Christmas panties in a wad because you're Charlie Brown's passive aggressive nemesis Lucy, and Richard is Snoopy who licks you on the face making you scream *Get the iodine! Call the doctor! Ugh!*"

"Okay, cut the Christmas crap! Who is he?"

"Who, Tim? I don't know what you're talking about."

"Yes you do, because Richard and I haven't heard from you in weeks, plus I had to hear from

371

Grace that you won't be home for Christmas. I even called Janet to check up on you and found out that she and Mark Cooper have both left Revlon and gone to Lancôme! Not to mention the fact that Dana Lebrowski is missing in action! So what do you have to say for yourself, Missy?"

"Well, now that you happen to mention it, I did sort of meet a man at the Revlon holiday party named Dan."

"Ah ha!"

"Tim, do you want to hear this or not?" Silence. "That's what I thought! His name is Dan Moore and he's Nina White's secretary's brother visiting from Pittsburgh. I met him at our annual employee Christmas gala about two weeks ago, but Tim, I don't even know if he's gay! But he might as well be with the amount of flirting he sent my way over cocktails. Dan's an actor who is kind of a cross between Kirk Douglas and Benjamin Franklin. I know it sounds strange but trust me, he's really yummy. I gave him my number and said *Dan, if you're ever back in New York, call me.* Tim, the reason I'm not coming home for Christmas is because I'm exhausted and I told Mother that, but of course she has to make a big deal of it."

"Well, queen, I'm sorry you'll miss Aunt Tillie's punch, and a little notice would've been nice since the day after tomorrow is Christmas Eve!"

"I'm sorry, Honey, and God knows I want to be with you and Richard right now, but things are really interesting at Revlon, so I'm a little uneasy. My favorite boss of all time Nina has been moved to Revlon marketing and my new boss Hilary, whom I haven't even met yet, from Chanel, has been totally unavailable, so I don't know what's going on. Please don't worry and I'll call you on Christmas Day. If my mother pressures you for information, lie and say that I was recruited by Bloomingdales' Santa Claus to deliver presents on Christmas Eve to the needy! Even Grace won't question charity work this time of year! Merry Christmas, my best friend, I love you, and a big kiss to Richard."

At 9:00 the next morning, I arrive at Revlon. The receptionist greets me: "Hi, Harvey. You have a meeting with the new VP of Marketing and I've been asked to escort you to her office."

As I enter and make myself comfortable in a chair facing her, this new VP whom I've never laid eyes on just sits and stares at me for a moment. Without any introductions she begins. "Harvey, you've had one of the most phenomenal years in your tenure at Revlon, and we're giving you an 8% increase for all your wonderful efforts, but unfortunately today we will also be discontinuing your position in the company." She proclaims this all in one breath.

"So you're saying that I've had the best year in my history here at Revlon and you're firing me right before Christmas?"

To put this into perspective, remember that I've worked for Revlon since I was nineteen years old and many things could've popped into my mind at this moment, but the universe chose to zoom in on my very first customer in the Belk's cosmetic department at the Revlon counter. Remember that old battle axe who didn't want a man to wait on her? Sitting here and thinking back on it now, I should have said, "*You know what, lady? You're a prejudiced, bigoted bitch with horrible dragon breath, and I think you should buy three tubes of Revlon lipstick in a shade that absolutely suits you called "KISS MY ASS!"* Probably not appropriate to ask her to buy three tubes at one time, but Sue always told me that a woman should buy one for home, one for her purse, and one just in case of emergencies. Old beauty habits never die!

This moment hurts as if someone is asking for a divorce after a long, interestingly difficult marriage. Miss VP with no name looks at me and says "Your severance agreement is in this envelope, so please look it over because you have an appointment with Human Resources in an hour." She leaves the room, and then it hits me that my career at Revlon is over in a matter of three minutes. As I'm in my office packing up my personal belongings, I meet my new ex-boss Hilary for the first time.

"Harvey I wish you and I could have worked together, and I know you must feel terrible with it being Christmas and all, so I've booked you a two bedroom suite at the Essex House hotel on Central Park South, just in case this has ruined your holiday."

"*Ruined my holiday*, Hilary?"

"You probably already have holiday plans, but you can go check in, enjoy the Spa, and charge Broadway Show tickets on us."

As I'm coming out of Hilary's office I run smack dab into Sherrill Webb. "You too? I didn't even know that you were here Sherrill, but isn't it ironic that we met at my first beauty school and now we're together on our last day as well? Want to make our final Revlon send-off poetic by joining me for Christmas and New Year's at the Essex House on Central Park South with Revlon picking up the tab? Champagne? Spa? Broadway Shows?"

As I walk out Revlon's revolving door for the last time with Sherrill, I reach into my bag to find my new cell phone and hand Sherrill some tissue because she can't stop crying. I dial and the phone is ringing and on the other end I hear *Bah Hum Bug! Leave a message.*

"Tim? Here's a happy Harvey holiday message for you. I just received my Christmas present from Revlon and it's official! Please tell Richard that I'm not the Revlon girl anymore. Sherrill and I are going to check into the Essex House on Central Park South through New Year's and we'll call you in between the champagne cocktails. Merry Christmas to you two, and as always, under no circumstances are you to let Mother know about the recent Christmas unpleasantness."

Walking up Central Park South the following Monday morning, after a few days of extravagance with Sherrill, I realize that I'm not in any rush and have plenty of time to get home. Actually, I have all the time in the world now. *Who am I now? I've been Harvey Helms from*

Revlon for a lot of the time I've been on the planet.
Now I'm just plain ol' Harvey Helms. What's next?
Well I know what has to be *immediately* next and
that is to go and do my Laszlo Ritual because I
haven't done my splashes in a week and it's
definitely showing in my pores. Dr. Laszlo would
excommunicate me!

As I'm looking through my bag for some
temporary oil control, my phone rings and I hear a
voice on the other end say, "Hi Harvey? This is
Dan. Do you remember me from the Revlon
Christmas party?" Do I remember him? *Meow*!
"Harvey I'm moving to New York to start a theatre
group and I'm wondering if it's okay to call you
again when I hit town?"

I just purr. "Sure Dan. Call me as soon as
you hit town!" *KABLAM!* I now know what I will
be doing! I'm instantly grateful for the generous
severance package from Revlon because it's going
to take all my time getting Dan to fall in love with
me. Is he gay? He has to be! He's an actor! He'll
be famous and I'll help him! We'll give fabulous
parties and become the new *it* couple! Harvey
Helms-Moore? I know hyphenated names are very
Lewis-Cartwright but I think it has a nice ring to
it, don't you?

My phone rings again as I'm walking, dreaming about becoming the new Mrs. Moore, and the voice on the phone flatly says, "Hello, Harvey? This is Jason Rockwell and I'm a friend of your friend Judy McGibony from North Carolina. I live in Washington D.C. and I'd like to visit New York for the first time in a few weeks. Judy told me to call you to see if I can crash at your apartment for a few days. Will that be okay?"

After Dan's call I think, *Why not?* "Sure you can!"

Jason asks, "Do you have an iron and an ironing board?"

"What? Of course I do!" After we hang up I wonder who is this Jason Rockwell thinking I'm so gauche living without an iron and ironing board? *Oh forget about that, Harvey, you have more important things to concentrate on, namely Dan Moore! Maybe you should stop at Bergdorf Goodman on your way home to look at china patterns because Mother always says "A girl can never be too prepared!"*

"What do I wear in bed? Why, Chanel No. 5, of course."
-MARILYN MONROE

It's 1:00 in the morning and I'm in the Four Seasons Hotel martini bar making out with Dan. Eight gin martinis later and I don't care about a thing, because his kisses are so passionate. Looking into his big loving blue eyes, I'm engulfed in the warmth of his mouth and touch. If he's not gay, he sure is a great actor! This is better than any movie I've seen or any book I've read. It's magic, and, no, it's not a dream! The server cautiously looks at us and says in a calm and gracious Four Seasons manner, "Gentlemen! Please! This is the Four Seasons after all." *Got it! Taxi to Riverside Drive!*

After much fumbling of clothes and accessories we end up in bed. The next morning, waking up, I know I am love. I prop myself up on a pillow. "Dan? Can I ask you a few questions?"

"Yes my love?"

"Were you ever in a fraternity?"

"No."

"Are you manic depressive or bi-polar?"

"No. I don't think so, but I don't even know what that means."

"Dan, you're really an actor, not a Federal Court Judge or secret political official?"

"What?"

"Dan, do you have something you carry around as an emotional crutch like a teddy bear, a pillow or something?"

Dan looks at me like I'm crazy. "No?"

"Okay Dan, I'm all good."

I collapse back on my pillow and think about the last dreamy weeks. Dan arrived in New York and is working temp jobs so that he can develop this troop of young actors. They meet in the evenings and I come along to help with their PR, new photos of the group, and overall styling. I love it mainly because it's great to see Dan in his element. With a kiss goodbye, Dan is off to pack because he's taking me away for a romantic weekend. I don't think I'm going to take my whole beauty arsenal, not wanting to scare him too soon! One little overnight bag and Dan will think I'm totally low maintenance. Well, not really, but it sounds good.

Jason, who needs an iron and ironing board, is arriving today from Washington D.C. and I can't entertain him because of my romantic weekend excursion. I know it's bad Southern hospitality and Mother would be mortified to hear that I'm leaving Jason alone here, but I can't help it. As I'm getting ready to put a key into an envelope for the doorman to give Jason, there's a knock on the door.

Standing in the doorway is one of the most beautiful men I've ever seen in my life. Like Eileen Ford Modeling Agency handsome. Six feet tall, dark hair, big green eyes with eyelashes like Bambi, and lovely young fair skin. No... I mean *really* young skin, or at least a lot younger than my beauty-withered, 28-soon-to-be-29-year-old skin! As he opens his mouth to speak I see a million dollar smile, after which he sticks his beautiful strong hand in my direction. "I'm Jason Rockwell and you must be Harvey." He has on the cutest gray Banana Republic pea coat.

"Hi Jason! Unfortunately, I'm kind of in a hurry, so here are your keys, and I'm sorry I can't spend any time with you this weekend!" I grab my overnight bag and shut the door quickly, but turning to reopen it because I forgot to tell him, "Jason, the iron and ironing board are in the

381

kitchen next to the linen cupboard! Oh! And it's nice to meet you!"

The romantic weekend in Mystic Connecticut flew by quickly, but I now am convinced that Dan is the one I'm supposed to marry. I just know it. Maybe now with my imaginary upcoming engagement and wedding, followed by a fabulous Italian Rivera honeymoon, I can turn my attention to finding my next beauty position.

As I'm dreaming about reinventing myself for whatever job will be next, I'm also spending a lot of time looking in the mirror because I have a birthday upcoming. I'm not getting any younger, that's for sure. Eventually I'll be looking for another job in beauty, so I need to look great. When I call Jeanine Recckio to invite her to my birthday party, she says she hasn't landed anywhere yet since leaving Revlon, but there are a few possibilities and she'll keep her eye out for me as well. She's such a doll!

Back in the mirror, I remember something that Donna Shapiro had said to me at Revlon. *"Exercise may not be enough, Harvey. The doctor may be necessary for a smoother, refreshed look."* Donna is absolutely right! The doctor! A little skin rejuvenation? Well, actually big rejuvenation with C02 laser resurfacing, which is actually a controlled second degree burn that erases sun damage and helps with acne scarring. It's not so much about aging, but these nasty acne scars that I don't want in my future wedding pictures with Dan!

I'll have the down time to recover in seclusion because Dan will be busy for the next few weeks rehearsing his new theatre company. My laser surgery will be performed by a plastic surgeon named Dr. Margaret Skyles, who happens to wear pearls with her scrubs.

As I lie there in pre-op with my backless hospital gown and tons of tubes connected to me, a nurse comes in and pulls back the curtain. She looks down at me and yells, "Girls, we got a young one in here. Don't worry, I'm the queen of veins and I have to put your IV in." She was right, I didn't feel a thing. Actually I couldn't feel anything.

The last thing I remember is Dr. Skyles coming in and asking me "Any last requests before I begin?"

In an overly medicated voice I plead, "Please, Dr. Skyles, make me beautiful because I used to be somebody."

I don't remember waking up, but Dr Skyles warned me before: *"Day 1 Harvey, you won't know where you are. Day 4 you'll want to kill me, and by Day 6 you'll want to kill my family as well. But by Day10, you'll have new incredibly smooth, pink baby skin."* She was right on all accounts. I had planned to arrive at my birthday party with new refreshed, acne-free skin and a loving Dan on my arm.

I bought tons of Veuve Cliquot champagne, food, and a wonderful cake, as well as a beautiful beige crepe suit with a fresh blue and white striped dress shirt from Bergdorf Goodman for my birthday gala. I'm still using the post-procedure skincare from a company called Biomedic which is the best post-any-plastic-surgery skincare. Dr. Skyles told me no Laszlo for a while because I didn't want to do anything to ruin the procedure. My skin is somewhere around the Revlon lipstick shade called "Love That Pink." Dr. Skyles told me I'd be this vivid shade of pink for the next six months. I don't care, because it's the smoothest my skin has been since childhood.

8 p.m. and people start arriving with fabulous gifts and well wishes. When my friend Jeanine shows up she whispers, "I heard about your "procedure" and you look fabulous! Screw

Revlon! Where's the champagne?" More people who aren't Dan keep arriving and I start drinking champagne. Of course you know me by now, so with every minute he's not here I have another glass of champagne. And another. All my guests but Dan have arrived! Two hours into the party the doorbell rings, and I pray *Please God, let it be Dan!*

I run down that long hallway and fling the door open. It's Dan all right, but he's with an actress who I recognize from his troop named Jessica. *Okay, so he brought her to my party, but that's okay because they work together, right?* I look at them and she has her arm through his and is leaning into Dan's chest. They look at each other. No, I mean THEY REALLY LOOK AT EACH OTHER! I know what's getting ready to happen because I've seen this on the Lifetime Network (Television for Women) a hundred times.

As I turn and walk back down the hall, my face feels like it's on fire. I turn into the bathroom and look at my face in the mirror, which is now the color of a fire truck. Laser, plus madness, plus 6 glasses of champagne has made my face the shade of Revlon's top selling lipstick "Love that Red!" Dan came to MY BIRTHDAY PARTY with this woman. I hear Mother's voice: *"Harvey.*

You have guests, so put your personal troubles aside."

As I walk back into my birthday party, I hear Jessica explaining how she and Dan fell in love through acting. Isn't that romantic? Just like Hollywood. Last weekend they had looked at each other and knew "It was fate!" They kiss right in front of me. *That bitch just kissed my Dan!* I guess while I was recuperating from my little procedure they fell in love. Mental Note to self- *Next plastic surgery procedure, keep boyfriend locked in his apartment!* I throw myself into a chair beside Jeanine and sigh.

"What's wrong, precious?"

"Jeanine, see that gorgeous blond man over there by the dining room table?"

"Yes, you mean the one that looks like he's a cross between Steve McQueen and Michael Douglas?"

"I hadn't thought about him in that way until right now, but yes. That's Dan, my new boyfriend. So Jeanine it would seem that while I was getting a little rejuvenated, he was here getting a little rejuvenation of his own. See that pretty brunette who can't stop touching him? She's replaced me as his girlfriend, so Happy Birthday to me!"

Jeanine sat up straight in her chair "No shit, Harvey? Wait here!" Jeanine came back with two bottles of Cliquot. One for me and one for her! "Here you poor thing! I found the good stuff so let's drink a birthday toast! MEN SUCK!" I sat with her and cried while I drank three more bottles of champagne. The tears really hurt this time. No, literally hurt.

Mental Note # 2 to self: *Harvey, if you ever have the C02 laser resurfacing procedure performed again, and start to cry because you break up with your boyfriend at your birthday party, remember that the salt water in your tears burns the crap out of your skin as it streams down your face. Happy Birthday.*

"Because you're worth it."
-L'OREAL PARIS

"Mother, I already told you, and I'm only going to say it one more time! Jason asked me out first. Not the other way around! And he asked me to marry him! I promise! We've been dating almost a whole year so I don't feel that I'm rushing into anything!"

"Harvey, I don't care if you've been dating Jasper for three years! This is just plain wrong!"

"My future husband's name is *Jason*, Mother!"

"Harvey, I don't care how many times you say it. He's only twenty years old. You're almost ten years older than him, have you thought about that? And marriage between two men? That's against God!"

"Really? God, Mother? And yes, I am ten years older and thank you for pointing that out, but I've also been waiting for someone to love me my whole life. Is that so bad? Don't you think I deserve love? When Jason first asked me out I said *No, you're too young for me.* The second time I again said *no*. Jason said *If you don't say yes, I'm just going to continue asking every day until you say yes so you might as well give in Harvey."*

"Well you should've just said NO!"

"Mother, are you really this selfish?"

"I only have your best interest in mind."

"I don't believe that anymore. I guess I've never really believed that to begin with, because you only care that Daddy doesn't get upset or that the neighbors will think we're not the normal American family. And you know that's a bunch of bullshit because no family is perfect."

"Harvey…"

"No, Mother. It's your turn to listen now. With the life I've lived so far I think very few people have had my best interest at heart. So this time if you can't be happy for me then let's just call it a day. I'm tired of this same conversation we've been having for 20 years. 20 YEARS, MOTHER! I'm gay. Period. No discussion. No justification. If that doesn't work for you then let's call it quits right now. I don't know how long I will be on the earth but I know I'm not spending the rest of my life trying to make other people happy at the expense of losing myself. If it hurts, I'm sorry, but I'm not compromising this time. Our

Commitment Ceremony is on Christmas Eve at Tim and Richard's and Richard will officiate. The dress is formal and Jason and I are registered at Bergdorf Goodman's in New York. If you're interested, I've chosen Rosenthal's Magic Flute china pattern and the customary gift from parents, Mother, is at least three place settings, plus a large serving platter and gravy boat."

"Well, Harvey, what should I tell your father? That you're going to marry a man?"

"Frankly Mother I don't give a damn what you tell Daddy. Bye-bye."

I know Grace is livid; not only am I marrying a man, I used Rhett Butler's exit line from Scarlett O'Hara in *Gone With The Wind* against her. It's somehow poetic justice because I feel like I just ended a Civil War of my own. When did I know I was gay? You've read my diary now! From the moment I remember thinking my first thoughts. Who has the right to tell me what to feel and how to be? Is being gay a choice? Not for me. Who has the right to tell me who I can marry? When the Universe passed out sexuality, I got a white wedding gown and Judy Garland's greatest hits.

Not all gay men are as feminine as me but they still deal with the same mess. I've fought this so long that I'm just tired from it—and don't kid yourself, this bias is not innocent, because as you know I was almost murdered over it. It can lead to death if ignorance is fueled by rhetoric. The Church? The Government? I'm not an average, *normal* person and I never will be what society thinks is *normal*. I hate the word *minority* because it implies that there are other people who for some reason think they can pass judgment on those of us who don't look or act like them. *Equality* is a funny word. Does it truly exist? It hasn't for me, so I guess I'll have to make the most of these moments of joy wherever I can find them.

I have that every day with Jason. I love Tim and Richard with all my heart, but Jason is the first person in my whole life who understands me deep down in my soul. I know that somewhere in the Universe our names are written side by side as soul mates meant to love for an eternity. So that's that, ladies and Gentlemen! On the evening of December 24th, I will now be known as Harvey Helms-Rockwell. Tim said it kind of sounds like a porn name, but that's okay. Look at me! I'm finally getting married!

No more time to think about Mother and gay wedding drama! First I have an appointment with the Guerlain perfumery at Bergdorf Goodman to have my custom wedding day fragrance mixed, and then it's off to L'oréal to meet Jeanine. She left a message asking me to meet her there for a job in product development, working on Ralph Lauren's beauty concept! I love Ralph, as you already know. After that, it's back to pack for North Carolina.

I'm a little late as I rush to the Guerlain counter. "Hi! I'm Harvey Helms, and sorry I'm so late! The East side traffic is an absolute nightmare today! I'm here for my custom wedding fragrance consultation and blending."

A handsome young man, dressed immaculately and sporting a little French mustache, says, "No worries, Mr. Helms. I've been expecting you. My name is Steve. Please have a seat so that I may ask you questions and test fragrance notes that will work with your chemistry for your special day. These notes will be the foundation for your custom fragrance, so let's begin by you unbuttoning your shirt sleeve so I can test each note on your arm. The first is Peony." Steve has so many bottles in front of him that I wonder how he'll know which one and how many to use. He dips a white paper strip into the Peony bottle and then swipes my arm with the clear liquid. "Please don't rub it, Mr. Helms, as it may bruise the fragrance and the oils from your hand could change the scent. It will take a few seconds to dry." I look at Steve inquisitively as he pulls my arm to his nose. "Too sweet. Now let's try Jasmine." My head is soon spinning from all these fragrance notes.

Steve dips and swipes about 20 bottles, and finally he asks, "Where are you getting married?"

"Charlotte, North Carolina. Obviously not *legally* married but we're having our Commitment Ceremony there."

"Congratulations Mr. Helms. That's interesting, I'm from the South too."

"Really? Did you work in fragrances in the South with Guerlain?"

"No, I started in cosmetics."

"I worked in cosmetics too for Ultima II at Belk South Park."

"I worked at Belk's at South Park as well for Clinique!"

"Steve it's such a small world! My best friend was from Clinique. Did you know her? Her name is Sue."

"Mr. Helms. hang on one minute. I need to prepare your skin a little more before we begin the next rounds of fragrance notes." Steve starts looking under his desk and through a few drawers.

"Steve, what are you looking for?"

"The Epilady."

Silence.

"*Sue?*"

"Harvey…"

"ARE YOU KIDDING ME!"

The entire department whips around to see the drama at the Guerlain counter. "*SUE!*"

"Shh! Harvey! It's Steve, please. Nobody knows about me here. They only know me as *Steve*, 'cause Sue died a long time ago. I'm sorry I haven't been in touch but I didn't know how you would react because everyone else has disowned me. I always knew I was a guy trapped in a girl's body but I couldn't decide what to do about it until I was in Atlanta working for Germaine Monteil. I had this amazing boss who told me to become what I wanted. I had the operation and hormone therapy in Sweden then I decided to move to New York where no one knows me so I could be whoever I wanted to be. Do you understand, Harvey?"

"Do I *understand*, Sue? I mean Steve! The only thing I wish in this moment is that Patti Garrison and Anorexic Blue Eyeshadow Debbie could be here, so I could tell them *I'm marrying a man,* followed by the finale of you dropping trousers so they could see your penis."

In the taxi on the way to L'Oréal I opened my new custom fragrance, dabbed some onto my wrist, and took a deep breath. *How appropriate from the Universe that Sue—I mean, Steve—would create the fragrance for my wedding day! You can't make this shit up.* Steve and I exchanged numbers, promising a dinner date as soon as I return from North Carolina.

The irony of life! The person who gave me confidence and love when I had none was back in my life, needing the same genuine understanding and compassion. *Thank you, God. Oh, here it is on the left.* I hand the taxi driver a twenty and say, "Keep the change." Might as well spread my karmic good luck around a little.

As I walk through the doors at L'Oréal , the receptionist asks, "Who are you here to see?"

"Jeanine Recckio."

"One moment."

Out of a side door walks a tiny brunette with a surly scowl. "Are you Harvey? Follow me." I'm lead through a long corridor not unlike that at Revlon with different photos and decor, but the environment feels strangely the same. " Please make yourself comfortable. Jeanine will be here momentarily." She gestures for me to enter an office and sit. I notice that the room is all Ralph plaid everything. Floor to ceiling. There's a huge desk with a chair facing the window with someone sitting in it and she looks like she's trying to open her palm pilot with a table knife. Who is this crazy woman?

I'm getting ready to clear my throat to let whoever's sitting in that chair know I'm here when I hear, "Harvey Darling! So glad to see you!" I get up to kiss Jeanine on both cheeks, but as I turn around, the desk chair is swiveling to reveal the mystery woman with palm pilot in her hand.

"Angela?"

"Hello Harvey. Welcome to L'Oréal . But please, next time call me Mrs. Cartwright.

"Tim, I'm only going to tell you one more time! Sue is now Steve and when the chair swiveled around the evil villain turned out to be Angela Lewis-Cartwright. Now get out of here! I'm getting married in five minutes. I love you." As Tim leaves, I look in the mirror and see a face that has been through some interesting stuff. I decided to take Elle magazine's advice and do a *blushed bride* look. Pinky neutrals that look like you're wearing no makeup. Kind of like the defunct Barely There Collection but with more blush, if you know what I mean. Jason and I decided on black tuxedos with matching black and white bow-ties.

I hear a light knock on the door. "I'm not ready yet."

"Of course you're not. You don't have something old, something new, something borrowed, and something blue." Mother is standing in the doorway dressed in Christmas red velvet.

"Mother, I..."

Grace walks over to me and puts her hand on my mouth. "Harvey, here's a blue handkerchief from your grandfather whom you're named after. That will cover the old and blue." As Mother's placing it in my pocket she says, "You know, when you were a little boy, people used to say *Grace, I know who's child that is* because we look so much alike. I guess, son, out of all of my children, you're the most like me. God help you. Now take off your right shoe. Here's a new shiny Penny to put in your shoe for good luck. And the something borrowed is my love to watch over you. May I wish you every blessing on your wedding day." Grace kisses me lightly on my forehead.

I hear the piano. "Mother, I guess it's time."

As we walk out of my bedroom door, I stop because Daddy is standing there with his hair all slicked down in his best Sunday suit. His eyes are blood-shot and he looks nervous as hell, but he pulls his arm up and grabs mine holding my hand hard. "Are you ready, son?"

I look over at my mother and knew that by some miracle from the Universe, she had changed. "I think so, Daddy." As I look down the aisle I see Tim (who is of course my Maid of Honor!) and Richard (smiling in his Holy Minister wedding robes). As I turn to walk down the aisle, I see the beautiful face of my soul mate Jason, beaming back love and tranquility. In this moment, I'm thanking God that I have on Maybelline's Waterproof Great Lash mascara. But now that you've my diary, I'm sure you're not surprised by that.

Made in the USA
Lexington, KY
07 September 2012